THE MAN WHO [...]
THE B[...]

Miles Morland was born i[...] [...] '[...] all over the place', but chiefly in Iran, Iraq and Jersey. He was sent back to England to be educated at Radley and subsequently read law at Oxford. After six years working in the city, followed by a further ten on Wall Street, he returned from New York in 1983 to run the London office of a leading American investment bank, from which he resigned in 1989. He now lives on a houseboat on the Thames with his wife Guislaine, and their two daughters, Natasha and Georgia, and is working on a historical novel. This is his first book.

MILES MORLAND

The Man Who Broke Out of the Bank

... and went for a walk across France

Fontana
An Imprint of HarperCollins*Publishers*

Fontana
An imprint of HarperCollins*Publishers*,
77–85 Fulham Palace Road,
Hammersmith, London W6 8JB

Special overseas edition 1993
9 8 7 6 5 4 3 2 1

First published in Great Britain by
Bloomsbury Publishing Limited 1992

Map by Neil Hyslop

ISBN 0 00 637 939 7

Set in Baskerville by
Hewer Text Composition Services, Edinburgh

Printed in Great Britain by
HarperCollins Manufacturing Glasgow

To Guislaine, the hero of this book

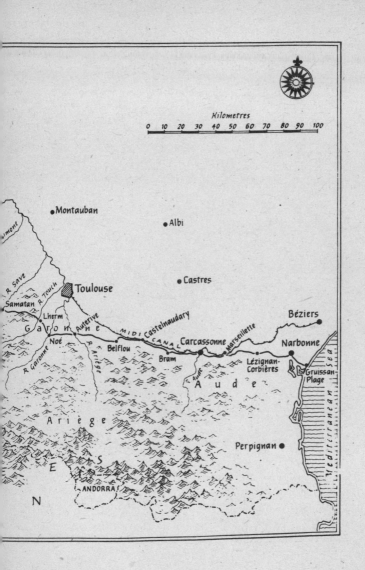

CHAPTER 1

The first thing that struck me about walking across France was how easy it was. We climbed over the boulders at the edge of the beach and there was the road ahead of us, straight as a ruler along the channel that led from the sea. All we had to do was walk. Easy, really. Here, one foot in front of the other, juggle the pack a little, breathe in the warm, sea-salt air and that's fifty yards gone. We had expected it to feel different. The Mediterranean to the Atlantic is an unthinkably long way for two middle-aged wrecks who consider a walk round the Serpentine exercise. I squeezed Guislaine's hand.

I don't think either of us, as we walked off that Mediterranean beach, thought that we would get as far as the Atlantic, three, or maybe four, hundred miles away; we had been careful not to measure too precisely in case the distance discouraged us. But whether we succeeded or not was less important than this moment. This was it. This, more than the day I gave up my job, this was the single moment that marked the division between Twenty-Two Years Shouting Down a Phone and a future as empty and unmarked as the open sea. These few steps took me over the watershed. Everything in the forty-five years up to now had been part of boarding school, Oxford, the City, Wall Street and only-another-fifteen-years-till-the-pension.

These steps began a different journey.

Most of the people I knew had asked me, 'What are you going to do?' in tones varying from admiration to jealousy to disapproval, voices that said more about what was going on in their own lives than in mine.

I had usually answered, 'Well, I think I'll take the summer off, have a nice long holiday, and then start my own firm in the financial world, you know, a little boutique where I'm my own boss.' Oh yes? It was easier than saying that I had no idea what I was going to do, apart from walk across France – for if I said that, people would smile knowingly as if they knew I was up to something but couldn't talk about it for competitive reasons. The start-my-own-firm story saved a lot of trouble. People believed it. They would nod and say, 'Mmm. Good idea. Keep me in touch. I wouldn't mind doing that kind of thing myself. I'm fed up with working for a big firm.'

And they were very curious, particularly people in the City. I was like the boy who had stolen into the headmaster's study to take a look at the exam papers. It really wasn't done but everyone else was secretly longing to do it too. Saying that I was going back into the City made it acceptable. I may have gone into the headmaster's study, but I hadn't actually looked at the papers and soon I would be back at a desk surrounded by quote screens Shouting Down a Phone. Of course.

The only person who didn't ask me what I was going to do was the one who would be most affected by it: Guislaine. (Everyone finds it hard to pronounce. She's half French; hence the name. It has a hard *G* and a silent *s*.) She was likely to go through as big a change in her life as I in mine, but in her case it wasn't because of a decision she had taken herself. She was going to change from being the wife of someone earning a large and regular salary doing a job that, five days a week, took him out of the house from before she got up in the morning till just before dinner, into being married to a man with no outside income and nothing to do all day, seven days a week. She told me her friends' reaction: 'What are you going to do with Him around the house all day? It'll drive you mad. I had Tom/Dick/Nigel home for a month when he was between jobs and we practically got divorced.'

Although they didn't usually say that to my face, it seemed a reasonable concern. I was as curious as they to know what I was going to do all day. In the few days between finally leaving the office and starting our walk I seemed to have been busy all the time but things would be different, wouldn't they, when the Walk was over and we were back in London.

And I worried about divorce.

Five years before, in our thirteenth year of marriage, we had split up. For me it had been as sudden and devastating as a hurricane. Like many men with demanding jobs I hadn't had my eyes open to the change in the weather and it came as a complete surprise. There were three years of mess and misery culminating in an untidy divorce. The hurricane passed on, and in the ensuing quiet things seemed different. A few months later we married each other for the second time. Giving up a safe job and walking across France, when we had never previously done anything together out of doors that would raise a sweat, would certainly do something to our marriage. We didn't know what.

Guislaine, who was on the receiving end of all the change in my life, was remarkable. I was so preoccupied with what was happening to me that at the time I didn't appreciate how remarkable. She encouraged me, but in a quiet way, to leave my job, because she felt that that was what I wanted and she must have felt that I had already crossed the bridge in my mind; she never once asked me at the time what I was going to do. We would talk in general terms and I would tell her that I didn't know and she would leave it at that. She asked me for the first time when we had been walking for over ten days, as we sweated over the thirty-seven kilometres of hills between Belflou and Auterive, but I didn't have an answer. I said something about how wonderful freedom felt. It did, but putting it into words made me feel I was speaking someone else's dialogue in a bad play. She didn't probe further. There was no 'Look, don't you think it's time you gave it some serious thought? I've got a right to know as well, you know. It affects me just as much as you.' All that was true, but she never said it.

I didn't ask myself the question either. It may seem strange that I could give up a secure and well-paid job at the age

3

of forty-five without a plan, but I did. The Walk would be a month of hard thinking about blisters, tonight's bed and tomorrow's route; there wouldn't be much space for 'What am I going to do with my life?' Although Guislaine says that I think analytically and logically – not compliments in her lexicon – I don't like thinking in abstract terms. The heart makes better decisions than the head and it doesn't keep you awake at night doing it but just announces one day what the decision is.

After so many years working for Wall Street firms I knew how American business people liked to take decisions. Get a bit of paper, put the pluses on one side and the minuses on the other; then see which column is longer. 'You gotta decide these things analytically, Miles,' they would tell me. 'Keep emotion out of it.' I had cheerfully exploited this system for years when I wanted to hire someone away from a nice, cosy firm where he was happy and doing his job well. I would encourage him to draw up a plus-and-minus list because I knew that, if he did, all the juicy things I could offer – money, cars, important-sounding titles – would outweigh feeling comfortable and being at home in a job. It wasn't always the wrong decision. There were many people I had hired, particularly the younger ones, who thrived in the highly-charged 'I can work harder than you, pal' atmosphere of a Wall Street firm. But in their cases the heart told them to do the same thing as the head.

In New York my firm employed a corporate psychologist, one of whose jobs was to give the branch-office managers tips on 'interviewing strategy'. We became friends and I remember her saying to me one day over a drink, 'You know, honey, all the worst decisions people make are the sensible ones. The smart guys are the ones who do what their heart tells them to do and forget the analysis.'

No one ever believed the Walk was Guislaine's idea. Guislaine was brought up on the Continent. She was shunted from school

4

to school in the course of a childhood during which she was sometimes in the care of Gael, her peripatetic mother – beautiful, artistic, and forever in the power of mysterious and sudden enthusiasms – and sometimes of Tony, her mother's sister, who was living in Strasbourg with her husband, Dunstan. The only time Guislaine wasn't in the care of mother or aunt was when Guy, her French father, came to take her to the movies and kidnapped her for days or months. Stories vary.

Education was a succession of *lycées* and convents all of which shared a conviction that you weren't at school to play games. Guislaine was never exposed to lacrosse, hockey, basketball, compulsory runs, tennis or gym. The only exercise that Gael, Tony, Dunstan and Guy all did was dancing. Guy's tango was more famous than his tennis – although Guislaine swears he was doubles champion of St Tropez in 1938.

I am the opposite. I have always wanted to be good at dancing but I'm not. I have, however, had much exposure to games of the British sort. At eight I went to a ferociously tough prep school set up at the turn of the century to feed boys into the Navy via Dartmouth. My father – who did go into the Navy – had been there. I was chubby and hopeless at games, but that didn't excuse me from every afternoon having to play rugger, cricket or soccer depending on the time of year. Not to mention boxing and gym, both of which I loathed. Gym was particularly bad, as I had an elder brother, Michael, at the school who was a superb athlete and 'Sarge', the PT instructor, would stand behind me as I struggled to do a chin-up, saying, 'That's pathetic. You're a disgrace to your brother.' It wasn't that I disliked games. I just hated being so bad at them, particularly at a school where sporting success was everything. I was overjoyed when, in my last term, I got into the First XV for rugger. This was because they needed someone heavy in the second row of the scrum. My cup was full.

When I was thirteen I went to Radley. There, the worship of the sportsman was even greater. You had to be either a 'dry bob', who played cricket and hockey, or a 'wet bob', who rowed instead. I became a wet bob, because I didn't want to compete with Michael who was constantly Saving the School with the brilliance of his batting. I was dreadful at rowing although I longed to be good at it. Not wanting to admit my failure as I sweated up the Thames in the lowest grade of tub, I would pretend I didn't care by fooling around and making jokes at the expense of all the hearty sportsmen. This resulted in my being frequently beaten for 'offences on the river', no laughing matter at Radley. I even tried to become a dry bob, a change that needed your housemaster's permission. Mine would sit behind the desk in his study with two canes on it, a thin, whippy one and a great thick brute. 'Look, boy, if you're going to argue with me I shall be forced to use the Big Chap,' he would say, fingering the thick one. When I asked to be allowed to give up rowing, I didn't get beaten but permission was withheld. 'Stick it out, boy. It's good for you to do things you don't like.'

Despite this, Radley was better than prep school because, even if you weren't good at games, you would be tolerated as an 'intellectual' if you were funny. Making fun of things was my game.

Then, in my third year, Ronnie Howard came to teach at Radley and to take over as senior rowing coach. Ronnie had been President of the 1957 Oxford boat that had won against all the odds and against the first of the American Boat Race mutinies. By the time he arrived at Radley I was over six feet tall and no longer quite so chubby, but still dreadful at rowing. He was a brilliant coach and he gave me a chance in a good crew. Entirely thanks to him and his coaching, I made the First VIII that year and was Captain of Boats the next. He introduced modern methods of training from Germany with the result that we became superhumanly fit. This was a new world to me. I had never been fit before and I felt for the first time the extraordinary pleasure of rowing in a good eight, with eight men moving in utter unison and wanting to push themselves beyond the limits of exertion and pain. Under

Ronnie's coaching that year we won the Princess Elizabeth Cup for schools at Henley and broke the record for it.

Life at Radley was transformed by my suddenly becoming one of Them, the sportsmen. I no longer needed to pretend I didn't care about games and to be the quick-tongued intellectual. More importantly, rowing showed me how much joy a sport can give you when you dedicate yourself to it. It also sharpens the competitive instincts: rowing and coming second is miserable. Once I had achieved my sporting ambitions I began having second thoughts about them, particularly when I went on with rowing at Oxford. I never felt entirely happy in my new role as a 'hearty', as sportsmen – especially oarsmen – were called at Oxford. I liked the fun of the sport and I liked winning but, now that I had succeeded at what I had always envied, I was uncomfortable. I wanted to go back to being the intellectual, not the rowing blue.

I say this not just to illustrate that I had been exposed to physical exertion whereas Guislaine hadn't before we went on our walk, but because I had the same feeling working in the City. Succeeding there, at least in the Big Bang world I was in, required many of the same qualities as winning the Boat Race – competitiveness, dedication and a willingness to push yourself to extreme limits – and in the same way there was acclamation for the winner. Non-City people think the satisfaction is in the money. They're wrong. Most of the pleasure comes from the sheer competitive intensity of the work. But when I became successful in the City, I had the same feeling I'd had at Oxford or Radley as a successful sportsman. I was wearing a suit that looked good, but hadn't it been made for someone else?

CHAPTER 2

The idea of the Walk was Guislaine's pre-emptive strike.

Guislaine has inherited not only her mother's distaste for Anglo-Saxon sports, but also her fear of flying. Guislaine remembers flying with her as a child. As the plane gathered speed down the runway, Gael would shut her eyes tight, grip Guislaine's hand and say, 'Don't worry. It's going to be all right. We're not going to crash. Think hard. There's someone out there who's praying for us. It'll be all right.' Not surprisingly, Guislaine's palms get wet at the sight of a British Airways advertisement.

I have always loved to travel; planes, boats, trains, I love them all. Two months before leaving my job I had to go to the Far East. This was a wonderful excuse for a round-the-world flight. 'What a bore,' I said to people, as I asked my secretary to book me to New York, Tokyo, Bangkok for the weekend, Singapore, Hong Kong, then on to Madras for three days' rest before returning to London. I said 'What a bore' because that's what senior people in the financial world always say. They make a show of hating travelling even if, like me, they can't wait to get on the plane. I always take a bag full of books and magazines on plane journeys but I never read them; gazing out of the window at a desert sunrise, or the Arctic, or even a cloudscape, has too much magic to leave time for reading. I never sleep on planes and have spent whole nights sitting on the steward's jump-seat by the door at the back of a jumbo looking through the little round window at the moon over a dark sea.

As soon as I had given up my job, Guislaine knew it would be only a short time before I suggested that the two of us go off round the world. She had visions of Tuesday in Tonga and Friday in Fiji, palm-fringed airport after palm-fringed airport. She knew how restless I was at weekends after a week of twelve hours a day in the office and foresaw that, now I'd been let out of the cage, I would want to do some roaming. I had not had more than two weeks' holiday at a stretch for twenty-two years, and some years I had had no holiday at all. Roaming and nightmare are synonymous for Guislaine. She likes to stay in one place.

She realized she wasn't going to buy me off with sitting in South Kensington. 'Why don't we take a little house in Spain in a village in the mountains and live there for three months?'

'What, and just sit there?'

'Well, that way we'd get to know the locals and become part of the scenery. We couldn't do that if we were travelling around.'

'Not for me, thanks. I mean, there are times when I'd love to spend three months in a little village in Spain but not now, not after twenty-two years at a desk.'

'How about Greece? You like that. We could find a house down in the Peloponnese, somewhere unspoilt, that peninsula Arlette is always talking about. You've always wanted to go there.'

'Yes, I know. It would be nice, but I feel like moving around. This is a great opportunity to see places we've never had the time to go to. We can go to Greece or Spain anytime. I was thinking about the Pacific: Indonesia, the Cook Islands, the Gilbert and Ellice Islands – I don't even know what they're called these days. Places like that. We could fly there and then go from island to island on a tramp steamer.'

Usually, if Guislaine doesn't like something I suggest, she will say no and I'll spend the next week trying to persuade her that if she knew more about it she really would like it. This never works, but I'm pig-headed enough to try. This time, she didn't say no but deflected me with a brilliant counter-stroke, pushing the ball back into my court. On the baseline. 'How about a walk?'

'A walk?'

'Yes, a walk.'

I was winded. I had been preparing for a travelogue on the South Pacific. 'Hmm. What sort of walk?'

'You decide. Anywhere pretty. Oh yes – as long as it's in Europe,' she added quickly. She knows the way my mind works and could see that my next move would be to suggest hiking round some insanitary part of India.

'That's not a bad idea. Yes, I'd like that. Where could we go? Are you sure you want to do it?'

'Yes, I think so. But I don't want to camp out in tents and things. I'd want to stay in a hotel or a house at night. But I'll certainly give it a try.'

I was overwhelmed.

We considered and discarded most of Europe over the next few days. We wanted to walk, not mountaineer; it didn't have to be flat, but a few rolling hills were as much as we thought we could manage. It had to be a walk that would provide us with somewhere we could get a bed for the night every twenty miles or so. This ruled out much of Greece and Spain. We eliminated northern Europe as we were worried it would be wet – although when we came to do the Walk, there were many afternoons when we prayed for a wisp of wind or a cool shower.

Most important of all, we wanted a real starting-point and a real finish.

We were still talking about it a week later when we went down to stay with Gael, Guislaine's mother, at her house in the Quercy, half-way between Bordeaux and Toulouse. Her wanderlust is as bad as mine. She was much taken with our scheme. 'Oh yes, what a good idea. Maybe I'll come with you for part of it.' She and I sat in her garden under the papyrus tree and bounced walks off each other while Guislaine looked miffed – after all, it had been her idea. But she had had less practice than Gael and me when it came to armchair travelling.

Both of us, if we're not actually on a journey, like to plot one. Guislaine doesn't. She regards guide-books as an intrusion and consequently arrives in places with an open mind and a fresh eye. I have usually read so many books about our destination, several of which I keep to hand when we arrive, that it's difficult not to be disappointed.

'I know. How about the Route Napoléon?' I said.

'Good idea; that's got a nice ring to it,' said Gael.

'I hate to be ignorant,' Guislaine butted in, 'but where exactly does it go?'

'Good question. I really don't know,' I said. 'It's after he came back from Elba. Didn't he land somewhere on the Riviera? And then he marched north, you know, the Hundred Days and all that, ending in Waterloo.'

Gael fetched the green Michelin guide for the Côte d'Azur. 'Here we are. From Golfe-Juan – that's where St Juan-les-Pins is – to Grenoble.'

I peered over her shoulder. There was a map of the first hundred miles of the route as far as Sisteron. The road ducked and dived round mountain peaks. We had stayed near Grasse the previous spring and I remembered how bleak and forbidding those mountains were.

'Who wants to finish up in Grenoble, anyhow?' Guislaine asked.

So much for the Route Napoléon. We thought about Alsace, from Strasbourg to Basle, maybe, through all the little wine villages. That would have a special nostalgic quality for Guislaine, as the only slightly stationary part of her childhood had been the years she spent in Strasbourg. A different green guide was consulted and Alsace was rejected as being too short. We had no idea precisely how far we could go, but we had put aside a month for the Walk, knowing that we had to be back by 5 July for the beginning of school holidays, and thought that we ought to be able to manage three hundred miles or so. That seemed doable. How about Robert Louis Stevenson's *Travels with a Donkey in the Cevennes*?

'You can be Modestine, darling,' I said to Guislaine.

'Mmm. That sounds rather sexy. Hey, wait a second. Modestine's the donkey.'

'Only joking.'

'Very funny.'

It's a wonderful book. I had often thought that following his path would be a trip worth doing, but we rejected it as it went through some of the most hostile country in France. Later we were glad we had, when we learnt that there are now guided tours following the 'Stevenson Trail'.

'I know,' said Gael. 'How about sea to sea, the Mediterranean to the Atlantic.'

Of course.

CHAPTER 3

I was so excited about the Walk – it already had a capital *W* – that I didn't have time to think about the implications of Not Working. The Walk took over.

We still didn't have a fixed route. The first decision had been to walk from sea to sea, the Mediterranean to the Atlantic. The second, to do it the shortest way. When we returned from our stay with Gael we spread the map of France out on our kitchen table. I stretched a piece of string over the waist between France and Spain to find out where it was narrowest.

I showed the map to Guislaine. 'There we are,' I said. 'That's it. The Walk. Perpignan to Biarritz.'

'What's that?' she said, pointing.

'What?'

'That dark bit.'

'The Pyrenees.'

'Are you mad? I'm not walking over that.'

Out came the string again. I moved it thirty or forty miles north of the Pyrenees to the area where the dark brown of the mountains gave way to white and green. 'There. How about that? It's not much longer and a lot flatter.'

'Well, where do we start?'

I peered at the map. The starting-place seemed to be a place we had never heard of, Gruissan-Plage, on the Mediterranean near Narbonne, and the finish somewhere north of Biarritz. We decided not to decide on a definite finishing-place. We'd see how we went. A place called Vieux Boucau looked as good a place to aim for as any. We didn't measure the distance exactly but I did match my thumb against the scale on the map. The end joint measured about forty kilometres; it was ten thumb-joints across France from Gruissan to the Atlantic. That was in a direct line; walking would be a lot longer.

Neither of us had gone on a Walk before. I had, it is true, marched the forty-odd miles from Aldermaston to London singing 'It's suicide to live along the Clyde and we dinna want Polaris', in the Easter holidays of 1962, my last year at school, but that didn't count as a real Walk. It had been more of a ramble to allow mums with prams and grannies against the bomb to keep up. But even then – and I had been fit then from rowing – it had been hard work. I had gone with three friends from Radley. We weren't certain about banning the bomb but I was a convinced communist and the Aldermaston March was a good way of showing solidarity. At that time I used to write to the Soviet Embassy for propaganda: there was no unemployment, no taxes, no crime and no poverty in the Soviet Union. That didn't stop my feet hurting like hell on the march. I had worn the army boots that we were issued with in the Radley CCF (Combined Cadet Force) and by the time we reached Trafalgar Square they had rubbed all the skin off my ankles and toes. The Walk was going to be about ten times as long.

Guislaine and I consulted friends as to what we should wear, particularly on our feet. This is a subject on which there are no agnostics. Everyone is an expert. Frank Neyens, a friend at work and a keen hiker, said that ankle support was essential. Boots were the only thing. Patrick Hughes, an epic walker when he is not painting, thought boots a waste of time. Only masochists walked in anything other than sneakers. No, no, said the Uribes. They run in the London Marathon and they should know. Julien worked with me and his wife Anne has been a friend since we were teenagers. I can't remember most of what the Uribes recommended as they take great pains over their equipment and their advice was so specific and detailed that it was impossible to take it all in. The tip Anne gave us that turned out to be a Walk-saver was about Second Skin. This is a miraculous American product that you put over blisters. But that was later.

In the end I went to Lillywhites and picked their most comfortable pair of walking shoes. These were made by Mephisto, a French manufacturer. They were made of real leather, which had been treated to give it that synthetic look the French like, and they had laces and eyelets all over them. Guislaine took one look at my Mephistos and, decided not to get new shoes at all. She had a pair of Noddy shoes she had bought years ago when we lived in America, which had been fine for walking in the woods round our house in Westchester County. They had been fine more recently, too, for her daily walk round the Serpentine. She would return, face radiant with health, saying, 'Four miles today.'

'Four miles???' I'd ask. 'Where did you go?'

'Oh, across the bridge in the middle and round the far end by the café.'

'Well, that's not four miles. Two, maybe two and a half at the most.'

'Yes it is. I measured it on the map.'

'If that's four miles, I'm the Pope.'

'It is. It took an hour and a quarter with a stop for a cigarette and I walk at four miles an hour . . .'

I'd then realize what I was doing and give her a kiss to admit defeat. It wasn't until just before I left the City that I became aware how aggressive that world makes you. The ethos of the part I worked in was half public school and half US Marines. You would never admit to taking anything seriously, and any weakness or eccentricity would be challenged and ridiculed.

We had a salesman in our office who had been there for years when I took it over. I'll call him Jock. He was a bumbling old bear of a Scotsman and I was under pressure from New York to sack him. I tried once, because he wasn't paying his way any longer and the other salesmen used to complain when we'd have big luncheon meetings for our clients and Jock would have a dram too much and fall asleep at the table until he woke himself with a loud snore. I told him in January one year that he had to find another job and gave him till June to do it.

July arrived and Jock was still there. I didn't have the heart to fire him, as I knew he wouldn't find another job, and I hoped that he could hold on until retirement without doing too much damage.

John Engels, my then boss in New York, called to ask, 'Got rid of Jock? It's July.'

'No, I couldn't do it, John. I told him he could stay till the end of the year.'

'You pussy.' If you'd been to Virginia Military Academy, as John had, being a pussy was worse than molesting children.

Jock started falling asleep in the afternoons at his desk. Once, the younger salesmen tied his shoelaces together while he was asleep and then one of them yelled, 'Jock, Jock, it's Mike [the man who handed out the orders at Jock's biggest client]. He's got an order. He's come in on the trading desk.' Jock woke up with a start, gave a roar of 'Tell 'im I'm coming' and leapt to his feet, only to come crashing down over one of the secretaries, knocking her off her chair.

Another favourite pastime was selling Jock cars. He would corner new recruits and tell them about the house he was going to buy in Perthshire when he retired and show them pictures of vintage Rolls-Royces he dreamed of buying to go visiting in. The recruits would telephone him on an internal line: 'Top Hat Motor Cars here, sir. We understand you're interested in a Silver Ghost?' Jock would look craftily around the office to make sure no one was listening and cup a hand over the mouthpiece before continuing. What he didn't know was that the whole call was being broadcast through a speaker on the other side of the office.

Guislaine would catch the tide going out in the evening from the office crossfire. I would come back from work charged up with competitive maleness ready to prove myself by snatching anything she said and making fun of it. I'd catch myself doing it and try to stop, but it must have been difficult for Guislaine.

Once we had our shoes for the Walk, the next question was training. We were both unfit. I had taken no exercise since January, four months earlier, when my Achilles tendon had snapped with an audible *pingg* while I was playing tennis. That meant an operation to sew all the bits of tendon back together. This is rather like sewing together two paint-brushes; it leaves you with a bulge at the back of your ankle, and leads to seven weeks in plaster, which in my case came off two months before we started the Walk. The tendon contracts while you are in plaster and it takes a few weeks before you can walk properly again. It was no longer painful and I hoped that it would hold up across France, but I didn't see any point in tempting providence by training. Guislaine stepped up her daily strolls round the Serpentine to include the Italian Garden at the north end, and put in an extra burst of yoga before going to bed.

We did do one training walk. The weekend before we left we decided to walk from South Kensington to my mother's house near the Sheen Gate of Richmond Park. I put on my new shoes and we strode out. We weren't wearing backpacks as we didn't want to overdo it. It was a hot day for May and by the time we reached my mother's we were exhausted. We put our feet up, sat in the sun in her garden and drank pints of water and a bottle of wine and ate some sandwiches. On the way back we had to stop on Putney Heath for a rest and a half-hour nap. We crawled home in the late afternoon and sank into a bath. We had walked thirteen miles. I had avoided working it out, but I had an uncomfortable feeling that, on the Walk, we were going to have to average several miles more than that each day. With loaded backpacks. We banned further training.

Maps to me are vodka to a Russian. I am a mapaholic. The Walk was what I had been waiting for all my life. In Long Acre in Covent Garden there is a map addict's dream: a shop called Stanfords, with drawers and shelves and whole rooms full of maps. It has everything from the Thomas Cook rail map of Asia to huge-scale military ordnance maps of every country in Europe and many beyond. France was a doddle. There was a whole section devoted to it. I would go to Stanfords and drool.

'You must use the Grandes Randonnées maps,' was universal advice. Stanfords sold me the thirteen that went from coast to coast along the Pyrenees. When I got home I looked more closely and noticed that, since we had moved the string north and decided on a flatter route, the maps were useless. They didn't cover our route. I gave them to Frank Neyens, my friend from work who had advised us to walk in boots, and cast around for something that would get us across France in fewer than thirteen maps.

I looked at the big-scale Michelin maps. Guislaine and I had used them often in the past, on weekend trips when we had taken the car across to France and sprinted round the country not wanting to miss anything in the short time available. These trips usually resulted in rows, with Guislaine wanting to stop somewhere and me determined to pack in another couple of hundred kilometres before it got dark, just in case there was somewhere nicer down the road. The Michelin maps were excellent for that, but they are motorists' maps. We were hoping to find paths where cars weren't allowed.

In England I use the Ordnance Survey maps. They are the Château Lafite of maps. Although we never go on long walks we use them often to plot out two- or three-mile strolls in the neighbourhood of our cottage on the north Norfolk coast. They tell you everything you need to know and nothing you don't. In theory, France has an equivalent: the maps prepared by the Institut Géographique National, which come in scales varying from the Série Bleue, at 1:25,000, to the Série Verte, at 1:100,000. There's a Brune in between, at 1:50,000, which is the same scale as the Ordnance Survey Landranger maps. The French maps had a very different look and feel to the English. They appeared more detailed but were more confusing. They did, however, use colour well, with grey smudge to indicate the side of a hill – the darker the grey, the fiercer the hill.

After four or five visits to Stanfords and some exploratory purchases I decided on the Série Verte, 1:100,000, one centimetre to one kilometre. The advantage of the Verte was that just four maps would take us across France. We could always buy more detailed maps in a *maison de la presse* on the way if we needed them.

The next big question was, where were we going to stay? My map addiction is matched by a craving for guide-books. We have shelves filled with Michelins, Gault-Millaus, Lonely Planets, Rough Guides, Cadogans, Companions, Blue Guides, even Fodors and Fieldings. I have probably kept whole publishing firms afloat in hard times. Some of these guides are for places we have visited and many are for places we haven't. Just in case. I like to read up about them, otherwise how will we know whether they're worth visiting?

Often someone will be telling me of a place they have visited, say, Mauritius, and I will say, 'Oh Mauritius, yes, wonderful. Did you stay at the Touessrok? Marvellous, isn't it, right down there on the beach . . .'

'Yes, we did. When were you there?'

'Never been there, actually.' I get some funny looks.

Guislaine views my compulsion tolerantly but without understanding. 'Do we really need eight Michelin red guides to France covering different years between 1971 and 1990? Couldn't we get rid of some of them?'

'Get rid of them? No, I don't think that would be a good idea at all. Don't you think they look rather nice sitting there all together?'

She has stopped asking. You might as well ask someone why they smoke.

There was a problem. The Walk would be a month of needing a place to spend the night in France. This called for an arsenal of guide-books. They would end up weighing more than our clothes. It wasn't as if we knew exactly where we were going to be spending each night. We knew our first night was to be in Gruissan-Plage, but from then on it could be anywhere. We didn't know if we'd be walking five miles or twenty-five miles a day and we weren't sure where we were going to finish up.

The solution involved doing something I had never done before: attacking a book with scissors. Guislaine and I love books. They are our extravagance. Wherever we live there is never enough room to put them all up on shelves, so that cellars and bathrooms always have an unpacked box or two in the corner. The thought of cutting something out of a book with scissors appalled me. Guislaine, who had been urging me to throw away surplus guide-books, was even more horrified than I at the prospect of cutting one up. But once the decision had been made and I had taken the first few cuts, the rest was easy. There was even the thrill of doing the forbidden.

I assembled all the possible guides – the Michelin red guide, the Gault-Millau, *Logis de France*, the *gîte* handbook for the Languedoc and a two-year-old copy of the Fontana/Hachette *Guide to France* that I found at the back of a bookshelf. I then unfolded the map of France again and asked Guislaine to stretch the string between Gruissan-Plage and Vieux Boucau while I drew a pencil line between them. I noted down the names of all the towns and villages along a broad band extending about fifteen kilometres either side of the line. This meant that we wouldn't be committed to any particular route but could choose an itinerary anywhere within the band.

The first bit, from Gruissan to Castelnaudary, via Narbonne and Carcassonne, ran along the plain of the Aude and the Canal du Midi. There were plenty of towns and villages and we would be able to pick and choose where we stayed. Castelnaudary was just over a quarter of the way, but after that everything petered out. Auch was the only place between there and the Atlantic that merited bold type on the Michelin map of France, and nowhere deserved capital letters. It looked like the Empty Quarter. This was on the whole a Good Thing, as the more rural our walk the better. We did, however, need somewhere to spend the nights. I carefully wrote down all the places mentioned on the map, but there were still some big gaps if we assumed that twenty miles would be the maximum we would want to do in one day.

We needed more detail, so I unfolded the four Série Verte maps on the kitchen floor. They covered fourteen feet, wall to wall. Guislaine and I looked at each other. We were going to walk across all that? It was almost like having an aerial view of the whole width of the country as we looked down on the expanse of map with its rivers and roads and hills. We felt daunted but proud at what we had decided to do.

One feature in particular caught our eye. The middle part of the journey had a series of charcoal-grey ribs across it. They were spread out like a fan held by the Pyrenees. These were the long rows of hills dividing the valleys of the rivers flowing north from the Pyrenees. On the big map of France you don't notice them, as your eye is distracted by the grey-black mass of the Pyrenees, but seen on the Série Verte on the kitchen floor they were very apparent. I wasn't sure whether to point them out to Guislaine, as I didn't want to discourage her, but I decided that she had a right to know what she was taking on.

She shrugged it off. 'Oh well, by the time we get there we'll be pretty fit. Anyhow, that's just the map. I'm sure it won't be that bad. Will it?'

'Oh no, I shouldn't think so,' I replied without conviction. I think I was more concerned than her. My map fetish means that maps come alive for me and I have only to look at them to picture the countryside in vivid detail. To Guislaine maps are bits of paper; a thing becomes real when you can smell it. But from then on the Fan – already with a capital *F* – lurked uncomfortably at the back of our minds. If our walk foundered, it would be here.

With the aid of the Série Verte I was able to fill in the holes in the Empty Quarter with names of little villages and hamlets. There was then the job of looking up these names in the guide-books to see if they listed anywhere to spend the night. When I found a place I cut it out. It took a long time. After three nights' work, up till midnight every night, I had a kitchen table covered in little slips of hotel entries. I arranged them in order, starting with Narbonne, sixteen kilometres inland from Gruissan, and finishing up with a sprinkling of places on the Atlantic coast around Vieux Boucau.

The backbone of the list were the Logis de France. These are a network of family-owned, family-run hotels. They tend to be small and intimate and the emphasis is on the food more than on the accommodation. The Michelin was helpful, particularly in the larger places like Castelnaudary. The Gault-Millau didn't contribute much. Gault and Millau discovered, some say invented, *nouvelle cuisine* and theirs is a good guide for someone driving around France looking for exquisitely presented and exquisitely priced meals; the hotel ratings pay more attention to gold-plated taps than they do to the warmth of the welcome. I culled some entries from the out-of-date Fontana/Hachette guide when there was a gap we couldn't fill with the *Logis de France* or the Michelin, but the best gap-filler was the *gîte* handbook. *Gîtes* are French bed-and-breakfast places, private houses that take in guests for the night. We had never used them before but there was a hole in the middle of the itinerary, Fan-country, where the other guides were blank. The *gîte* entries were appealing: '6 guest rooms in a castle surrounded by 13 ha. wood'; '2 guest rooms in a large XVIIth-century farmhouse surrounded by flowers'; '1 room in Lauragaise farmhouse with greens'.

Once the entries were arranged in order I Sellotaped them to pieces of paper and had them photocopied. There were seven sheets in all, weighing virtually nothing, to put in my backpack and five well-sliced heavy guide-books to leave in London. We had at least one entry every twenty-five kilometres or so, usually a choice of half a dozen depending on which route we took. There was just one gap in the middle where, however I juggled the routes, it would be difficult to avoid a thirty-five-kilometre walk if we wanted a bed for the night. Something would crop up when we got there, I was sure. I didn't tell Guislaine. (And nothing cropped up.)

I was curious about how far we were likely to walk in total so, once the hotel sheets had been done, I made a trial itinerary. It came to twenty days' walking and added up to 465 kilometres, or 290 miles, an average of around fifteen miles a day. (The reality, once we were on the Walk, turned out to be worse. We followed the trial itinerary for the first day, to Narbonne, but diverged after that by branching off on a more southerly route.)

Working out distances was easy. I had bought a wonderful tool at Stanfords. It looked like a large plastic orange thermometer. At the bottom, where the mercury would be, was a little wheel. There was a scale on one side of the 'thermometer' with distances on it. As you ran the little wheel over a route on the map, a red line mounted opposite the scale allowing you to read off the distance covered. This 'thermometer' became my third-best friend after Guislaine and my shoes. Only walkers realize how important distances are.

CHAPTER 4

I still have my diary for 1989; it's one of those slim cheque-book-sized things that will fit in an inside pocket. Looking back in it I see there is nothing special on 26 May. It doesn't say 'Stop work'. Like the dog that didn't bark in the night, the lack of appointments is the only giveaway. Up until that Friday it is scribbled full of meetings and appointments.

I had spent the previous six years running the London brokerage office of First Boston which, despite its name, has nothing to do with Boston: it is one of the leading Wall Street investment banks. The name is a historical accident and refers to a long-dead connection with the First National Bank of Boston. I had been working in New York for a competitor for nearly ten years before that and had been hired by First Boston to come back to England and build up their London office.

In those six years the office had grown from a sleepy little operation of a dozen people to 130 shirt-sleeved tearaways all sitting in one enormous room and all Shouting Down a Phone at the same time. By 1989 I hardly ever Shouted Down a Phone any more. Instead I sat in a glass-walled office trying to link the tall stacks of computer print-outs that appeared daily on my desk with what was going on on the other side of the glass.

Sometimes I would be outside the glass walls watching the movement and someone would shout over the noise, 'Hey, Miles. It's Luis. For you.' Luis was the volcanic Cuban I reported to in New York. He was a legend on Wall Street, largely for his willingness, with hardly more than a few seconds' thought and a grunt of acceptance, to take risks involving hundreds of millions, sometimes billions, of dollars.

I would pick up the phone in my office and hear the familiar growl: 'Hey, chief.'

I was 'chief' when I was in favour, 'Moll'n' – his way of saying Morland – when not. Occasionally, when he wanted to be really nice, I would be promoted to 'OK, asshole'. If the phone rang and I heard that, it was going to be good news. Only once did he greet me with 'OK, you screaming asshole'. That was when he telephoned to tell me I was going to become a partner. The conversation began, 'OK, you screaming asshole. You get on the goddam Concorde tonight, OK, and you be in Buchanan's office tomorrow at ten. He got something to tell you.' Buchanan was the head of First Boston, tomorrow was my birthday, a week before Christmas, and the day partners were made.

When Luis first became my boss he would call to browbeat me into hiring more people. That was in 1987, the glory days when Wall Street knew no boundaries, and the talk was always of expansion.

'Hey, chief.'

'Yes, Luis.'

'You hired a sales-trader yet?' They had sales-traders in New York. Their job was to feed information to the traders at the client organizations, take them to the Superbowl and buy them dinner at Christ Cella, a New York steakhouse where a steak cost thirty-five dollars. I had resisted hiring a sales-trader in London.

'Er, not yet. We're talking to a couple of people though.'

'You better be. Mumble, mumble, 1 June, OK?'

'OK, Luis.' Much of Luis's conversation was a menacing mumble, mumble. I would call up Dominick Scianandre, Luis's *consigliere*, after talking to Luis, to find out what he had been saying. Dominick was calm, articulate and unemotional; he would interpret Luis's wishes to his managers.

By 1989 things had changed. The junk-bond artists were going bankrupt and the risk arbitrageurs were being dragged off trading floors in handcuffs. Wall Street was leaking, First Boston more than most.

I had called Luis in January to discuss plans for the year. I had heard rumours of lay-offs. 'Are you going to be cutting back in New York?' I had asked him.

'Nah. No focking cut-backs in my department,' Luis had growled.

'Good. I'd been hearing rumours. Glad they're not true.'

'Right. You tell them in London that we're not going to cut back, OK? Just gonna do some selective upgrading.'

Selective upgrading? This was Luis talking? 'What's that, Luis? Upgrading?'

'Yeh. We're gonna upgrade by twenty people in the department. I told Dominick I want names by the end of the week.'

'I see. So you're going to upgrade by hiring twenty replacements who are better? Shouldn't be difficult. There are plenty of good people on the Street looking.'

'Who said hire people? Hey, chief, you're not listening. There's a hiring freeze. You know that. We gonna hire nobody. We just gonna upgrade. Twenty people. Gonna upgrade them out. Don't worry. Your office is OK. We're not gonna upgrade anyone in London.'

I was in a funny position in London. The office I ran was a branch of First Boston in New York and did stock-brokerage business. But we had an affiliate in London, Crédit Suisse First Boston (CSFB), that was owned jointly with Crédit Suisse, the giant Swiss bank. CSFB did all the other investment banking functions, apart from brokerage, like raising money, dealing in bonds and giving financial advice to companies and countries. They employed six or seven hundred people in London to my office's 130. Although my masters were in New York and that's where I reported to, I was in CSFB's building in London.

CSFB was an extraordinary firm. It was run by a group of twenty or so very aggressive and very talented people – Swiss, Dutch, French, Italian, German, Australian, even a few English. I enjoyed working with them and found them more interesting than most of my First Boston colleagues. They were also the best team of business-getters in the international banking world and were hated and feared by their rivals for their hard-nosed approach to business. At the top of this group was the diminutive and Napoleonic figure of Hans-Joerg Rudloff. Rudloff has at different times been called the most influential businessman in Europe by the *Wall Street Journal* and appeared on the cover of *Euromoney* as the devil, horns and all.

The group of people running CSFB gave Rudloff complete loyalty. In return he rewarded them well. The firm was run on the feudal system. Rudloff was king; the senior executives were barons, all equal. If one showed signs of getting ahead of the pack, Rudloff would wait for an opportunity to humiliate him in public. As I was a partner of First Boston, not of CSFB, I didn't go to their meetings but I'd hear, later in the day, 'Lucky you weren't there this morning, Miles. Rudloff beat up Chris/Luigi/Michel . . .' They all got beaten up from time to time just to make sure that no one got above himself. As one of them said to me after a particularly savage beating, 'At CSFB they don't stab you in the back. They invite an audience and do it with an axe.'

I was glad not to be part of this. My chats with Luis were enough. The problem for me in sharing offices with CSFB was that Rudloff hated Americans. Consequently everyone at CSFB hated Americans. And I worked for them. 'Zese fucking Americans, zey know nothing,' Rudloff would say, to preface a comment about First Boston. 'How's the little German?' people at First Boston would ask when they called me. I seemed to spend half my time saying to the Americans, 'Actually Hans-Joerg's not a bad guy, you know,' and the other half trying to persuade Luis that we and CSFB were on the same side.

As the two firms grew we began encroaching on each other's territory. First Boston would parachute merger specialists into London to do gigantic mergers without telling anyone at

CSFB, and CSFB would send teams of suave European bankers round Ohio and Pennsylvania to chat up First Boston's clients and suggest they do some financing in Europe without First Boston's help. To try and solve a part of this confusion, I was put in charge of the grandly-named International Equity Group. This was a joint venture between CSFB and First Boston to build an international brokerage firm dealing not just in American shares but in European ones as well. The idea was that I would report jointly to Luis and Rudloff.

Luis would come over to London to negotiate with Rudloff, who would agree a day and time for the meeting and then arrange to be in Geneva, where he also had an office, by the time Luis arrived. Luis became a volcano in a state of constant eruption. I could do nothing till the two of them agreed on a plan. I suspected that both sides were waiting for the other one to blink, when they would nip in and steal the whole franchise.

Rudloff refused to see me in London as it was 'too noisy' in the office, so he told me to come and have lunch with him one Friday in 1988 when he was in Geneva. Over lunch he oozed affability and laid out an ambitious plan for domination of the European brokerage business. 'But of course,' he said, 'I can do nothing. I just follow orders. Until zesefuckingamericans can agree on a plan we can do nothing.' I didn't have the courage to say that it was difficult for zesefuckingamericans to agree on anything as Rudloff always cancelled his meetings with them.

It was never dull. At the end of that year, CSFB and First Boston merged under the umbrella of Crédit Suisse. The Swiss, in their logical way, as the major shareholders, had thought that a merger was the best way to bring about harmony in the group as a whole. Under the merger CSFB and First Boston kept their respective spheres of influence, but the idea was that as partners of the same firm we would be one big happy family. As part of this agreement, Luis and Rudloff's joint responsibility for the International Equity Group was dissolved. Rudloff got responsibility for dealing in European shares worldwide and Luis for American shares worldwide, including in Europe.

I had the option of going with either, but one of the first rules of Wall Street firms is that you must have a 'rabbi'. Without a rabbi, in Wall Street terms, you're dogmeat. A rabbi is someone who looks after you and makes sure you get paid at the end of the year. Luis was my rabbi, so I threw in my lot with him and became Head of American Equities in Europe – I forget the exact title. But the fun had gone out of the business. I had enjoyed my time at First Boston. It had been like rowing in a good crew: hard work, frustrating at times, but exhilarating in a lunatic way. In my new job I wasn't working so hard; it was less frustrating now that I just had one boss, but the exhilaration wasn't there either. And I had stopped learning. I felt I could do the job in my sleep. When you stop learning, the arteries start to harden very fast. It's the lack of discovery that ages people in the financial world, not the pressure.

In January 1989 I telephoned Luis and told him I was resigning. It wasn't fun any more.

'Listen, asshole. You're not resigning, OK? I take care of it, don't worry. I give you a bigger job. I get back to you, OK? Don't do nothing. I gotta square it with some people first.'

'OK, Luis.'

Luis took care of me; he was my rabbi. He called back a few days later and told me I had been promoted. I was no longer Head of American Equities in Europe, I was now something like Supreme Global Commander of American Equities. That wasn't the exact title but I know that 'Global' was in there somewhere. They liked 'Global' at First Boston; 'International' was considered sneaky and Rudloffian. 'Global' had a good ring to it and seemed to include the Pacific in a way 'International' didn't.

Luis had plucked this job out of thin air to keep me happy, but hadn't actually thought of what I could do. By then he had his own problems. The upgradings were so frequent that visitors were no longer taken to see First Boston's great trading floor in New York. A year earlier it had been like a battle scene, people screaming and shouting, screens flashing, traders standing on desks and the smell of war. Now there were empty desks and a low murmur. The salesmen were on the phone to headhunters and girlfriends as the clients didn't have much business to hand out. They would quickly hang up and dial a 'player', as clients were called, if Luis walked by, in case he overheard them and they got upgraded.

Luis told me my first task in my new job was to come up with a Long-Term Global Strategy for Equities. I went off on the world tour but my heart wasn't in it. I liked talking to clients, doing trades and, most of all, hiring young people and watching them develop till they did those things better than me. That was fun. Writing business plans and going to long meetings weren't.

At the end of April I telephoned Luis again.

'Whaddya want, chief?'

'Luis, I'm really not enjoying it. This time I am going to resign.'

'OK, chief. If you're really sure that's what you wanna do. I talk to Hennessy, see what I can do for you.'

Jack Hennessy had succeeded Pete Buchanan as head of First Boston. I had signed a partnership agreement at the time of the merger with CSFB, and unravelling that was complicated. Luis was a good rabbi. He spoke to Hennessy and the way out was made easy. First Boston, despite their war wounds, was fundamentally a decent firm.

Luis called back. 'OK, chief. I taken care of it. They gonna do everything I asked them. You can go, but we're trusting you not to go and work for the competition. You're not gonna work for those fockers at Solly, are you?' 'Solly' was Salomon Brothers, the school bully of Wall Street.

'No, don't worry, Luis.'

'Hey, chief.'

'What's that, Luis?'

'I'm gonna miss you like hell.'

'Me too.'

'OK. So what are you gonna do?'

'Take the summer off. Walk across France.'

'You know something. You're crazy. Good luck, chief.'

Modern tradition has it that as soon as your resignation is accepted or you are fired in the City or on Wall Street you are given a black garbage-bag to empty your desk into, stripped of your corporate credit card and the keys to your company car and escorted off the premises by a uniformed security man. Maybe I was lucky, but I escaped that. My resignation was accepted at the beginning of May and I stayed on till the end of the month putting the finishing touches to the Long-Term Global Strategy for Equities. I said that there was no point in drawing in your horns when times were bad, and that this was exactly the time we should be going out and hiring as the opposition would all be cutting back. Consequently my report suggested that Luis's department should expand its international presence.

The people who were now doing well at First Boston were the ones who were good at firing people, the 'professional managers', as they liked to call themselves. I expect my report was put in the shredder, although no one was rude enough to tell me that. Luis was disappointed by it, as he had hoped that it would recommend the transfer of business from our Geneva and Zurich offices to London. The Swiss offices were run by Max Schneeberger, an amiable and easy-going veteran, who was regarded by Luis as being a crony of Rudloff's. Luis was hoping that my report would give him an excuse to cut back Max's fiefdom in favour of London, thus taking business out of Rudloff's sphere of influence. I knew I was meant to recommend this but I didn't. Max's only crime was his friendship with Rudloff and he was doing well in difficult circumstances in Switzerland. But I heard later that

New York's view was that 'Miles has gone soft on Max. They must have got to him.'

I liked Max. When I had gone to see him he had taken me home for dinner and a tour of his personal computer set-up in the bomb shelter under his house. He knew that with Rudloff's protection he was safe from Luis in Switzerland. I admired the way he treated the bureaucrats in New York. They would send us directives asking for positive assurance that we were complying with Federal anti-discrimination laws or enquiring when we were going to attend the seminar at New York University on 'AIDS in the Workplace'. 'Ach, my dear Miles,' Max said, as we sat drinking brandy in the bomb shelter, 'there is only one way to deal with these people in New York. I tell them to fuck themselves.'

I must have spent my last week after handing in the report packing up my office and saying goodbyes. I don't remember any of it. I know I packed up my office because I have the boxes, still unpacked. There are only two of them, not much after twenty-two years, but I didn't see the point in taking a lot of things I didn't expect to use again. All I had were a few souvenirs and a boxful of baseball caps with company names on them. American companies liked to hand out baseball caps to everyone involved in a deal.

And I must have gone around both First Boston and CSFB – still resolutely apart despite the merger – saying goodbye, although I don't remember that either. I had managed to keep out of the civil wars and, as far as I knew, had made no enemies at either firm but had got to know a lot of people I had great respect for and was very fond of. I still am.

CHAPTER 5

'When are we going to tell the girls?' Guislaine had asked me. Our two daughters, Tasha, then fifteen, and Georgia, twelve, were at a boarding school near Ascot. They knew that I was thinking of giving up my job but I had asked them not to tell anyone. Several of the people I saw in the City had daughters at the same school and I didn't want word leaking back before I had told Luis.

As soon as I had told him I was resigning, Guislaine had called the girls at school to let them know that there was no longer any secret about it. 'You can tell anyone now,' she said to Tasha.

'Oh don't worry, Mummy. I don't think anyone would be interested.'

Both girls showed polite interest in my resignation but seemed to regard it as a passing phase. My fads and enthusiasms were a family joke and this was just another example of something I would soon get bored with and then everything would return to normal. I thought I had been quite bold in giving up my job. Tasha and Georgia saw it as skipping work without a good excuse and not to be encouraged. It made their lives more complicated. It was one thing, when someone asked what their father did, to say he was Something in the City. Having to say, 'Well, er, sort of nothing. He goes on walks,' didn't have the same ring.

Later, a week before we left for the Walk, I went to pick them up for half-term. I was wearing the new, synthetic-look, eyelets-and-laces Mephistos which I wanted to break in before we left. I was secretly proud of them and keen to show them off. I arrived at the school, still driving First Boston's Mercedes, and parked by the main door. There was a throng of girls waiting for their parents, Tasha and Georgia in the middle. I opened the car door and got out.

Tasha rushed up. 'Daddy, Daddy. Get back in the car. Those shoes. Someone might see them.'

I don't remember my last week at work but I vividly remember the first week of Not Working, not because I was thinking about the change in our lives that Not Working would bring but because I was so busy. I was much too busy to think about anything other than the immediate future. I had the feeling that the success or failure of the Walk might well depend on our being properly equipped. But with what? There was a week to departure day, 5 June, and I had bought nothing for the trip apart from Mephistos and backpack. I knew there were a host of essential things we would need on the trip. I didn't know what they were.

I had already been haunting bookshops, hoping to learn from the masters, great walkers of our time. *A Time of Gifts*, the story of the first part of Paddy Leigh Fermor's epic walk from the Hook of Holland to Constantinople, we had both read. He had been tougher and younger than we were now. I treasured the image of him striding off from the Hook along the polder, with his greatcoat flapping in the wind, as skaters swooped in and out of the mist on the frozen canal. We had lost our copy of the book but I seemed to remember he had taken few clothes with him and had lived off the land, relying on his charm to get things mended on the way by the adoring women who invited him into their schlosses. Wasn't he also often in a dinner-jacket? I don't think he had that in his rucksack either; it must have been borrowed off the brothers of the adoring women.

Most walking books are light-hearted until it comes to talking about equipment, when they adopt a Victorian tone and warn sternly against the awful things that happen to people who go on walks without compasses, or Gore-Tex outerwear, or moleskin trousers. Hypothermia is an obsession with people who write walking books. Sunburn would be more of a problem for us. The more I read, the worse it got. We would need a wheelbarrow in which to put all this equipment. Talking to people was no better. Everyone was an expert and no two agreed. You would think that there would be agreement as to whether it is better to walk in short or in long trousers. Frank Neyens swore by lederhosen. Patrick Hughes, our other walking guru, said that in shorts we'd get chafed legs, sunburn and scratches; anyhow, long trousers were cooler. This made sense. As a boy I lived in the Middle East and I remembered how the Baghdadis would wrap themselves up in jellabas in the terrible summer months and take off a layer or two when it got cooler.

The most sensible advice came from Peregrine Hodson's book, *Under a Sickle Moon*. Peregrine is a remarkable man whom I had met three years earlier when he was looking for a job. He is an oriental scholar who after leaving Oxford spent time in Japan; he speaks good Japanese. He went on to work in the financial world and then, between jobs, he disappeared into Afghanistan during the worst of the fighting against the Russians and lived with the guerrillas, the Mujaheddin. He covered a thousand miles, mainly on foot, was bombed and shot at and nearly drowned. The book is about his experiences in Afghanistan.

It is a masterpiece. I felt absurd when I was introduced to Peregrine and he asked about the possibility of working at First Boston. It seemed unthinkable to me that a man of such talent at writing should want to become an investment banker. Thinking now about it I realize that he wanted to make the same journey I was making, only in reverse. His motivation was probably as difficult to put into words as mine.

At the beginning of Peregrine's book is a list of what he took with him to Afghanistan. That was a good starting-point for us. Here is his list:

3 pairs of cotton socks	1 pair of plimsolls
3 pairs of woollen socks	1 pair of boots
3 pairs of pants	1 jumper*
3 shirts	1 handkerchief
needles and thread	Swiss army knife
assortment of pills	phial of iodine*
2 rolls of bandages	glucose tablets*
talcum powder	plasters
money belt*	water bottle
camera and lenses	micro tape recorder*
film	pens and pencils
Walkman*	notepads*
pocket Bible*	Farsi dictionary*
maps	comb
soap	toothbrush and toothpaste
spare bootlaces*	tapes (Bach, Vivaldi, The Doors, Bob Dylan)*

* I packed everything except for the items with an asterisk.

The Farsi dictionary, the jumper, the iodine and the money belt were needed for the Afghan highlands but would not be for south-west France in June. We thought about a Walkman and decided against it, partly on grounds of weight, but mainly because a Walkman cuts you off from your surroundings.

The Bible was a tempting thought. Neither of us is religious but we have reached the age when we are getting curious; I hadn't picked up a Bible for years, apart from dipping into the Book of Job when Guislaine and I split up on the 'there's always someone worse off than yourself' principle. And the Old Testament is a rattling good read. Another attraction was that it is easy to find good-quality pocket Bibles, whereas other pocket books – the Everyman Library and the small Oxford Classics – have disappeared from everywhere but second-hand bookshops.

We didn't take a Bible. Books are heavy and I decided to

restrict myself to one thick paperback. I took *Pendennis* by Thackeray. I had enjoyed *Vanity Fair* at school and thought that *Pendennis*'s nine hundred pages should last for a good part of the Walk. I knew Guislaine was taking *Moby Dick*. I had read this when we lived in America but looked forward to reading it again, provided that we both finished our books at the same time and could swap.

I added the following to Peregrine's list:

3 pairs of trousers	sun-block
1 pair of shorts	scissors
sun-vizor	blister treatment
sun-hat	pocket torch
2 (more) handkerchiefs	travelling clock
shaving brush	bandana
razor	swimming pants

Peregrine's list is trouser-free and would have you think that he joined the Mujaheddin naked from the waist down, unwise in a country where the peach-like quality of a boy's bottom is a popular subject for song. Particularly inadvisable for Peregrine: *peri*, he says, means 'fairy' in Afghan. He wisely called himself Abdul. It may be that 'pants' on his list is used in the American sense to mean trousers. The photographs in the book show him on the march wearing pyjama bottoms, which are a sensible and popular form of clothing throughout the Middle East. I took three pairs of trousers, two for walking and one for changing into, and a pair of shorts just in case. I also made some substitutions. I took American moccasins instead of plimsolls; these were light and comfortable and were for *après*-walk. I took three polo shirts, and only one ordinary shirt, a short-sleeved non-iron affair I bought specially for the trip, to wear in the evening.

The night before leaving we had a dress rehearsal with the backpacks. Neither of us had ever used one before. Buying them had been a complicated business. A secretary at First

Boston, who had spent a couple of summers Eurailpassing round Europe and knew about backpacks, sent us to the YHA shop between Covent Garden Market and the Strand. YHA stands for Youth Hostels Association. The shop is almost as good as Stanfords for browsing. I hadn't realized how complicated camping and walking were. There are three warehouse-like rooms of tents, sleeping bags, groundsheets, boots, sneakers, ice-axes, crampons, fluffy anoraks, moleskin trousers (of course), mattresses, blankets made of cooking foil, ropes, primus stoves, first-aid boxes, compasses, whistles, balaclavas, thick socks, do-it-yourself splints and snake-bite kits. I was glad we weren't going to be camping out.

Half a room was devoted to backpacks. I was amazed to see how many varieties of backpack there were. Guislaine and I spent an hour trying them on, not knowing what we were looking for. Many of them were expensive. We asked the helpful but overly knowledgeable assistant what the difference was between a German backpack at £110 and an English one that seemed to offer the same combination of pockets and flaps at one-third the price. 'Ah, quality. It's made out of glxpzsplin fibre.' We asked how long the 'low-quality' English one, which had the YHA's own name on it, would last. 'Oh, years and years.' That was good enough for us. We bought a matching pair in blue.

Size was another problem. Backpacks come in litres, which meant nothing to us. Patrick Hughes had given Guislaine some good advice. Don't get a big one. You'll only fill it. Ours were medium-size, either thirty-five or forty litres; I'm not sure which. Guislaine swears they were forty. They were about two feet high when loaded and had two side-pockets for water bottle, knife, camera and salami and an easy-to-get-at top pocket for maps, book and blister stuff.

We crammed as much as we could in at the dress rehearsal the night before leaving and found that only half would fit. We then discarded luxuries like towels, extra shirts, mirrors and things we could buy *en route* such as sunburn cream. Finally they were packed. We put them on. There were straps over either shoulder and a wide belt that went round the waist. We weren't sure how tight or loose to make the straps, but we would have time enough to experiment on the road. The weight of the pack felt strangely comforting. We looked at ourselves in the mirror. We were walkers now.

CHAPTER 6

We didn't know what to make of 5 June, our day of departure. We were excited but nervous. Our plane was scheduled to leave Gatwick in the early afternoon, giving us a long morning to get ready and to worry. Leaving at dawn would have been easier. We fussed about details, all of which we had already taken care of. Who was going to feed Kimbers the cat? Should we leave the answerphone on? Had the telephone bill been paid? Was it too late for me to buy a rain-jacket? It wouldn't fit in my pack but I could always tie it on the outside as Guislaine had done.

The one thing we didn't talk about was the Walk. The night before, we had each asked what the other's biggest unspoken worry was. Guislaine's was that I would want to push on too far every day. She remembered our motoring trips. Months later she confessed that her real worry, which she hadn't told me, was that I would want to take short cuts – hitch a lift, jump on the bus. I was amazed. My worry was that she would tire and tell me to go on by myself and she'd catch up later. Neither of us voiced the thought that the whole undertaking was crazy. I could remember the pain of my Aldermaston blisters, and that had been after only three days; I also remembered the only serious walk we had taken in the last few years. We had gone with Tasha and Georgia to Majorca at New Year for a remarriage honeymoon in Deya. There are serious mountains in Majorca and we had taken a walk up one of them. It had been hard work, especially for Guislaine; she had faltered a couple of times, but gritted her teeth and made it to the top. That had been just half a day's walk, though admittedly a tough one, and it had almost been too much for us.

Filling the backpacks, getting dressed and having breakfast took much less time than we had allowed. By nine o'clock, we found ourselves at the kitchen table having our third cup of coffee, breakfast finished, and wondering how to fill the time. We leafed through the papers and talked about theatre reviews. The doorbell rang. It was Ian Gordon, our best man seventeen years earlier, dropping in to say goodbye on his way to work.

'What's this?' he said, gesturing towards our packs.

'Our packs.'

'I can see that. Where's the rest of it?'

'The rest of what?'

'Your luggage.'

'That's it.'

'That's it? I take more than that out to lunch with me.' He prodded the packs and shook his head. 'I couldn't do it.'

'What, the Walk?'

'No, that's no problem. Anyone could do a walk. It's the packing. I've never managed to go anywhere with less than four suitcases. Oh well. I suppose you know what you're doing. Give us a call tomorrow. I'd like to hear about the blisters. Good luck. *Bonne chance*. Bye.'

'That reminds me,' I said as the door closed. 'I'm not sure we've got enough Second Skin.'

'But you bought some yesterday,' said Guislaine.

'Well, you never know. Just in case. We probably won't be able to get it in France.'

The Second Skin meant a trip to Kensington High Street and another forty-five minutes gone. Then it wouldn't be long till midday and time to leave for Victoria. Once we were under way I felt sure the worries would go. It was like the morning of the Boat Race. You read the papers, went for a walk, told jokes, talked about the Easter holidays, about anything but rowing against Cambridge. And with every five minutes of inactivity your stomach drew another notch. tighter. Then the bus came to take you to Putney; the worrying stopped and the momentum took over, each action leading seamlessly on to the next without the need for thought in between. The important thing was to keep doing something – getting changed, putting the boat in the water, it didn't matter what as long as you didn't have to think about the impossibility of the task ahead of you.

Noon. Time to catch the taxi to Victoria. Our plane was at half-past two. Bob, the house-painter, by now almost a member of the family, took a photograph of Guislaine and me, rucksacks at the ready, on the front steps. I hailed a taxi on the corner of the square and jumped in, carrying my pack like a suitcase. I held the door open for Guislaine. She, braver than I, had strapped her pack on. She manoeuvred her way in with difficulty and I shut the door. Before she could sit down we were off with a jerk and she was tumbled to the floor. She knelt there, pack on back, like a camel. We both laughed. The driver did too. He had been laughing ever since he let the clutch in.

When we reached Gatwick I wasn't sure what to do with my pack. Were you meant to wear it indoors? Walking round the terminal with it in position didn't feel right. But then nor did carrying it like a suitcase. Tasha has a little red knapsack. She slings it nonchalantly over one shoulder when she goes off down the King's Road with her friends in the holidays. I tried that with my pack. It kept slipping off and ending in the crook of my arm. I didn't want to look amateurish. Like all men, I hate being found out doing something for the first time; I want to be the old pro.

I was also hoping that someone would ask us where we were going with our packs. 'Going hitch-hiking are you?'

'No. Walking across France, actually. Sea to sea.'

But no one asked.

When I had been getting the Second Skin at Rock and Snow in Kensington High Street, I had told the assistant where I was going.

'Across France, eh? Interesting,' he had said. 'I did the

Himalayas last year. Wouldn't mind doing an easy one like you, though. Lots of plonk, eh?'

The packs felt heavy, whatever position we carried them in. They hadn't seemed too bad when we weighed them at home on the bathroom scales – about twenty pounds each. I gave up on finding a comfortable way to carry mine and got a luggage trolley. 'Don't worry, darling. I expect they'll feel lighter when we get used to them,' I said without conviction.

We were booked on a flight to Toulouse where we expected to arrive with a couple of hours in which to get to the station for the 6.40 p.m. train to Narbonne. Dan Air announced that the plane would be slightly delayed; this turned into over an hour. We would have twenty minutes at most to get from the airport to the station. But the trance had taken over by now. We were on our way, and if we missed the train maybe there would be a later one, or we could hitch. Somehow we would reach Gruissan that night. A month earlier I would have been buttonholing the stewardess, demanding train timetables and rental cars. Now it didn't seem important.

We were sure we had no hope of catching the train when our taxi pulled out of Toulouse Airport and into the rush-hour traffic.

'When is your train?' the driver asked.

'6.40, the train to Narbonne.'

He laughed. '*Merde*. 6.40. No hope. That train is always on time.'

By now we were jammed at a junction where five roads met.

'Where are you going with those packs? You are hitch-hikers, *hein*?'

At last someone had asked. '*Non*. We don't hitch-hike. Tonight, if we catch the train, we go to Gruissan-Plage, on the sea near Narbonne. Tomorrow we start to walk and in a month we will be at the Atlantic.'

'*Insh'Allah*,' murmured Guislaine.

'*Mon Dieu*. I too am a walker. Don't worry. I'll try to

get you to the station in time for your train.' He mounted the pavement, jumped a red light and skidded off down a side-road. 'I walk in the Pyrenees,' he said, gesturing to the south. *'Avec mes amis.* We go for three days, we walk, we have good times and we leave our wives in Toulouse.' He glanced at Guislaine in the mirror and bellowed with laughter.

We careered through Toulouse backstreets. The town was dry and dusty. The water in the Canal du Midi had almost dried up. We asked about the weather.

'Ah, this year it is hot. It hasn't rained for weeks. And once the weather gets like this it doesn't change. Madame will get a good tan.'

He cut through a stream of traffic on the inside, rounded one last bend and we were at the station. It was 6.33. I gave the driver a big tip.

'Ah, that's not necessary. Good luck. *Courage.* See you in a month.'

We scuttled into the station, packs on backs, taking the bends crab-style. Moving with a pack was new for both of us. The weight gives you extra momentum when you come to a corner and you find yourself in a Tom-and-Jerry scrabble to get round. It's the same feeling as driving on ice. There was a queue for tickets; Guislaine took one line, I took the other. 6.35. At last – 'Two for Narbonne.' Another wait while the ticket clerk checked which platform we needed and we were off again. Scuttle, scuttle, corner, grab the railing, down stairs, adjust the pack, corner, up stairs and there was the train. By now we were starting to get the hang of this and we clambered aboard with surprising ease. We slipped off the packs once we had found seats and I slotted them up in the racks with a practised air. Nothing could stop us now.

I took out *Pendennis* but was too excited to start it. I fumbled around in my pack and found 'Toulouse–Albi' and 'Béziers–Perpignan' instead. The maps were all named after two of the bigger towns at either side of the territory covered. This made each map sound like a dynasty. We would be

44

starting on the Mediterranean with 'Béziers–Perpignan', going through Cathar country with 'Toulouse–Albi', trudging on – if we got that far – across the Gers using 'Tarbes–Auch' and finally making our way over the great plain of the Landes and, please God, to the Atlantic, with 'Bayonne–Mont de Marsan'.

I spread the first two out on the table. The railway was a thin black line snaking along the Canal du Midi. Our train stopped at Castelnaudary, roughly half-way to Narbonne. I checked on the map. 'We should be here in a week or so,' I said. 'From here on, this train journey'll be through country we're going to walk through.'

Soon we were in Carcassonne, another intended landmark on the route. 'Half an hour to Narbonne,' I told Guislaine, who was gazing out of the window at the plain of the Aude, all gold and green in the evening sun. 'And three days to walk back.' I was busily trying to match the map on the table to what was whoosh-whooshing past the window, but we were going too fast.

We slowed but didn't stop at a village. 'Look, look. Maybe we'll stay there.' Guislaine pointed at a hotel with geraniums on the window-ledge and a vine-covered trellis, but the name of the village and the hotel passed in a blur and ten minutes later we were pulling into Narbonne.

Now it was just a taxi ride to Gruissan-Plage. I scrabbled through my maps in the back of the car to see if the driver was going anywhere close to tomorrow's walk, but he took the main road out of Narbonne towards la Clape, the six-hundred-foot-high chunk of limestone that squats between Narbonne and the sea, and then skirted its base to Gruissan. That wasn't our route for tomorrow. We were avoiding main roads and hoped to drift through the marshes on a country lane.

Gruissan is a pretty little fishing village coiled round Barbarossa's Tower, an old pirate stronghold. Nowadays it is almost two kilometres inland and Gruissan-Plage has sprung up on the sand-bar between it and the sea. We had booked ourselves into the Hôtel la Plage, which we had found in the Michelin. We liked the thought of spending our first night in a hotel on the beach listening to the waves of the Mediterranean. It was not to be. La Plage was not on *la plage* but three blocks away from the sea with neither sight nor sound of it. Gruissan-Plage itself seemed to be closed. It was a grubby little town of two-storey concrete buildings laid out in a grid of identical blocks set at an angle to the beach. It was getting dark when we arrived, and our hotel was the only place showing a light. All the other buildings were boarded up or closed.

I knew a little about this coastline. We had visited it briefly almost twenty years earlier when they were starting to build these concrete towns. It was difficult to believe, but Narbonne, now ten miles inland, had once been on the sea. It had been the Romans' favourite city in France. But about six hundred years ago the Aude, which at that time flowed through Narbonne and on to the sea near Gruissan, changed its course to the north and the old delta turned into a marsh. The mosquito came to breed in the stagnant pools and the meadows became swamp. Malaria took the villages. Soon only wild flowers and marsh birds flourished where the Romans had had their villas. It became a Mosquito Coast where no one went for pleasure.

Then, in the sixties, the beach-mad French found they had used up all the available land on the Côte d'Azur. They looked west. Here was a virgin beach the size of Brittany. Who cared about a few mosquitoes; you can't see a mosquito in a brochure. The Côte Vermeille was born. The plans they used for these new resorts might have been borrowed from the moon cities that the French were throwing up at that time in the Alps – Tignes, les Menuires, Avoriaz. Their seaside cousins were similar but didn't have the snow to soften the edges and hide the bits that no one had bothered to finish.

Gruissan-Plage might look better in high season with some bunting and neon signs and busy shops and restaurants. We had forgotten how short the season is in France. Six weeks of bedlam from *le quatorze juillet* and then up go the shutters for the rest of the year. We had been worrying that we might find places fully booked in early June; our new worry was, were they going to be open? Our hotel didn't have a restaurant. We asked Madame where we could go and she gestured vaguely up the road towards the only other light we'd seen. That was a restaurant, but by the time we got there it was nine o'clock and they were closed.

What the hell. We'd walk to Gruissan village. It was only a couple of kilometres and at least that was a proper village, not a six-week wonder. It never entered our heads to get a taxi or a bus. We were walkers now. The village was very different to Gruissan-Plage, a real Mediterranean fishing village, sitting under its tower at the end of a canal to the sea. It was quiet but we found a bar that was open and happy to serve us some food. I have no idea what we ate but we had a wonderful time. We drank a couple of bottles of La Clape, the wine from the hill we had driven round earlier that evening. It was cold and fresh; the sea and the limestone the vines grew on gave it a nice bite.

It was a night of stars as we walked happily back after dinner. When we reached Gruissan-Plage we decided on a midnight reconnoitre. We picked our way over the rocks to the beach. It looked flat and brown, even at night. We could hear a ripple at the water's edge. No wind, everything was still and quiet. We sat on the beach looking up at the great starry darkness.

'I'm glad we're doing the Walk this way round,' I said. 'I wouldn't have wanted to end our walk in Gruissan-Plage. Think what an anticlimax that would be. I want to hear the crash of surf when we arrive.'

'Shhh.'

We fumbled over the rocks and on to the road. Not a dog was moving as we walked through the boarded-up streets. When we reached the hotel Madame was waiting. She opened the door a crack and hissed instructions at us. I couldn't follow as my French wasn't good enough, but Guislaine nodded conspiratorially and the door was opened for an instant to allow us in.

'What was all that about?' I asked.

'Mosquitoes. I wasn't really listening.'

It was too late. We had left the window of our room open, hoping to cool it down while we were out at dinner. The room was no cooler but the mosquitoes had arrived in force. Word must have gone round that the first tourists were here. We closed the window and got ready for bed before counter-attacking. We stood on chairs, we stood on the bed, we jumped and pounced, Guislaine armed with the *Spectator*, I with *The Economist*, until finally the room was mosquito-free. We must have killed forty. We slipped into bed and turned out the light.

I was just starting to dream, something about an empty yellow beach with the Atlantic surf crashing down on it, when I heard a thin whine. It couldn't be. It stopped. Then it started again. The hell with it. What did real travellers do I wondered, in the jungle?

By four in the morning, I knew. Real travellers let them bite away.

'Are you awake?' I whispered.

'Mmm.'

'I wish it were morning.'

'Mmm.'

CHAPTER 7

I must have slept. The room was cooler and there was no mosquito but it was still a relief to see Madame at 7.45. She cruised into the room carrying a tray in one hand. With the other she swept our carefully arranged belongings – maps, first-aid kit, books and Guislaine's hair-drier – on to the floor to make room for the coffee and burnt baguette.

'*Voilà, pour les Anglais!*'

She looked at our scattered things on the floor and added that it was necessary to protect the carpet.

We dressed excitedly. This was it. The real thing. Jerry was over the Channel. Scramble . . . Scramble . . .

No more rehearsals. Better get it right. One pair of socks or two? One. Long trousers or short? Long. White T-shirt. Mephistos. We were quick and efficient and talked quietly as we gulped our coffee and packed.

I had brought a black dustbin-liner for packing. First I put alarm clock, torch and some socks into the moccasins. Those went at the bottom of the pack. Then I carefully folded shirts, trousers and pants and slipped them into the dustbin-liner which I wrapped tightly around the clothes to make a parcel. I eased this into the pack on top of the moccasins and then stuffed the remaining things – sponge-bag, sun-hat, odds and ends – into the corners. The pack felt full but closed easily enough. I saved the top compartment for maps and books so I could take them out without unpacking. The water bottle, filled for the first time, went in a side-pocket, as did map 'thermometer', camera, sunglasses and sun-block cream. I had a white sun-vizor with the First Boston badge on it – a blue clipper ship in a blue globe – a memento of our corporate tent

49

at Wimbledon; this I tied to the back of the pack ready for use. Guislaine's style was different. She had lots of little polythene bags. She segregated her things in small, categorized sausages and pushed them in individually.

Thirty minutes after Madame's knock on the door we were ready.

Leaving was easy. Pay the bill and walk out. It was a strange feeling not having to pack the car or wait for a taxi. Just walk. Where you like. When you like.

We followed last night's steps over the rocks and on to the beach. It was flat, the sand almost mud, a dull brown. A breakwater of jumbled boulders guarded the entrance of the canal and a wooden lifeguards' hut sat on stilts half a mile away; otherwise the beach was empty and without feature. This wasn't a place for heroic gestures but we had at least to get our feet wet. I gave Guislaine the camera, inched into the water and gently dipped my Mephistos in a ripple at the sea's edge. I couldn't think of anything to say, so first I looked east out over the sea and then turned, struck a pose, pointed westward and grinned. We swapped positions. Guislaine did better; she sang a sturdy verse of the 'Marseillaise'. Emotional moments bring out the French in her.

We both threw coins into the Mediterranean and kept a silence while we wished for good things.

'OK. That's enough sentimental rubbish,' I said – my response to emotional moments – 'let's go. The next time I get my feet wet it had better be in the Atlantic.'

Climbing on to the road with loaded packs was awkward. We had hardly noticed the rocks last night. We scrambled down, gave each other a complicated hug and started walking. This was easy. The packs, so heavy before, sat comfortably on our backs and our tread was smooth and light as we followed our shadows west along the road to Gruissan village. Its surface was already shimmering in the heat although it wasn't yet nine o'clock. There were no people, no traffic, just a solitary trawler chugging home up the canal with the distinctive 'boog-boog-boog' noise that wakes you up at five o'clock in fishing villages all over the Mediterranean. Tiny white butterflies flitted over the scrub by the road's edge.

'This beats the morning meeting,' I said.

Nine o'clock, eight in London. The meeting would just have started. There would be a brief review of what had happened the night before from the late man who had stayed till ten to catch the New York close; then Nigel Pilkington and Sambo Lewis, the two people now running the office, would give the salespeople and traders their priorities for the day. 'Prioritizing' is a favourite Wall Street word. Top priority was humping deals; this meant selling new issues – far more profitable for the broker than normal buying and selling on the stock exchange.

There weren't many new issues around any longer, but I still felt a surge of adrenalin thinking back to the times when we'd had two or three big ones going at the same time. Everyone was on the phone, pushing, pushing and then, suddenly, one salesman would throw down his phone and leap to his feet with a cry, 'Hey, OKAY, I got a big one. Where's the book? I can use half a million. Whooo-ee!' I used to encourage the chest-beating. It built momentum and put pressure on the other salesmen to get orders. The one who had just succeeded would march round the office slapping palms with the other salesmen, who'd say, 'Hey, who's better than you? Half a million. Size. You're Size.' Being called Size was the ultimate compliment.

Every day the state of the deal would be reviewed in the morning meeting and the salesmen would be questioned as to why their big players weren't in yet. God help you if we heard through the grapevine that one of them had given his order to a competitor who was a co-manager of the deal.

'I hear that Mercury gave Solly an order for a million.'

'They did?' the salesman would splutter. 'They couldn't have. I spoke to them three times yesterday and they said they wouldn't be deciding till they'd had their meeting this afternoon. And they promised I'd get the order if they came in.'

'Oh yeah?'

If the morning meeting was managed right, the salesmen would run out of it, charged with a mixture of fear, greed and excitement, to be first to start Shouting Down a Phone.

'Do you miss it?' Guislaine asked.

'What do you think?'

Gruissan was now behind us and we were following a little by-road through the marshes. The only noise was the burble of a pigeon and the faraway hum of a vineyard tractor. Our road ran between two hills. A mile or more to the right was our old friend the Montagne de la Clape whose wine we had drunk last night, and on our left stood the little Crête de Penelle. That too was thick with vines. Most of the wine from the area round Narbonne is dull, which is why these wines with their sea-salt and limestone tang are prized.

The road to Narbonne was a surprise. It looked boring on the map, but the map knew nothing of the scent of salt marshes and vines and wild flowers. Soon, as June wore on, the wild flowers would fade, but now they were everywhere, white and yellow and blue, thick by the roadside and scattered in thick clumps through the marshes.

'What do you think those ones are?' I asked, pointing. 'Do you recognize any of them? I can do the daisies and the buttercups and the thistles but I get stumped after that.'

'No. I wish we'd brought a book to tell us. Maybe we can find a little pocket one in Narbonne.'

'Look at the poppies. Poppies everywhere.'

Guislaine smiled. 'Matou's poppies,' she said.

Matou is her name for me. It means 'tom-cat' in French, or so she says. I've noticed that French people always give me a funny look when they hear Guislaine call me Matou and then they giggle. 'It's not really like "tom-cat" in English,' she says. 'It's different. More like "pussycat". I can't translate it.

52

There's something rather warm and cuddly about it.' 'OK, OK, I believe you,' I reply before she comes up with anything worse. By now I've forgotten it has any meaning at all. I like being Matou. Let them giggle.

Poppies are my flower. I thought of the weekend before we left, when we'd gone up to our little house on the marshes in Norfolk. There had been poppies there, but poor lonely things in their ones and twos where the farmers had forgotten to put herbicide. Here it was different. Whole fields were gashed red, acre on acre of poppy.

We stopped for a rest. We had been going for an hour and a half. This, we decided, would be a good length for each leg of the Walk. Stopping every hour would be too frequent and would break the rhythm, while two hours in this heat would strain us. We couldn't decide whether to stop for five or for ten minutes, so we compromised. I had heard that armies on the march take a five-minute break every hour. We would take seven minutes every hour and a half. That seemed like a good rhythm. We eased our packs on to the ground and sat on a boulder by the side of the road. The first swig at the water bottles. The water still had a delicious coolness. I fumbled in a side-pocket for the 'thermometer' and ran it over our route to see how far we'd come. We had covered just over six kilometres in just under ninety minutes. I had been curious to know what our speed would be. It worked out at around four and a half kilometres an hour or three miles an hour. Not bad for the first day, particularly as we had made frequent stops for photographs and flower identification.

'How are you doing?' I asked Guislaine.

'OK,' she said, summoning up a smile. 'OK. Bit stiff, that's all. Shall we go on? I'm ready.'

As the hills fell behind, the twin towers of Narbonne Cathedral peeked up over the vines like an owl in the rafters. There is a special magic in the sight of a distant cathedral over flat fields. Like poppies, they make the heart sing. Most cathedrals are now hidden by buildings until you get close, but there are a few that have escaped and float distant above the fields like great ships of the plains. Ely is one; Chartres is another. And here Narbonne. We see them as their builders did.

We walked on in silence, the sun hot on our backs. Here was another reason that walking this way round, towards the Atlantic, was better. If we'd been aiming for the Mediterranean we would have had the sun in our faces all morning. As we found later, those afternoons that found us still on the road were made doubly hard by our having to face the sun.

I asked Guislaine if she had brought any books apart from *Moby Dick*. She had Michael Ondaatje's *In the Skin of the Lion* and Gerard Manley Hopkins's *Poems and Prose*, both in paperback. Hopkins was a recent discovery for her and she was enchanted by him. I knew him from school and have always liked him.

'Is "The Windhover" in there?' I asked.

'Not sure. I think so.'

I fished around in her pack while we went on walking and took the book out. There, on page thirty, was 'The Windhover'. All morning we had watched hawks, 'kingdom of daylight's dauphin', tower and strike over the marshes. My new life found an echo in the poem, 'My heart in hiding stirred for a bird'.

'I'm going to learn it by heart,' I said.

I had tried years ago to memorize it and failed. It's a difficult poem to learn because Hopkins's sprung rhythm, his invention, is no help to memory, unlike the regular beat of an iambic foot. But that is the joy of the poem and what gives it its extraordinary energy.

We had our second rest. It was midday and the heat took us by surprise. We hadn't expected it to be this hot. We clambered over a railway line and found some shelter at the edge of a vineyard. We were almost in the suburbs now. We had low expectations of Narbonne. Years earlier we had visited it on one of our breakneck motoring holidays. I don't remember even spending the night there. It was just a detour from the autoroute, all dust and traffic.

We trudged on from the vineyard. The suburbs were depressing. Roundabouts, billboards, empty lots, dust. The cathedral disappeared from view. We had telephoned the previous night and booked a room at La Résidence. This was another Michelin clipping from the photocopied hotel sheets. We had chosen it because it should have been easy to find, tucked in behind the cathedral; it was cheap and, said the Michelin, it had '*bel aménagement intérieur*'. I was following my nose, as the map wasn't much help when it came to towns. All we had to do was walk in the general direction of where we had last seen the cathedral.

'How much longer?' asked Guislaine. She was hot and looked as if she might be about to crumple.

I was fraying too. My feet hurt. The Mephistos, so comfortable in London, were agony now. There was a spot of fire on the ball of each foot. I tried to walk on the edges of my soles to alleviate the pain but it didn't work. 'Oh, just a kilometre or so,' I said as cheerfully as I could. I was guessing.

'This is dreadful.' I wasn't sure whether Guislaine was talking about the pain or about the suburbs of Narbonne.

Then we turned a corner; we were out of the suburbs and entering a network of twisty little mediaeval streets. We hadn't seen this when we drove through. The already narrow streets were made narrower by the overflow from the shops of fruit and flowers. Lunch was getting under way in the restaurants. There was a smell of grilling meat. Both of us perked up and quickened our stride. I caught a glimpse between buildings of the cathedral, only a few hundred yards away now. We ducked into a tunnel which turned out to be a covered bridge over the canal and emerged in a great square. Seen close up, the cathedral, on the other side of the square, was a strange building. It was taller than it was long. It had a huge façade topped by the twin towers that had been our guide and beacon all morning. The back half of the cathedral was missing. Whether it had fallen down or had never been built, I don't know. Our hotel was tucked away where the missing part should have been.

We checked in and stumbled up to our room on the first floor. Packs off. Fall on bed. We'd made it.

We giggled with pleasure and relief; we slipped off our shoes and felt the exquisite pleasure of waving our feet unshod in the air while we lay on the beds. I ran a bath. We sat on its edge and dabbled our swollen feet in the cool water and looked in admiration at the newly forming blisters.

We showered. Aaaaah.

We put on clean clothes. Mmmmmm.

We slid our feet gently into soft shoes. Oooooh.

And we limped out to lunch.

Narbonne was delightful. We crossed the big square and wandered down to the canal that cuts through the middle of the town. By it was a lawn and a dignified walk where the locals were strolling and gossiping under the plane trees. We sat at a table in the shade, ate salad and an omelette and drank a couple of bottles of rough red Corbières from the same hills we would be walking through tomorrow. We ached and we were stiff but we'd survived our first day and we felt good.

By the time we were half-way through the second bottle of wine I was feeling almost perky. Guislaine was jotting furiously in her notebook. I never know what she writes in there.

That's not quite true. I looked once in England. It was a record of her dreams, together with some comments about what a difficult man I was to live with. I was outraged. I was torn between wanting to defend myself – I wasn't really like that, it was so unfair – and not wanting to admit I'd been reading her notebook. In the end I told her I'd had a look. This made her so angry that I never did get a chance to explain that she'd got it all wrong. I gave her my word that I wouldn't do it again and I haven't. But I do get curious.

Whatever she was writing now, it wasn't dreams and I don't think it was about me. The dream-and-Matou book had been left in London. This was a new notebook specially for the Walk. She had abandoned the stiff-covered black books with red corners and spine that she buys at the French stationer in South Kensington in favour of a small, bendy book that she could keep readily to hand in the little zipper pouch she wore on her belt. As we walked she would take it out and write whenever a flower, or a bird, or the angle of a view caught her notice.

I stretched back in my chair, thirst finally slaked and feet luxuriating in the softness and lightness of moccasins; Guislaine began a second page of notes about the lady with fat thighs and a big bag of groceries who had plonked herself down on the bench opposite, and about the courtly old men in black suits who were completing their third turn up the walk, deep in grave discussions.

Guislaine had always wanted to write but didn't begin in earnest till we split up. She wrote short stories about her life, family, friends. Food has always been important for both of us, so meals and cooking played a big part in the stories. She is a passionate cook. Chatto and Windus, the first publisher to whom she showed the stories, were enthusiastic and said they would like to publish them as a book. One small thing: could they have recipes at the end of each chapter? When they received the final draft they said yes, that's very nice, but we'd like to cut out some of the stories and put in more recipes.

Guislaine fought. She didn't want to write a cookbook, but without more recipes and fewer stories Chatto weren't going to publish it. And, one more thing, they didn't like the title. Guislaine wanted to call it 'Cassoulet in June'. I had suggested – we were back on speaking terms then although we were still apart – 'Love among the Onions'. Chatto called it *The Food of Love*, perhaps hoping that people would think it was about aphrodisiacs. Another publisher brought out a book with the identical title the same month. Guislaine's book came out, was well reviewed and sold only modestly. We, naturally, blamed this on Chatto's marketing.

It deserved to sell better. Everyone who read it liked it. (Except my mother, who thought it 'too personal – you should save that sort of thing for the psychiatrist'.) Guislaine's writing draws the reader into the middle of what she is describing so that he can smell, feel and touch it. I didn't see the book until it was almost finished, as it was only then that we re-established diplomatic relations. She gave it to me with trepidation and I accepted it worrying that I was going to have to think of polite things to say, mindful of the teenage poetry she had shown me years earlier. I read the book with astonishment. Tears, partly of relief but more of admiration and joy, came into my eyes. She had, and has, a talent for pure and lyrical description that a writer can only envy.

A blue-black North African was executing a little dance in the middle of the walk. Guislaine gave him an appraising look and began to write energetically.

'Always scribble, scribble, scribble, eh?'

'Oh shut up.'

'You should be flattered. That's not mine. It's what was said to poor old Gibbon when he presented the last volume of *The Decline and Fall* at court.'

I had a project of overriding importance for the afternoon. Buy some new shoes. It was that or the train to Biarritz. I couldn't walk a second day in my present ones. I had discovered what was wrong when I took them off in the hotel. The soles were cleated. One thick rubber cleat was so placed that it bore directly on the ball of the foot and, each time I put my foot down, it concentrated the weight on a tiny area. I had a big, puffy blister on the ball of each foot.

Guislaine drifted slowly back to the hotel while I hobbled up and down the rue Jean-Jaurès, a busy little street behind the Archbishop's palace, where the shops were. I went from shoe shop to shoe shop. The French like hiking and they love buying sporting equipment almost as much as the Americans. There was a good choice of shoes and boots – until they asked my size. '*Ah, monsieur! Quarante-six! Non, non. Désolé.*' I shuffled on painfully to the next shop. At last I came to a scruffy little one that knew nothing of modern inventory policy. '*Quarante-six? Mais oui, pas de problème.*' A cheerful lady brought me out shoes that George Orwell might have worn to Wigan Pier. These, too, were Chaussures Mephisto but these had a smoothish sole with a tread on it. No cleats. I tried them on. It was like slipping my feet into eiderdowns. Heavy in the hand, they were blissfully light on the feet. This was too good to be true. But what if they were the same size as the shoes I already had? Those had not only mauled the ball of the foot; they had also been half a size too small for prolonged walking, although they had felt just right in the shop. As did these.

Back to the hotel. Back to the shop carrying the old shoe for comparison. The perfection of the new shoe was confirmed. *Quarante-six* vs. *quarante-cinq*. I floated out of the shop. Guislaine had joined me by now. She was looking jealous.

The old shoes were mailed back to London. I couldn't bring myself to throw them away – they might be good for gardening (not that we had a garden) – and I certainly wasn't going to carry them all the way to the Atlantic. We drifted lazily around Narbonne for a little longer, in and out of the funny cathedral and the quiet stone cloister next to it, and back to the hotel. We sat for a moment on the bed while we decided how to spend the rest of the afternoon. By the time we woke up it was 8.30; we were ravenous. We found a little Moroccan restaurant where we had a huge couscous and two bottles of cold Moroccan rosé.

There is a great peace at the start of a long journey. The end is so far away that all you see is the journey itself. You think of nothing else.

CHAPTER 8

I love sailing. Today was like waking up at sea, the first day out of sight of land. All the fluster of loading and leaving port was forgotten and there was nothing but a big sky and an empty ocean. We helped each other on with the packs. They felt as familiar as old saddles.

Today was going to start with a hill climb as soon as we were out of Narbonne. I had spent a long time the night before studying the maps. I had even bought two of the Série Bleue in the rue Jean-Jaurès, the 1:25,000 extra big-scale maps, in the hope that their additional detail would allow us to find a way out of Narbonne that dodged both the hill and the main road, the N113, that ran from Narbonne to Carcassonne. But I couldn't. We chose the hill.

The Institut Géographique National divides roads into three categories, red, yellow and white, according to size – red being the big trunk roads like the N113, white the tiny country by-roads and yellow somewhere in between. There are also a variety of broken and unbroken black lines denoting different types of track, from *laie forestière* to *sentier muletier*. (We walked on several of these but never met the mule.) Our strategy was simple. Avoid red roads at all costs, treat yellow with circumspection and seek out white. We liked the idea of the paths but wanted to wait and see how reliable the maps were before committing ourselves to one of those.

Guislaine was, for once, taking a keen interest in my maps, or at least in the new Série Bleue pair. As we left Narbonne behind and began climbing between fields of vines I mentioned that the Bleue was so detailed that it even named the individual fields, never thinking that this piece of map maniac's trivia would interest Guislaine.

'Really?' Out came the notebook. 'What's that one? The one with the stone wall?'

'Er, les Muscats.'

'And that?'

This was becoming a bore. 'Hang on. I can't look up the name of each damn field. I know. I'll find you some good ones for your notebook. What about these? Let's see. Le Bâtardel. La Femme Morte – poor lady. La Turque – I wonder how they got here. And that one with the big oak, les Potences. What does *potences* mean?'

'Gallows.'

The broom distracted her. It was getting too high and rocky for vines. Instead the fields and hedgerows were a mass of yellow broom. Broom is Guislaine's favourite plant; it reminds her of Spain.

'Oh look, look. Smell this one. Smell. They don't smell like this in England.'

I stopped to take a photograph. I can't resist photographing landscapes of flowers. We have cupboards at home full of five-by-threes of lavender in Provence, daisies at Kew, poppies in Normandy, poppies in Picardy and sunflowers in Spain. I needed the wide angle for this. My camera had been a last-minute find in London. It fitted into the palm of the hand and yet had interchangeable lenses. It was second-hand and rare. I dug around in my pack for the wide angle. I had wrapped it and the telephoto in a silk handkerchief and wedged them in a side-pocket of the pack. The pocket was open and they were gone. Disaster.

Then I realized what had happened. Walkers often suffer from chafing of the thighs, particularly ex-oarsmen with big thighs. Pat, Guislaine's yoga teacher, had given us a tip. To prevent chafing, rub Vaseline into your thighs. We had forgotten to do this when we set off that morning, until we reached the outskirts of Narbonne where we branched off from the N113. Here we had stopped by the roadside and I had taken the pot of Vaseline out of the side-pocket. Both of us had put a generous dollop on our fingers and massaged it into our thighs. I don't know what the passing motorists on the N113 must have thought seeing us bent over with our flies open and a hand inside our trousers rubbing vigorously. I must have forgotten to do up the pocket when I replaced the Vaseline.

'Shall we go back?' asked Guislaine.

'No. It must be over two kilometres. There and back would be an hour. More, maybe. I know. I could rent a car after we've checked in at Lézignan this afternoon and drive back.'

'That's cheating.' We had agreed to go on foot the whole way. No hitching.

'No it's not. Not really. We will have done our day's walk by then. I'll just be retracing our steps.'

'Well, even if it's not cheating, it's the wrong spirit.'

'You're right. Well, I hope someone enjoys them.'

We trudged on upwards. I was too dejected to take a photograph with the remaining lens, the normal one. Now we were faced with a new problem. The map quite clearly showed one uninterrupted black line finding its way between the peaks of two hills. According to the map this was a *chemin d'exploitation*, a quarry track. We couldn't go wrong. In real life, the single black line on the map turned into three identical paths, then four, and finally, everywhere, little paths criss-crossing the hillside. The maps were no use. The new Bleue I had bought for just such an eventuality had a single line dissolving into a mass of whirls and dots which I couldn't match with the hillside. It did tell us that we were lost between the peaks of la Grèce and le Pain de Sucre. I passed this on to Guislaine but she had stopped writing by now.

We had chosen a path at random that pointed in the right direction. It became steeper and steeper. I was walking behind Guislaine and sensed that she was struggling from the way she hesitated slightly each time before she picked a foot up for the next plod up the slope. We reached a saddle in the hills and stopped. Her breath was coming in big sobbing gulps. She was winded.

'Don't worry,' I said. 'Let's take a rest. It'll get easier from here.'

We sat on a lump of granite and sipped our water. Guislaine was beginning to get control of her breath. I left her sitting on the rock while I climbed up higher to reconnoitre. We had a choice. Either we could take the path leading west, our direction, which climbed further, in the hope that once we were over the brow of the hill it would be an easy descent to the Bizanet road, our immediate destination, or we could follow the path that curved round to the north, longer but downhill.

I returned to Guislaine. She had stopped panting but she was still looking very frail and small.

'Sorry,' she said. 'I'm OK now.'

'Don't be silly. There's nothing to be sorry about. It's the damn map. This should have been easy.'

'Which way?'

More climbing was out of the question and I didn't feel like taking a detour to the north. 'Down here.' I launched myself confidently down the hillside, where there was no path at all, just scrub.

'But there's no path. Are you sure you know where we're going? I don't like the look of this. Can I see on the map?'

'Don't worry. The map's a bit complicated. We've just got a bit of cross-country and then as soon as we're over that wall I think there'll be a path the other side.'

'Oh God.'

We stumbled down the hill. I gave Guislaine a hand over some of the rougher bits and we pulled and pushed each other and our packs over the wall at the bottom. At least we were in a vineyard. This was easier walking. I picked a path going west. After another forty minutes up and down we saw a road with traffic. I was hoping that, if my navigation was right, we

63

had cut across the elbow of two roads and saved ourselves an hour's walk.

I was wrong. We were back on the N113. I located us on the map. We were three kilometres from the outskirts of Narbonne; we had spent two hours going in a semicircle.

Walking on the N113 was bad. The ground trembled from the passing *poids lourds* and, as with so many French roads, there was hardly any verge to walk on. We were thankful it was only a kilometre to where we turned off. But even after turning off we had another uncomfortable hour on a busy yellow road. We were walking, as all the books on walking tell you to, facing the oncoming traffic. Each time a truck hurtled past we had to make an effort to stop ourselves jumping into the ditch. We were in single file, Guislaine ahead. I could see her stiffen and her hands shoot out like starfish each time a truck passed.

'The hell with this. Let's cross over. At least that way we won't have to look at whatever it is that kills us,' I said.

We waited for a gap in the traffic and scampered across. Now the trucks were coming from behind.

'Don't look round,' I said. 'If you do they'll know you've seen them and they'll expect you to get out of the way. Just keep walking and looking straight ahead. That way they'll have to move.'

It required some getting used to not to turn each time we heard the thunder approaching from behind, and at first there was a prickling feeling in the small of the back, but after a while we got used to it. It wasn't pleasant but it was better than facing the monsters.

At last we were in sight of our turning. Another hundred yards and we turned on to a little white road that meandered gently between the vineyards. The thunder became a growl and then there was silence. Birds and flowers.

My new Mephistos were a spectacular success. I had lanced and dressed my blisters the night before but had worried that as soon as I started walking again they would blow up. It didn't feel as if they had. We had been on the road for over three hot, hard hours and, apart from some footsoreness, I felt good.

'OK?' I asked Guislaine.

'I think so. I'll be all right.'

'Remember the old T.E. Lawrence thing when he put his hand in the flame and was asked what the trick was – not minding the pain.'

'Oh sure. I've tried thinking that. It doesn't work. It was OK for him. His trick was he *enjoyed* the pain.'

Our path ran on through the vineyards towards a little yellow farmhouse. There was a sign at the turn saying 'Labastide – Muscat – Dégustation – Vente Directe'. We'd had a muscat yesterday in Narbonne before our dinner. Here, and all over the South, they drink the sweet muscat, *vin doux*, as their aperitif. In England it has gained notice with the appearance of Muscat de Beaumes-de-Venise on fashionable wine lists. That comes from the Rhône valley and is considered flashy in this part of France. Here, many of the little villages make their own. It's made from several different grapes, but most notably the muscat itself, fat and scented as a harem queen. Sometimes a richer and less scented wine is made with *malvoisie*, the grape that the Greeks with their sweet tooth spread throughout the Mediterranean. It still survives in their old colonies. Crete, Sicily, Rhodes and the Dalmatian islands all have their Malvasias and Malvazijas. Even the butt of malmsey into which Richard III had the Duke of Clarence bundled was the same grape under a different name.

'You know, it's a funny thing about aperitifs,' I said as we passed the 'Muscat' sign.

'What?'

'In the North, in England, we drink dry aperitifs – sherry, gin, whatever – and sweet after-dinner drinks – port, Sauternes, 'stickies'. Down south, it's the other way round. Muscat or *porto* before the meal and then, after, eau-de-vie or marc as a *digestif*.'

We were interrupted by two old orangey dogs loping out

from the farmhouse to bark in a desultory, only-doing-my-duty way.

'Quick. Quick. Use the alarm,' Guislaine hissed. She is a cat person. She had consulted my mother's dog psychiatrist before we left, for advice on How to Ward off the Dogs of France. People who have written books about walking in France are obsessed with dogs; they advise large sticks. We didn't like the thought of carrying something extra and I worried that waving a stick at a dog would only enrage it. So we had the dog alarm which the canine shrink had sent us. It looked like an aerosol. When pressed it gave out a shriek of unimaginable loudness. This was agony to human ears, despite the frequency's being pitched so high that it was meant to leave humans unmoved while turning Rottweilers to jelly. We hadn't yet found out if it worked. We had tried it on Kimbers the cat before leaving: Guislaine and Georgia screamed and Kimbers sat there unmoved, looking fat and superior.

'Go on. Go on, for God's sake use it,' Guislaine said now.

A shutter opened in the farmhouse. Madame had heard the barking and was watching us through the kitchen window. I tried to imagine her reaction if I loosed off a noise like a lifeboat siren at her old dogs. What if it worked?

'Bonjour, madame.'

No answer. She was busy doing something below the level of the window-sill, while not taking her eyes off us. Loading the shotgun? We hurried on. The dogs trotted off and went back to sleep.

We had been on the road for nearly six hours by the time we reached Ornaisons. There were clouds in the sky but it was another murderously hot day.

'Please God, let there be a restaurant. I promise I'll never tell a lie again,' I said.

I had passed the hour since the shotgun lady thinking about lunch. The fantasy had a shady tree, a comfortable chair and a table with maybe grilled chicken, maybe an omelette on it, and wine and bottles of cold Evian. There was a sign to

66

the Restaurant Octaviana as we entered the village. It was closed. There had to be somewhere to eat. This was a biggish village. We hobbled on towards the village square and there was my fantasy come true, even down to the shady tree and comfortable chair. Inside the restaurant half a dozen people were stuffing themselves at a big table piled with food. We dumped our packs on a table outside and hurried in.

'Two Evians, no make that four Evians, a *citron pressé*, a beer and, let's see, grilled chicken, perhaps? And a salad?'

'*Non.*'

'*Non?*'

'*C'est pas possible. Vous ne pouvez pas manger.*'

What? Why not?

We were too late. There was no more food. Those people over there were family. *Désolé*. But we could have our drinks.

That was better than nothing. We took our drinks outside. I went off in search of somewhere to buy a sandwich or some ham while Guislaine sat at the table, too worn to care. The village shops were all closed for lunch. Everyone closes for lunch in the country in France; in Ornaisons even the restaurant did. I gave up. At least we had our drinks and it was only about six kilometres to Lézignan-Corbières, our destination for the night.

Guislaine had perked up when I returned. She had been looking so forlorn that the son of the owner had taken pity on her and had agreed to scrounge some bread and pâté for us and maybe a bit of cheese.

In the square was a travelling circus. There was the big top, a blue-striped tent which could hold forty villagers if they squeezed, a roaring-lion poster advertising that night's show, a red and yellow trailer with two layers of cages on it, two caravans for the circus folk, and a dancing bear on a chain. The bear was muzzled and tied to a tree; he paced up and down jerking at the chain. In the cages were a Chinese pig, two chimpanzees, a lemur, a baboon and two or three striped and spotted creatures half-way between a cat and a leopard in size. A group of village children stood, holding their bikes, in front of the cages but they weren't interested in the animals. They were grouped round the circus strong man, all tattoos and biceps, who was promising amazing feats at tonight's performance.

After lunch we went in search of a place to lie down. We found the school playground. It was empty. 'INTERDIT AUX PLUS QU' ONZE ANS' said the sign. There was grass and a shady tree. We lay under the tree with our packs for pillows and watched the puffs of white cloud through the leaves.

'You know, if we do this walk again it won't have the same magic,' I said.

Guislaine grunted.

An hour later we rose slowly and stiffly to our feet like two ancient clubmen levering themselves up from their leather armchairs. There was two hours' walk ahead of us. We marched slowly back through the square, past the circus and out into the country again. There was no shade; the road itself was radiating heat, its surface soft as warm putty in the sun. The route straggled through vines and poppies and wild garlic. Less than half a mile away the Autoroute des Deux Mers ran parallel to our track for a mile or so. The wind was from the north and blew the noise away. We watched car on car, truck on truck silently flick by.

'Where are they going?' said Guislaine. 'What's the hurry?'

I thought of myself a week earlier on the M11 to Norfolk, windows closed and speedometer at 110 miles an hour.

We walked deeper into the afternoon. The heat got worse and Lézignan was still four kilometres away. I was hot, but comfortable enough and bouncing along thanks to my new Mephistos. Guislaine was hobbling. I tried making jokes to take her mind off the pain of walking but I could see that she was close to melt-down. She had on a fixed, brave smile. That was a bad sign.

'Let me take your pack,' I said.

'Oh no. I'm fine. Anyway, you can't carry them both.'

'Why not? Let's give it a try.'

'OK. Just to the end of this hill. Thanks.'

She undid the belt-catch and I slipped it off her back. How do you attach two packs? I tried one hitched over each shoulder. No, that didn't work. I would have to wear it across my chest. I strapped it on so that I now had packs fore and aft. It was surprisingly comfortable. I reminded myself that the forty pounds I was now carrying would be considered light by an infantryman on the march. Guislaine seemed six inches taller and was bounding along the road.

It wasn't far to Lézignan now. We had telephoned the night before from Narbonne to book. We were relying on an entry in the out-of-date Fontana/Hachette guide as no one else mentioned anywhere in Lézignan. They gave the Hôtel Tassigny and accompanied the entry with a sign that looked like a pouting pigeon; I had no idea what that meant but assumed that, like Michelin's rocking chair, it denoted '*hôtel tranquille*'. I thought of lawns, trees and maybe even a stream.

'Could be Cleveland, Ohio,' I said as we walked past an abandoned ironworks and the municipal dump. There were no road signs and a nightmarish pattern of intersecting truck routes. We were tired. Guislaine had taken her pack back by now and both of us longed to be through this tangle of noise and smell. Our hotel was, said the guide-book, in the place de Lattre de Tassigny; that had a leafy, quiet sound to it. Fatigue overwhelmed us and we decided to take one more rest before going on. We stopped where we were and sat down in the dirt by the edge of one particularly noisy and hellish roundabout while I pulled out the map to find a way into town. I looked up to see if there were any road signs. Opposite was a grimy building.

'Oh no. I don't believe it. It can't be,' I groaned.

'What? What?'

'Over there, that building. Look at the sign. Tass-i-gny.'

'Jeepers. We can't stay there. There must be somewhere else.'

I pulled out the hotel sheet. 'Well, there is the Grand Soleil. It's from the same guide. 32, avenue Foch. It can't be worse than this. Come on, let's give it a try.'

We picked ourselves out of the dust and stumbled on. We tried a few stiff-upper-lip jokes but they didn't work so we walked on in silence. A tunnel under the road, a street of peeling buildings, a market – mainly Algerians selling to Algerians. We asked. Grand Soleil? Down there, second on the left. Nearly there.

We found it. The building looked dishevelled and the front door was locked. We went in through the bar at the side. The room stank of beer; there were two drunks propped up on their elbows at the bar.

'Do you have a room?' Guislaine asked the barman.

One drunk nudged the other and whispered something.

'Follow me,' said the barman.

The stairs were uncarpeted and smelled of sick. He opened the door to a room.

'Une double.'

Our eyes travelled from unmade bed to bare floorboards, to a broken cupboard, to the middle of the room where there was a bidet on wheels, attached to the basin by a hosepipe. We shook our heads. He showed us another room. This had two unmade beds and a bidet in the corner tucked under the basin.

'How long do you want it for?' he asked.

The usual answer was probably forty minutes. 'Er, no thanks. We've changed our minds.'

'I can make you a special price.'

'No. No thanks. Just remembered something.'

We fled. Back to what Guislaine had christened Thunder Junction, and the Tassigny. All was forgiven.

Our room was at the back and away from the road. It was quiet. There were three beds, one for me, one for you and one for the luggage. There was even a bath. I filled it to the top and lay in it with just my nose above the surface while Guislaine took up what she called the 'dead-beetle position' on her bed. This involved lying on her back, knees clasped to her chest and feet in the air.

Later we had dinner. A loaf of pâté left on the table for us to help ourselves, a huge, bloody steak — we had to have red meat — *frites*, salad, cheese and two puddings, ice-cream and *tarte aux poires*.

Back in our room I played around with my maps. I was still annoyed at how we had gone astray in the hills by Narbonne. I took out the 'thermometer' and ran its roller over the route we had covered.

'How far do you think we've been today?' I asked Guislaine, who was looking sorrowfully at the toes on her right foot.

'How much did we do yesterday?'

'That was eighteen kilometres, Gruissan to Narbonne.'

'Well, today was longer. Twenty-three? Twenty-four?'

'Twenty-nine.'

'Jeepers.'

CHAPTER 9

'Attack the hill.'

'Huh?'

'Attack the hill. It's something I learnt when I used to row. We'd have to go back early before the Lent term started, for Boat Race training. We'd stay at Henley for a week at the beginning of January and twice a day we'd have to run up Henley Hill. The idea was to start getting fit after the Christmas holidays. It was awful. We'd all run up together and you didn't want to be last. Most of the time you wanted to throw up. Ronnie, the coach, always used to say, "Attack the hill." It works.'

We had started the day with another hill climb. At least this time it was on a proper road. Guislaine had been in bad shape when we got up that morning. If yesterday had been our first day out of sight of land, today we felt as if we'd been through a hurricane – frayed and bruised but afloat, just. I had been worried that the crew might mutiny when I saw it sitting on the edge of its bed examining its toes.

'How do they feel?' I asked.

'I don't know yet. Wait till I walk on them. Did you sleep?'

'Not much. I had restless knees.'

'Me neither.' Guislaine walked gingerly over to the mirror. 'Good God.'

'What?'

'Look at my eyes. They're dreadful. And my face. It's all puffy. Oh this is awful. My hips hurt. Oh Matou, I don't feel good.'

I didn't say anything about a climb until after breakfast.

72

Two cups of coffee and a croissant later, Guislaine was ready for the road and looking determined. 'Today should be shorter,' I said. 'Around twenty kilometres. That's only a couple more than we did the first day. Oh, by the way, we've got a bit of a climb to start with.'

'Oh goody,' said Guislaine, with heavy sarcasm. 'As long as you don't get lost like yesterday. And please, no more climbing over ditches.'

'OK, OK. It wasn't exactly my fault. How was I to know the damn map was wrong? You wouldn't get that with the Ordnance Survey. Typical Frogs.'

I told Guislaine the 'Attack the hill' story just as we started our climb. It worked. She went up ahead of me, head down and accelerating. I couldn't swear to it but I thought I heard her growl.

The Walk was difficult for her and I admired her courage. It was much easier for me, thanks to rowing. Most importantly I had had a chance to learn that pain isn't necessarily bad. In fact, if it hurts that's good because it means you are pushing yourself hard and that's the point of any competitive sport. We had talked about this at dinner the previous night in between mouthfuls of steak and *frites*. Guislaine had been amazed. It was a new concept for her and she kept returning to it. 'I've never thought of it that way,' she had said. 'I've never done any sport. For me, pain has always been a signal to stop doing whatever you're doing. I've never thought that it could be something to be pushed aside and overcome. I'll have to think about that.'

Our first hour-and-a-half leg had elapsed before we got to the top of the hill, but we decided not to take a rest till we reached the summit. The road twisted more and more sharply as it neared the top and with each bend a new view would open up. Then we were over the brow of the hill and the plain of the Aude lay before us. We slipped off our packs and sat on a mound. A slight breeze blew up from the valley and into our faces. We drank from our bottles; the water was still cool.

Two hours had passed since we had set off and we decided to award ourselves a ten-minute rest, three minutes longer than the regulation seven. Our stiffness had gone; Guislaine was smiling and looking healthy.

'Thank you,' she said, 'for what you told me last night. About pain. That it doesn't necessarily mean stop. You don't know what a revolutionary thought that is for me. And it's a big help. I was thinking of it on the hill. Pain is the Beast and you've got to shoulder past it.'

'Mmm.'

'So where are we going now?'

'Oh it's easy now. Along to Montbrun, the little village over there, and after that it's all downhill to the plain.'

Behind us the hillside was yellow broom and goat pasture, dotted with scrub oaks. The air was hazy, but three miles to the south it was possible to make out the grey ridge of the Montagne d'Alaric. There are many places in the Languedoc named after him. This was Alaric II, the great Visigoth king whose kingdom stretched from the Loire to Gibraltar. Narbonne was his capital and his favourite city. Clovis, King of the Franks, envied Alaric's peaceful and prosperous kingdom and found a pretext – religious, as usual – for war. Alaric was killed and his army destroyed in a savage battle in AD 507 outside Poitiers, only a few miles from where, eight hundred years later, the Black Prince would rout the chivalry of France and take prisoner John the Good, their unfortunate king.

The barbarians loved this part of the world. Many of them passed through here, not just the Visigoths. The Suevi on their way to Galicia, the Alans to Portugal and the Vandals to southern Spain, where they left their name, (V)Andalusia. The barbarians are unkindly dealt with by history because it was the other side, the Romans and the Greeks, who wrote it, but the more I learn of them the more I like them. It came as a surprise to me to find out that the barbarians who sacked Rome had adopted Christianity well before the Roman aristocracy. The popular vision of Rome safeguarding

74

the chalice of civilization and Christianity from the barbarian hordes is rubbish. It was the other way round. A decadent and pagan Rome was invaded by clean-living Christians from the North. In fact, Alaric II's ancestor Alaric I was the first barbarian to conquer Rome. The only defeat he ever suffered at the hands of the Romans was when they took advantage of Easter Day, a day of peace and prayer for the Visigoths, to attack him. Despite this dubious victory they then panicked and, among other desperate measures, recalled the Twentieth Legion from Britain to help defend Rome. That was the end of Britannia's days under the Pax Romana.

Of course, not all the barbarians were clean-living God-fearing folk. No one has ever called Attila Christian. But then he was a Hun.

Our route was rich with a history of which an English education had told me little. I had read up about Alaric II in a bookshop in Narbonne. I resolved that when we returned to England after the Walk I would find out more about the barbarians.

Another educational black hole concerned the Albigensian heresy, the creed of the Cathars. We were in Cathar country; the ruins of their castles were everywhere. The green Michelin guide, consulted in the same bookshop, said that the Cathars were crushed by Simon de Montfort. When Béziers, a Cathar stronghold, was being put to the sword, de Montfort's lieutenant asked him how they would know who was a Cathar. 'Kill them all,' said Simon, 'God will know his own.' They did. Not a baby escaped. Could this be the same Simon de Montfort I had learnt about at prep school, who, I vaguely remembered, was the leader of the barons and the 'Father of Parliament'? No. I looked that up later, in a bookshop in Carcassonne. It was his father.

Cathars never came to England and the name has only the vaguest of associations for me, but Guislaine says that, in her family, they still lower their voices when the word is mentioned. She had a great-grandfather from round here.

Whether he was for them or against them she isn't sure, but she has been delving into her family history and means to find out. A book about the Cathars still sits by her bedside at home waiting to be read.

Our time was up. The ten-minute rest had stretched a minute or two longer but we felt we had earned it. We skipped down towards Montbrun. A car passed us going up the hill. The driver took both hands off the wheel and clapped. We were pleased. Our first applause. Motorists weren't that bad after all.

Montbrun was soon behind us and, to our relief, the road levelled out. The jolt, jolt of going downhill had been uncomfortable and jarring, but now we were on the flat we could swing out. Unless we wanted to walk alongside the autoroute we had to cross the Aude. This we meant to do at St Couat, but we had a roundabout route to get there.

I peered at the map and pulled out the new Série Bleue purchase, brother of the one that had left us in the lurch the day before. 'You know, there's a path that cuts through those fields up ahead. If we take it we'll save a couple of kilometres.'

'Oh no. Not after yesterday. Let's take a bit longer and stick to the road.'

'No, really. This one will be all right. Look, it's quite clear here on the map. We can't go far wrong and it's not as if there are any hills or anything. Even if it is wrong, all we have to do is follow our noses. Have a look. There's just this one path and then it joins up with a proper road, the white one. See?'

'Oh Matou, I really don't want to. I'm getting tired and I can't face any more climbing over walls.'

'Don't worry. It'll be all right. Trust me.'

An hour and a half later we were stumbling along a dried-up watercourse, our legs scratched and bleeding from the brambles. There were plenty of paths through the vineyards; most of them were dead ends and none of them was on the map.

We came to a wide ditch, brambles at the side and mud at the bottom.

'I'm sorry. I can't get across there. I can't. We'll have to go back.' Guislaine was close to tears.

'Give me your pack. And then we'll get you across.' I ferried the packs to the other side and then gave her a hand. 'Bloody IGN,' I muttered.

Guislaine wasn't interested in my excuses. The tears were running down her cheeks. We tramped on through the vines. At last through the sweat I saw the church spire of St Couat d'Aude. It bobbed up and down over the vines and never seemed to get any closer. Our road went every way but towards the village. It was 11.30. We prayed that there was an *épicerie* in St Couat where we could buy a picnic lunch. The village didn't look big enough to have a restaurant. Whatever there was, it would close at noon. We had just under half an hour.

I took Guislaine's pack and strapped it across my chest as I had done yesterday. That atoned a little for having dragged her over the ditches and through the brambles. I tripped on a vine-root. With the pack in front of me I couldn't see where I was walking.

'Oh my God. It's ten to. We might just make it if we hurry.'

We broke into a shambling jog. The packs bounced up and down, the straps bit into my shoulders, sweat trickled into my eyes and the first day's blisters were hurting. Guislaine looked heartbreakingly unhappy.

And then we were out of the vines and in the village. Three minutes to twelve. We asked about a shop and got some vague instructions. Oh please let it be open. Up the hill and left. There it was. We skidded in as the church clock began to strike. It was air-conditioned; our skins tingled with pleasure.

'Whew, that was lucky. Just made it. Quick, let's get something before they close.'

'No hurry,' said the lady behind the counter. She smiled at us; we must have been quite a sight. 'We don't close

77

till 12.30. And some days we don't close at all. Take your time.'

We went mad. It was self-service. We took a basket and filled it – baguette, two kinds of cheese, sardines, ham, peaches, big bottle of Evian, bottle of Corbières, salami, tomatoes and a bar of Cadbury's Fruit and Nut.

We hopped and hobbled out of the shop with our goodies. For once the map didn't let us down. It showed a track leading down to the Aude. We followed it through tall trees to a clearing on the bank of the river where we found a flat rock to sit on, took off our shoes and socks and dabbled our bare feet in the stream. I wedged the wine in some gravel at the water's edge to cool. We ate our picnic slowly and watched the fish swirl for pieces of baguette in the river. When I had finished eating I took off my trousers and waded up the stream while Guislaine lay stretched out on the rock. The water was cool and soothing against my legs. I bent down and splashed some on my face. I was tempted to swim but decided against it; this was good enough.

After lunch we came across a disused railway bridge that offered a short cut across the river. Our luck was turning. We found a hollow in the woods and lay down, put our heads on our packs and slept for nearly two hours.

It was still another eight kilometres to Marseillette, but after the picnic and the sleep even the afternoon heat was bearable. In a moment of over-confidence I took us on another short cut along one of the IGN's 'paths'. There is a memory of brambles and a disappearing towpath. Somehow it didn't matter.

The Muscadelle sat by the roadside a kilometre before Marseillette. It was one of the Logis de France network. Like all Logis it was family-owned and family-run. Mme Van Meenen was in the kitchen and Monsieur at the bar; they were from Belgium. Several of the places we stayed in on the trip were run by people from the North: we met innkeepers from Belgium, Holland and Alsace. The room Madame showed us had a tiny double bed in it, hardly more than three feet across. After three days' walking both of us wanted room to twitch and thrash in bed; we weren't sleeping well. We took two rooms, one each. At ninety francs a room it didn't seem extravagant.

Dinner was the best so far. The Van Meenens liked having English guests and made a fuss of us. I had a cassoulet – the first of the trip – although we were not quite in cassoulet country yet. It was crusty on top with rich duck *confit* underneath. Guislaine had an *andouillette*, a sausage that is too close to the farmyard for me. She also had some roast onions, which looked delicious. Madame saw me admiring them and a minute later I had four of my own.

Before dinner I had walked through the village, as we wouldn't be going through it tomorrow and I didn't want to miss anything. There was little to miss: one street, a pretty church and a Café des Sports. Beyond the village the road dipped down to the Canal du Midi. I followed the towpath back towards the Muscadelle. A big holiday barge was moored by the lock. On board was a party of Americans: three plaid jackets, two flowery frocks and a pair of Bermuda shorts sitting under a parasol on the after-deck. The English captain was serving them gin-and-tonics while the English cook was telling them what was for dinner.

'*Bonjour,*' cried a plaid jacket as I walked past.

'*Bonjour,*' I shouted back, delighted to be taken for a Frenchman.

CHAPTER 10

The Van Meenens had been so nice that we asked them to pose for a photograph before we left. They were shy. Madame took off her apron – just for a moment you understand, I'm very busy, it's breakfast – and stood in the middle; Guislaine, arm linked with Madame's, is wearing khaki trousers and a white T-shirt. She is already tanned. I don't know what she was thinking about; she has a broad grin and an air of scandalized amusement as if someone had just pinched her bottom. This was a new Guislaine. There hadn't been any laughing the morning before when we left Lézignan.

The photograph was taken behind the hotel in front of a little windmill so small that Guislaine would have had to stoop to get through its door. It had two windows the size of tea-trays, and geranium window-boxes. Over the door was a horseshoe.

Guislaine saluted this as we walked past the windmill, packs now in place, to start the day's journey. She likes to salute things. Magpies are her favourite. I was brought up in a family that didn't hold with any of that superstitious nonsense. Guislaine is the reverse. Nana, her grandmother, who lived in New York, did the Tarot cards and cast horoscopes. She was French and had moved to New York after the War together with Papa, as Guislaine's grandfather was always known, who had business there. The marriage foundered: Nana came down with arsenic poisoning. Stories swirl around the family to this day. She survived the arsenic but had to spend a year in bed. During this time she taught herself astrology, her own brush with death having sharpened her interest in the world beyond. She was a grandmotherly figure when I came to know her, with twinkling eyes and apple cheeks. By then she had recovered completely and was positively spry. Her skill with the cards and her horoscopes became well known in New York. She lived in a little apartment near the United Nations, and sometimes when we went to visit her we would meet a diplomat from Belgium or maybe the Côte d'Ivoire who was just leaving after a consultation.

Guislaine was a favourite of hers and learnt much of Nana's lore. When we were about to be married, Nana did my horoscope. I think her affection for Guislaine caused her to doctor it in my favour, as it said nothing but good things about me and my future. I was going to be an important diplomat. Nana wasn't able to resist adding as a footnote, *'C'est dommage qu'il est anglais.'* Guislaine never did the cards seriously, although when we had people to dinner in America they would often ask for a reading afterwards. She stopped doing this when her forecast of a neighbour's husband trouble turned into a painful divorce.

We never saluted magpies in my family. Guislaine only does it when there is an odd number; if they are in pairs you can safely ignore them.

We slid down the path that led from the windmill to the Canal du Midi. For the next few days we would be coasting along it to the other side of Castelnaudary where we would bear left and start the crossing of the Fan. We passed the holiday barge I had seen the night before. The parasol was now folded and there was no sign of the Americans. I told Guislaine of meeting them and we agreed that they didn't know what they were missing.

'Lazy buggers, still in bed,' I said.

This was unfair. Further on we passed the three men, now in tracksuits, doing a stately jog along the towpath. The flowery-frocked ladies we met later; they were balanced, also now in tracksuits, on folding bicycles with tiny wheels. We *bonjoured* them all enthusiastically and gave an extra *'Allez, allez'* to the ladies on wheels. Bermuda shorts must have been still in bed.

We came to a bridge and stopped while I looked at the map. We could clearly see paths running along both banks; the map didn't give either of them. This being a canal, common sense said that there had to be a towpath on at least one side but there was unlikely to be a path on both sides. One of the two we could see would peter out and if we chose the wrong one we would be marooned in the brambles for the third day running.

After the Walk was over I was so annoyed at the trouble the IGN had caused us that I wrote to them asking why they left so much vital information off their maps. I got back a charming letter from the Directeur Commercial, M. Grelot. He extended his warm *félicitations* on our *'belle entreprise'* and then went in for three pages of explanation which showed why the French have no rivals when it comes to the Civil Service. I had specifically mentioned this bit of towpath's non-appearance on the map and asked why they hadn't put it in. It was, said M. Grelot, *'sans fonction'* and therefore not worthy of an appearance on the map.

'Left or right?' I asked Guislaine. 'You choose.'

'Hmm. Let's take the left. I like the way the trees lean back from the river that side.'

I should have asked her the way more often. The left was flat, hard towpath all the way to Castelnaudary. After a mile the far side disappeared in a thick tangle of underbrush. The canal was easy walking but we never warmed to it. It had a dead quality. The water was dark green and still, under a high arch of plane trees so thick that the sun hardly penetrated. Either side of the canal was dense undergrowth giving only an occasional window to the countryside beyond. It was pretty enough in its way but the dominant impression was one of melancholy. Taking a barge holiday must be disappointing. The French canals cut through the world's most beautiful countryside and all you see from the barge is undergrowth and green water.

The impression of deadness was heightened by the absence of flowers. The grass grew thickly by the towpath and the hedgerow was strong and healthy, but never a flower, no fleck of colour to break the green. Nor were there any birds, not a coot nor a duck. The vineyards had been full of birdsong.

We did see a fox. A mile beyond Marseillette a big red dog fox stole out of the undergrowth thirty yards ahead of us and stood there as if to say this was his towpath. We stopped. He looked at us appraisingly for a few moments, sniffed the air, and slipped noiselessly into the brush. We were probably the only walkers he would see all day.

Walking along the canal was untaxing after the hide-and-seek of the last two days. If you don't mind the melancholy it's easy walking – no climbs, no forks in the road, no dead ends and you're shaded from the sun.

We would walk side by side unless we were on the verge of a busy road and had to go in single file to avoid the traffic. I had wondered before we started what we were going to talk about. Would we get bored? The scenery changes very slowly when you are on foot. Would the slowness of our pace irritate us? With all these unfilled hours ahead of us on the road the one subject we were bound to discuss at length was my career, or whatever it was now to be called.

We didn't. We were too interested in the Walk to talk about what would happen back in London. That was for later. We chatted for maybe half the time while we were on the road and the other half was a comfortable, easy silence. Sometimes, like yesterday, it was Alaric the Goth or the Cathars; later the Black Prince and Wellington popped up. They'd all done bits of the Walk and we came to know them well.

We talked a lot about food and drink. It was usually drink while we were walking – not alcohol, but how many bottles of Evian we were going to have when we arrived – and food once we'd stopped – cassoulet, steak, *confit, civet de lapin*, wouldn't some fish be nice for a change? And then there was Guislaine's craving, which became embarrassing, for blackcurrant sorbet.

We turned into obsessional hypochondriacs. Our bodies

were the machines to get us across France and deserved close attention and much discussion.

'Oh, my hips,' Guislaine would say, 'they're awful today.'

'My tendon. Oooh,' I would reply. 'I think it gave a sort of tweak.'

'The small of my back's agony. It's the pack. I can't seem to get the weight comfortable.'

'You know, I don't think I slept more than an hour last night. And just as I was finally dropping off some damn truck woke me up.'

When we reluctantly left the fascinating subject of our health we would usually talk about what we saw in the fields and the woods. Neither of us knows much about flowers and trees but we have the city-dweller's fascination with the countryside. Guislaine knows slightly more than I and would take shameless advantage of this.

'What a pretty tree,' I would say.

'Yes, isn't it? It's an acacia.'

I knew she was bluffing but as my tree recognition stops at horse chestnut I was at a disadvantage.

The very slowness of walking allows you to see the texture of things in a way that you would miss on a bicycle, let alone in a car. Those things we couldn't identify we soon gave names to. There was a 'fern tree' and a 'pipe-cleaner tree'.

We were often tired, irritated, thirsty, hot, lost and sore, but never bored.

At Trèbes we left the canal. It took a wide horseshoe loop into Carcassonne. We would save an hour by walking across the mouth of the horseshoe, and would rejoin the canal after Carcassonne. Our short cut started with half an hour on the N113. After the lifelessness of the canal, it was almost fun to be on a busy road. There was even a pavement some of the way. When that ended and the road narrowed it was less fun. We were the only pedestrians and there really wasn't room for us. We couldn't even walk in the ditch, as the road was in a cutting and had a wall on either side. We crept up the hill, pressed to the wall and terrified. A small road popped up on the right and we dived for safety.

'No more red roads,' said Guislaine. 'I don't care how much out of our way we have to go to avoid them.'

'No more red roads.'

We were back on a tiny country lane, noise and smell far away. Carcassonne was no more than four kilometres now, less than an hour's walk, but we couldn't yet see it. The road climbed slowly up a never-ending hill. We prayed for each bump to be the brow of the hill and a view of the famous skyline. We could sense the city getting closer. The country road was acquiring pylons and down-at-heel houses. At last, a dip in the road and a slight rise and there it was.

Guislaine collapsed. 'I need a rest. Let's take a stop. It's only a couple of kilometres or so and we've plenty of time. I've had it.'

She had chosen a rubbish tip by a gypsy encampment for our stop. 'OK. Let's take five minutes. What a good place.'

Carcassonne was another town, like Narbonne, that we had visited in a whirl of heat and dust the first time we went to France as a couple. We were just married then.

Our early life together had had its ups and downs. We met in New York in 1970 at a dinner party. Debby, our hostess, felt sorry for the young Englishman who had just arrived in New York and knew no one. She asked me to dinner and sat me next to Guislaine, who was then married to but separated from a well-known New York black sheep.

By the time the main course came round I was in love.

I asked her out to dinner the next night. She accepted in an absent-minded way. I think she was pleased that I pronounced her name right. She gets quite frosty when she is called 'Jillayne', as she often is in America. 'No, no. It's a hard *G*.'

I booked a table at Elaine's. I didn't particularly like it but it was starting to become fashionable and I wanted to make a good impression. I was looking forward to the two of us tucked away together at a little table in the corner. Guislaine had other ideas. She invited six of her friends to join us; we sat at a big circular table in the middle of the room and I wasn't even sitting next to her.

Elaine's has always been a noisy place. It's almost impossible to make yourself heard across the table over 'Who gets da veal?' from the waiters and the general singsong of New York at dinner.

When the espresso came I leant towards Guislaine and shouted through the empty bottles of Valpolicella, 'Marry me.'

Stephan, next to her, raised a weary eyebrow. 'Oh please. Not here. Would you mind doing this somewhere else?'

Guislaine smiled vaguely at me and shouted back, 'I can't hear you. What did you say?'

'Will you marry me?'

'I am married. Don't be ridiculous.'

Stephan pushed his chair back. 'Er, I think it's time we were all going. Hard day tomorrow,' he said, helping Guislaine up.

Stephan had a keen nose for a lady in trouble. He himself was involved with several. Before I knew what was happening we were all outside, there was a whirl of cheek-kissing, handshaking and cab doors slamming and I was alone on the sidewalk.

I walked slowly back to the studio apartment on Park and 86th that I had sublet for the summer from a Mrs Gold, away in Marbella till September. Despite its tiny size Mrs Gold had put in chandelier, emperor-size divan covered with green brocade bedspread and satin cushions, green flock wallpaper and two Venetian glass mirrors. I felt like Liberace.

The dinner at Elaine's had not been a good start. I needed advice. I met Stephan for a drink at Gino's on 61st Street.

'Stephan, what shall I do?'

'Ah, you English boys. Always in such a hurry. Relax. There

86

are plenty of women in New York. The trick is to let them come to you. Never fails. Here, have another martini. And, Miles . . .'

'Yes?' He was going to tell me the real trick. I leant forward.

'No more of this silly marriage talk. They don't like it.'

'Oh.'

'Listen. Enjoy New York. Come out to Southampton this weekend.'

I did. And met Guislaine again. The summer flicked past like a page in an album. In November I had to go to London. Either I hadn't listened to Stephan's advice or it hadn't worked. Whatever the reason, the romance had faded with the summer.

The next July I was going to New York on business. I telephoned Guislaine, to whom I hadn't spoken for six months, from London.

'Hi, it's me, Miles.'

'Oh. Goodness. Hello.'

'Look. I'm going to be in New York next week. It would be nice to see you. How about lunch?'

'Yes. Why not? That would be nice.'

'Good. I'll see you at Gino's. One o'clock on Tuesday.'

I sat at the bar waiting for her and nervously counting the zebras on the wallpaper. She arrived. I can't remember what she was wearing or what we said. I know it was all nonsense because 'lunchspeak' became a private word of ours from that day on. We had dinner together that night and lunch again the next day.

I had to return to London after that, but the following weekend I was back in New York to see her. I took a cheapie charter flight. Very cheap. On Donaldson International Airways, who had redeployed a propeller-driven Bristol Britannia from the Biafran airlift to the New York run for the summer. The flight over took eleven hours and the flight back, two days later, was delayed for five hours because 'the pilot wants to get some sleep before flying the plane back'.

The week after that, Guislaine came to London. She arrived the week before my brother Michael's wedding and stayed on for it. Guislaine and I shared a taxi with my mother to Michael's wedding at Chelsea Old Church. I hadn't told my mother what was going on but she knew something was in the air. I sat on the jump-seat while the two of them chattered on like old friends.

'Ma?'

'Yes, my son.'

'Guislaine and I are going to get married.'

'Oh I wouldn't. Why don't you just shack up for six months and see how it works.'

Which is what we did.

We had decided the night before to get married. 'What a wonderful week this has been,' I had said. 'You were right about all that marriage talk of mine in New York. Now that I'm not interested in it any longer things seem so relaxed between us.'

Silence. 'Miles?'

'Yes?'

'Ask me to marry you.'

'Oh, OK. If you insist.'

I was so excited the next day that I almost wrecked Michael's wedding. He had asked me to be his best man. When it came to speech time, I said at the end that it was a special day for me because not only was my brother getting married: I had got engaged. I was so wrapped up in Guislaine and me that it didn't occur to me for a moment that the last thing a woman wants on her wedding day is her guests all saying, 'Where's the girl?' and not meaning her. I don't think Chrissie has ever forgiven me; I didn't even realize till six months later what a *faux pas* I'd committed.

We couldn't get married yet as Guislaine's divorce from Bobby still hadn't come through, although they had been separated for six years. We had to take my mother's advice and shack up for six months. On 10 March 1972 we got married. It was touch and go with the divorce. That came through on 8 March. We had been wondering whether to go ahead with the ceremony and commit bigamy or cancel it if the divorce hadn't come through.

My mother, who has been married three times – 'One to have you, one to support you and one because I loved him' – took Guislaine aside beforehand: 'Good luck, darling. We've always said Miles's first marriage would be for practice but I'm sure it will be different with you.'

Meanwhile Tom, my stepfather, took me aside: 'I know she's only half French but you have to be very careful with these foreigners. You might think you can trust them but they're after your money. I'm not saying I don't think she's very nice but watch out.'

At the time the only thing I was watching out for was an overdraft, so I felt safe in ignoring Tom's warning.

When later my mother saw that the marriage wasn't just for practice, she and Guislaine became very close. She'd never had a daughter and enjoyed acquiring one so painlessly.

We took our honeymoon that March in a lovely house in Italy which Stephan's parents lent us. Later that summer I took a long weekend off work and we went to France. We flew to Marseille, rented a car and drove like escaped convicts in a great circle to Arles, Nîmes, Montpellier, Narbonne, Carcassonne, Cahors and back through the Gorges du Tarn. All this in four days – so it was not surprising that we remembered little of the places we'd been but traffic, heat and dust. Carcassonne was one of those places. We had stayed in a grand hotel a few miles from the town. I remembered the striking view of the ramparts from a distance and a vague impression of unfriendliness.

Twenty years later we were back. Our memories of Narbonne had been equally unpromising and it had given us a pleasant surprise. Carcassonne didn't.

We sat by the rubbish tip looking at the mediaeval city three kilometres away, with its massive walls and pointed Camelot towers. All it lacked were Lancelot and Guinevere. And they probably appeared at the *son et lumière*. It looked too good to be true.

It was. The old *cité* was rebuilt in the nineteenth century by Viollet-le-Duc, the man who 'improved' Notre-Dame. He insisted on getting things right. The old plans – if there had ever been any – had been lost; it had, after all, taken a thousand years to build the place. The Visigoths had built the first wall. Viollet-le-Duc worked out exactly what they would have, or should have, built and with Napoleon III's support set an army of labourers to work on the dreaming ruins. The restoration was perfect. Viollet-le-Duc had created the first Disneyland.

We checked into our hotel, half a mile from the East Gate (drawbridge, portcullis and all) of the *cité*. After a shower we went into the old *cité* to look for a bistro for lunch. For two hundred yards we pushed through Japanese and American tourists, past postcard stands and heraldic-shield shops. There were plenty of restaurants but they were the type that had menus written in Gothic script on 'parchment'.

We pushed our way back to the East Gate and caught a bus down the hill to the new town. Once we were checked in and had done our walking for the day we were allowed to catch buses for local transport: that wasn't cheating. The new town is as new as New College, Oxford, having been laid out in its present form after the Black Prince sacked it in 1355. He shared our view of Carcassonne. He arrived there half-way into his Grande Chevauchée of pillage and destruction across the Languedoc. He looted and burned the lower town although the tradespeople put up a stout defence. The rich folk and the nobility were safely holed up in the *cité*. The Black Prince had no hope of taking the *cité* without a siege much longer than he had patience for, but the burghers didn't know that. They were so scared that they sent an envoy out to offer the Black Prince 25,000 gold écus to go away and leave them in peace. 'I conquer towns. I don't barter them. Keep your money,' he said, clattering off with his army to sack Trèbes.

The inhabitants haven't got any nicer. We had a disgusting lunch in a brasserie and I spent over an hour afterwards trying to cash some American Express traveller's cheques. Banque Nationale de Paris said *désolé*, but they only cashed their own ones. Crédit Lyonnais held them up against the light as if they were Albanian banknotes and said try Crédit Mutuel. They gave a big smile; there was nothing they liked better than cashing American Express cheques, what a pity it was one minute past three and their 'Change' closed at three. Other branches of the same banks in other towns cheerfully cashed my cheques.

Our only success in Carcassonne was in the shoe shop. Guislaine had been watching me float along on my Mephistos with increasing jealousy. Her cries of 'No really, these are just fine' about her Noddy shoes bought eight years earlier in Charles General Store, Katonah, New York, were becoming fainter. She found a pair like mine. They didn't have any ladies' sizes; these were men's. She didn't want to get them: they would make her feet look too big. She tried them on and that broad smile of pleasure known only to Mephisto-wearers spread across her face. Noddy shoes went in a bag to be sent back to London.

We took a bus back to our hotel, La Vicomté. We had seen enough of Carcassonne and looked forward to spending the rest of the afternoon in our room. La Vicomté was a bland, Holiday Inn-style place. Normally we are rather snooty about staying in places like that but, four days into the Walk, we were thrilled. Our room had a television; the bathroom had a proper bath, full-size bath towels and a built-in hair-drier; there was a sliding glass window out on to the lawn. This was luxury. Guislaine spent the afternoon sitting on the bed admiring her shoes and dipping into Hopkins while I watched tennis on the television. It was the French Open.

We decided to eat in. We would dress for dinner. Guislaine had some pyjama-style trousers; these were baggy and, left to themselves, floated about. Guislaine would tie them in different places to achieve varying degrees of formality. I had some dark-blue lineny trousers that now came out for the first time; they had taken on a fashionable crinkly look after four days in the pack. I accompanied them with the short-sleeved, light-blue, non-iron shirt bought specially for the trip. This was made for someone narrower, and forced me to keep my shoulders hunched up.

We bathed, showered, washed our clothes, washed our hair, played with the dimmer switch and glided arm in arm down to dinner feeling terrific. The dining room was filled with a group of American tourists. We were shown into the partitioned-off ballroom where a few tables had been set up for people not part of the group. Only one other table was occupied, by four men. Three had leathery tans, bush shirts and South African accents, the fourth was French and in a business suit. They were just within earshot. I pretended hard not to listen – something about parachutes.

I leant over to Guislaine, scribbling in her notebook, and whispered, 'Arms dealers.'

'How do you know?'

'Listen to them. Toulouse is where they make all the stuff. They thought they'd come here for a meeting where no one would see them. By the way, I know what you're going to order.'

'What?'

'Duck.'

'No. Don't feel like it. I think I'll have something a bit lighter. Let's see the menu.'

She looked. It was a set menu. Starters were *foie de canard*

– duck's liver – or *salade de gésiers* – a salad of duck gizzards – and the three main courses were all made of duck.

'The duck sounds good,' said Guislaine.

'Mmm. Think I'll have it too.'

We asked the waiter if the chef had died. He ignored us at first, but as soon as the manager disappeared we received several chapters of hotel history: how the place was owned by a chain; there wasn't any proper management; the cooking was done by microwave; this was cassoulet, not duck, territory but it was what the tourists expected, what could he do?

Guislaine had two blackcurrant sorbets to compensate.

CHAPTER 11

Our ill feeling towards the hotel evaporated overnight. Dinner it was true had been revolting, but – in the words of Hoffnung's famous postcard – in bed they were terrific. The room was quiet, there was a breeze through the window and the mattress was just right. I had forgotten what it was like to wake up after a night's sleep. We sat on the bedside attending to our private preoccupations, Guislaine with her feet and I with my maps.

I finished drawing a green line to mark progress so far. It crossed the whole of 'Béziers–Perpignan'. I put the map down on the floor and opened it out to its full width to admire the length of the line. I traced out Gruissan-Plage to Carcassonne with the roller of the 'thermometer', carefully following the route. 'Heavens. Eighty-eight kilometres so far. How about that?'

Guislaine peered at the swelling between her left big toe and the one next to it. 'Uh-huh.'

'Well, today it's on to the second map, "Toulouse–Albi". What do you think of that? We've covered a whole map. Do you realize we've walked further than London to Oxford?'

'Really? Gosh . . . It hurts just here.' She pressed the ball of her foot with a finger.

I had a look at Guislaine's blisters. 'Mmm. Coming along nicely. They'll be ready to pop soon. They need another day or so to ripen.'

Guislaine shuddered. She stuck on corn plasters and pulled on socks and new Mephistos. 'Well, with any luck these will pinch me in a different place.'

We tried giving the hotel her Noddy shoes to post back to London. They had been wrapped in a brown-paper parcel and neatly addressed. We said we would pay in full for postage. Quite out of the question, said the manager. Why not, we asked.

'*Monsieur*. It is not our policy.'

This meant a detour through Carcassonne to the post office. We had hoped to skirt the town. Ah well. The shoes were duly posted and we walked on through the town. It looked better this morning; it was market day in the place Carnot, the big square with the fountain. Stands, stalls and vans stood shoulder to shoulder under their awnings. We find markets anywhere, but particularly in France, irresistible. We browse for hours between the mountain hams and the goat cheeses and the baby aubergines: 'Gosh, look at these pâtés', 'Why can't they have markets like this in England?', 'I'll just get a few slices of *saucisson*'. Not today. We'd had enough of Carcassonne. We gave the market a quick look and kept walking.

We started off well enough. We picked up the canal again and followed it for a kilometre or so out of Carcassonne. We would have followed it further, but once again the map said nothing about a towpath and we didn't want to guess which side it was on, so we took a road through the vineyards. It had once been the avenue to a grey stone château that we could see outlined in the trees ahead, the Château de Serres, said the map, happy to tell us things we didn't need to know. Our path made a semicircle round its garden and gave us a glimpse of cut lawns and pollarded trees. On through the vines. Soon it would be cereals. We were coming to the end of the wine country.

Our trip so far had taken us through the most prolific and, many would say, most undistinguished wine area of France. This is where the Common Market's 'wine lake' comes from. It all happened because of a fluke of politics. These vineyards were planted in the middle of the last century by refugees from the phylloxera beetle which had killed all the good vineyards to the north. The Languedoc was not only still beetle-free, it

95

was also an easy place to grow anything. You didn't have to worry about the climate. You could plant any old grape and turn out something red and not too alcoholic more easily here than anywhere else in France. The only problem was that it wasn't very good to drink.

At much the same time France was colonizing North Africa and the *pied-noir* was discovering that Algeria was a good place for making rough red wine. Whereas the wine from the Languedoc was thin, acidic and low in alcohol, the Algerian red was highly alcoholic – but like so many wines from hot places, it had as much character as a water-melon. It needed acid to give it balance. Laurel, meet Hardy. Before long the western Mediterranean was busy with tankers shipping Algerian red to the Languedoc, where it was mixed with the local wine to give a balanced wine of medium strength. This was sold under a brand name for a few francs at every food shop in France, the *vin ordinaire* of which a litre or two went down every French workman's throat every day.

France joined the Common Market. Algeria didn't. The wine-growers of Italy and Spain soon put a stop to the import of cheap Algerian wine. The Algerians, who being Muslims don't drink themselves, were left with whole *départements* of surplus vineyards hoping that their new friends in Russia and East Germany would acquire a taste for it. Meanwhile the Languedoc found itself with millions of gallons a year of near-vinegar. The wine-growers here were luckier than the Algerians, as the Common Market paid them to go on producing it regardless of whether anyone actually wanted to drink it. Hence the wine lake.

To its credit, the French Government is doing all it can to encourage the farmers to improve their wine by replacing the old vines with lower-yielding but higher-quality grapes. Fitou has already made a name for itself and it's not difficult to find drinkable Corbières and Minervois wines in an English off-licence. On the whole, though, we found them boring wines. It wasn't until we reached Madiran, two-thirds of the way across France, that we came across an interesting wine. For the most part we drank rosé on the Walk. Rosés don't need to be robust and full-bodied to be enjoyable, and the colder they are the better.

We ambled on and the last vineyard fell behind. Our little white road merged with a thundering red and we had to assume single file and try to ignore the traffic for a couple of kilometres.

'Do you mind if I get your Hopkins out?' I asked Guislaine. 'I might do a bit of learning to take my mind off the trucks.'

'Go ahead.'

I fished around in her pack and found the book. I had had a couple of sessions with 'The Windhover' but still hadn't mastered it. I remembered Tasha telling me that she had had to learn it at school as a punishment. Now I saw why. It wasn't easy. But the magic deepened with each repetition:

> . . . then off, off forth on swing,
> As a skate's heel sweeps smooth on a bow-bend:
> the hurl and gliding
> Rebuffed the big wind.

'Would you mind whispering?'

'Oh. Sorry. Didn't think you'd notice over the traffic.'

'Well I do. And it's very annoying to hear someone repeating the same lines over and over again.'

'Sorry. "Fall, gall themselves," ' I whispered, ' "and gash gold-vermilion." Isn't that a wonderful word, "gold-vermilion"?'

'Hmph.'

We took a detour. It added a kilometre but put us back on an empty white road, walking side by side. We crossed the river and stopped at a garage in the hamlet of Villesèquelande. An Alsatian leapt out of the garage scrap-yard and came at us, teeth bared and gurgling with rage. A chain pulled it up a yard short of my trousers. The owner wandered out and patted it.

97

'*Hein?*' – this to us.

'Do you have any food for sale?'

'*Non.*'

'Er, is there anywhere here we can buy some?'

'*Non.*'

Oh God. Half-past eleven and two kilometres to the next village, Ste Eulalie. Another jog with packs fore and aft. At least this time it was on a road and there were no vine-roots to trip on.

We never knew whether or not a village would have a shop or restaurant, but we were developing a system. We used to look up the population on the map. The IGN puts this in tiny letters next to the village name. Our system went like this:

Village population	*What to expect*
300+	One all-purpose shop
500+	Shop and café, occasional pharmacy
700+	2 shops, 2 restaurants, garage, pharmacy, *maison de la presse*
200	Forget it

It was the ones around the three-hundred mark that were the problem. Even when there was a shop, the owner was often out tending his vines. Ste Eulalie, bobbing up and down over the maize as we jogged towards it, was three hundred.

We puffed into the village square at five to twelve and were pointed to a shop down an alley. We knocked on the door; the shop was in the living room. It was dark as the shutters were closed but we nosed around and found ham, fruit, sardines and a bottle of wine.

'And bread, please.'

'Bread. *Mais non*. You get bread from the breadman.'

Of course. And where is the breadman?

Madame looked surprised that we didn't know. 'As usual. Midday in *la place*. You will hear his horn.'

We trotted back to *la place* with our purchases, happy for the rest. There was a particularly comfortable bench by the war memorial where we stretched out; it had the *mairie* behind it and in front, like a stage set, was a semicircle of houses. The arrival of the breadman, or Boris the Baguette as we had christened him, was apparently a high point in the day. Doors opened and housewives popped out wiping hands on aprons. Soon there were three, then five, and finally six.

Important gossip was taking place. Guislaine followed it all; my French wasn't that good but I could understand the gist. Being a housewife was no picnic. Worked all morning, got lunch ready, then the baker was late. Bah. Men were always late, particularly husbands. Husbands, bah. Never on time. Drank too much. And they were dirty too. My Michel doesn't wash his hands half the time when he comes in from the fields. Your Michel. What about my Jean-Paul? Talk about dirty.

An old fisherman wandered up from the river wheeling his bike. Smiles all round.

'*Bonjour Pierre*. Everything goes well?'

'Yes, thank you, *mesdames*. Can't complain.'

'And the fishing?'

'The fishing? *Ah non*. The trout are all asleep.'

It was now 12.20. I was getting restless. We couldn't wait all day for Boris. Today was a long walk, over twenty-five kilometres, and, pleasant though it was to sit on the bench and hear the gossip, we would have to move on. We agreed to give Boris another ten minutes. Half-past came. Even the women were giving up. Michel's wife had gone back to her stove after clouting her ten-year-old on the head for playing with a tennis ball.

We were just picking up our packs when – 'PAAAAARMP,

PAAAAAAAAARMP.' A car was racing up the road the other side of the church, with its horn on fire.

Guislaine and I looked at each other and said simultaneously, 'Boris.'

He stopped at the other end of the village while we waited. Mme Michel reappeared. More paaaaarmping and Boris was among us, skidding his little white van into the square in a spray of dirt and gravel.

He jumped from the van, strode to the back and threw open the doors. He was young and blond, wearing check trousers and a sleeveless vest.

'Mesdames, bonjour. Voilà.'

The baguettes were arrayed in layers, fat and thick at the bottom, long and thin at the top. The women stood round in a semicircle. He favoured Guislaine with a special smile. She returned it coyly and pointed at a long and thin. He handed it to her with a flourish while the others pushed forward to examine the display. I helped Guislaine into her pack and we hurried off to find a picnic spot.

'Fertility rites are one thing, but that takes the biscuit,' I said.

'Gosh, yes. I hadn't thought of that.' Out with the notebook.

We hoped to find a shady, bug-free place for a picnic. As we left the village we heard Boris and his horn, on his way to anoint the ladies of the next village.

After two kilometres Guislaine stopped. 'This looks OK. My feet are agony. Let's stop here.'

Something about the place said 'ants'. 'Could be buggy. Why don't we try a bit further?'

'You always say that. I'm stopping here.'

Something about Guislaine said 'don't argue'.

We sat down under a tree. That felt good, very good. We opened the wine, spread out bread, cheese, salami, cut up a tomato and took the lid off the sardines. There is that wonderful picnic moment when you have finished getting everything ready and there remains only the decision of what to start with. I had just slipped half a sardine into my mouth when they attacked. An army of creeping things and some flying. We stuck it out for a moment or two but to stay was impossible. We scraped up what we could of the picnic and straggled on in the heat, munching morosely as we went.

Guislaine, poor love, was looking bad. Her new Mephistos had come too late to save her; the Noddy-shoe blisters were too advanced. She was hobbling by now and had her brave smile on. The map showed that a short detour would take us into Alzonne. With a population of 1,200 this was certain to have everything we could need, certainly a comfortable place to have coffee and Evian and maybe a snack to make up for our lost lunch.

We walked into town, cowboys too long on the range.

There were two bars. One was closed, the other was the Disco Paradis, a gloomy cavern that smelled of ammonia. Four or five motorcyclists in studded leathers lounged against the bar, picking their teeth and scratching their crotches. Music pounded. The bikers stared hungrily at us as we hovered in the doorway. I looked at Guislaine. She shook her head. We backed nervously out of the Paradis.

We had to rest somewhere. We found a dusty area between the church and the village hall that had a little grass and some benches. On one side men were playing *boule*; they looked at us suspiciously. Guislaine lay down on the grass; I stretched out on a bench and was soon asleep. How much easier it was to sleep during the day than at night.

I heard a noise from Guislaine. I looked over. She was crying softly.

'What's the matter, darling?'

'Oh nothing. Well, it's my feet. They're not too good.'

'Let's have a look. I expect those blisters are ripe by now.'

'No, no. I'm all right. I'll be fine.' Guislaine didn't like anyone looking at her feet; she was sensitive about them.

'Just a quick look,' I said. 'It can't do any harm.'

Reluctantly she came and sat on the bench and took off shoes and socks. The *boule* players stopped to watch. I took the first-aid kit out of my pack and spread it out on the bench between us: a miniature sewing kit from the Helmsley Palace in New York, complete with scissors, thimble, three rolls of thread and four needles stuck in a piece of black paper; a box of matches for sterilizing the needles; a polythene envelope with corn plasters (useless); cotton padding; a roll of stretch sticking plaster; antiseptic ointment; and Anne's Second Skin.

Guislaine had never had to deal with blisters before. For me they were old friends from rowing. By the end of a summer's rowing we used to have hands like shoe leather, but achieving that state was painful. Early in the season we would put layers of gauze, lint and sticking plaster on our soft hands, hoping the blisters would turn to calluses before they went septic.

Guislaine looked on unhappily while I lit a match and tried to keep it alight long enough to sterilize the needle. I handed her the blackened needle. She had a big swollen patch on her left foot at the join of the big toe, the second toe and the ball of the foot. I looked away while she lanced it. It is surprisingly painless and satisfying to pierce your own blisters but I'm too squeamish to watch someone else do it. I busied myself cutting up the Second Skin. We hadn't used it before and I was impressed by its cool, soothing consistency. Anne had said that all the marathon runners used it. Guislaine whispered that she had finished work with the needle and the blister was drained. I pressed Second Skin on the place and covered it with a piece of sticking plaster which I had shaped with the scissors to go between her toes.

Voilà. The *boule* players had crept closer but were pretending not to look. We gave ourselves another ten minutes before setting off. We sat on the bench and shared some apricots and a bar of chocolate Guislaine had found in a side-pocket. I was praying that the blister surgery hadn't made her foot worse.

Rest over. Packs on. Two more hours to Bram. If Guislaine could walk. Gingerly she tried her weight on the left foot. She took a few paces. And another few. Please let her be all right. She looked back at me. Gone was the brave smile. This was a grin of sheer pleasure.

Now that Guislaine's foot was taken care of we could think about other things. How tired we were. How hot it was. How thirsty we were. This was our hottest day so far. We passed a thermometer on a pharmacy wall. Forty-six degrees. Roughly 115 Fahrenheit. That was in the sun; it must have been well into the nineties in the shade. What shade? We were glad to meet the canal after half an hour and to have the towpath to walk on. Melancholy it may have been, but the deep shade of the plane trees was a thing of wonder.

Our destination was the Auberge de la Gare in Bram. Guislaine had called them the night before from Carcassonne. They were sorry but they had no rooms. There was a motel on the autoroute. They would have rooms. We could go there.

But we couldn't, said Guislaine, we were on foot, that was too far. Surely you can't be full.

'*Non, non.* We're not full. We're empty. But tonight we have a big wedding and no one's going to sleep. There will be music and dancing. We're a small hotel.'

'We'll sleep. One double room, please.'

'Very well. If you're sure you don't mind.'

Arrival in Bram may have been the peak of 'thank God our friends can't see us now'. Our clothes were streaked with dust and sweat. Our feet were so sore that each step used up another fragment of our fading willpower. We toyed with the idea of one more rest, but we saw a level crossing only a kilometre from the canal and decided that the de la Gare couldn't be far beyond it. It was a long kilometre but at last we were across the railway and turning left towards the station. Ahead of us, next to the shunting yard, was the auberge.

Checking in could wait for later. We walked in a trance into the bar, dropped our packs on the floor and slid on to bar-stools. We had arrived. Now we could savour each moment. We had kept going over the last kilometre by telling each other what we would order. We had it off pat. Two litre bottles of Evian for starters, a large *citron pressé* for Guislaine and a litre of *panaché*, the French shandy, for me.

All the able-bodied staff were cooking and preparing for the wedding that night. Papa had been brought out of retirement to tend the bar; he'd forgotten where everything was. He muddled about, picking up bottles, examining them and putting them down again. Every so often he gave us a smile.

'Please, just the Evian. Forget the rest. Please,' I begged.

A brisk young waitress rushed in to get something.

'They want Evian,' said Papa.

She saw the state we were in and in a matter of seconds Evian, *panaché* and *citron pressé* were on the bar in front of us.

'We are the Morlands,' Guislaine said quickly before we lost the waitress.

'*Mais oui.* Madame is coming.'

Madame clicked into the bar on six-inch heels. The table was laid for a hundred wedding guests; now she would show us our room. Two weeks earlier we would have laughed at anyone who suggested we spend the night in it. I thought of times we had rejected rooms because the view of the sea was oblique, not straight on. Our view at the Auberge de la Gare was of the main-line railway track, twenty feet away. This view could be had only by peering through a crack, as the wooden shutters had been wired shut from the outside. The bed was another single-double, useless for two people suffering from Walker's Twitch; a mattress was brought and put on the floor.

'*Alors, ça va?*' asked Madame, polite but impatient to return to the *hors-d'œuvre*.

'*Oui, oui madame. Ça va très bien.*'

With an effort of will we forced ourselves to unpack and wash ourselves and our clothes before falling on the bed. Our unvarying ritual was:

> Unpack – slide out the dustbin-liner parcels and ease the folded clothes out and into a drawer, if available;

spread books, maps and first-aid kit on any convenient surface.

Shower – at least five minutes. Lift foot to spray water on the sole. Aah.

Wash clothes – T-shirt, pants and socks – in the basin and hang out to dry.

The ritual had to be observed. The temptation to lie down was too strong to be trifled with. This afternoon's ritual took longer than usual; every time we wanted to go into the bathroom we had to lift the extra mattress which was blocking the door. Finally, ritual over, we stretched out and listened to the thumps of the wedding band tuning up and making sure the amplifiers were working. They were.

Before dinner we had a drink in the bar and watched the wedding guests arrive. There were men in crinkly white satin suits and maroon bow ties, or in baggy black dinner-jackets with sequinned lapels, and women with heels like marlinspikes and tight dresses that pushed everything up and out. The men ordered complicated cocktails for the women. Papa, still behind the bar, had given up. He chatted with us and told them to make their own drinks. The band – three teenagers and Sidney Greenstreet – had finished their practice and were playing furious bar football.

'What are you giving the wedding guests for dinner?' asked Guislaine. 'With a hundred people I suppose it's cold.'

'Cold? For a wedding! *Jamais*,' said Papa. '*Foie gras* – that will be warm – with Sauternes, then a special *lotte à l'armoricaine* for fish, *tournedos Rossini* for the main course, *salade* and *pêche Melba*.'

'*Bravo*,' said Guislaine. 'Do the caterers come from Carcassonne?'

'Please, *madame*. Jean-Pierre, my son, cooks alone.'

Jean-Pierre even found time to prepare for us, and three other tables of people not going to the wedding, home-made rough pâté, fish soup, a delicious salad with lardons and croutons, steak, *frites*, cheese and something that was like summer pudding without the bread.

We went to bed early. On the way upstairs we peeped round the door of the party room. The band was warming up. They had six amplifiers, each the size of a refrigerator.

We may have slept. Each time a train wailed past it felt as if the shutters were going to be sucked off their hinges. Now we saw why they were wired shut. The band struck up at ten. The metal frame of my bed thrummed every time the bass on the electric guitar twanged. At midnight I switched on my pocket torch and opened up *Pendennis*. I hadn't got far yet but far enough to know that Thackeray had, as usual, lost his heart to the villainess. Wily little Blanche was going to steal the book.

CHAPTER 12

Next morning there was still pink and blue confetti on the road. We had been worried that we wouldn't get any breakfast as the wedding had gone on most of the night. Just as we were about to leave our money on the front desk and slip out we were hailed by a cheerful figure in a cook's apron. '*Bonjour*, what can I get you for breakfast? Some eggs for the English, maybe?' he asked with a wink.

'Oh no. Just coffee and some bread will be fine.'

'Hah. No appetite, eh?' He served us and went back to his own breakfast.

'The hotel's been cleaned up very quickly,' Guislaine said to him. 'The staff must have been up late.'

'*Madame*, the party ended at five. I am the cook. After my breakfast I will go to bed.'

So this was the man of a hundred dinners. He turned over a page of his *France Midi* and began whistling. I had spent the night half awake and half dreaming. Somewhere Blanche and Major Pendennis had been getting on the Toulouse Express; there had been raucous music and rattling shutters and blisters and a fox.

'I'm sorry. All this cheerfulness is too much. Let's go,' I whispered to Guislaine.

It was strange weather. The past few days had started grey, so grey that you couldn't tell where haze stopped and cloud began. Mornings that in England meant rain. Guislaine had come prepared with a lightweight green rain-jacket that she had bought in London. The whole thing folded ingeniously into one of its own pockets, leaving a parcel the size of a pound bag of sugar with two straps to form a belt. Guislaine wore this round her waist, ready for rain. The parcel bounced up and down on her bottom. When I was walking behind her I would sometimes find its rhythmic bounce charming and playful; at other times I would get hypnotized by it and it would drive me mad. My reciting 'The Windhover' probably did the same to her.

The rain never came. There was a hint of drizzle in Carcassonne but not enough to wet the road. It hadn't rained for three months. The jacket made an excellent groundsheet at picnics and a less good pillow afterwards. I didn't have a rain-jacket. Stuffed in the bottom of my pack was a transparent poncho like a knee-length condom. I threw it away after Carcassonne. I was longing for rain. I had fantasies about walking in falling sheets of cool wetness.

We hadn't expected such heat. Even when the day began grey, the sun would burn through by noon, a reddening fireball in the haze. On clear days when we started early we saw a different sun, sherbet-yellow, sometimes silver, in the cool of the morning. The heat was a shock. I had thought we would be walking through a perfect English June, a never-ending Laurie Lee summer's day. But it was an unusual summer all over Europe. The afternoons reminded me of being a small boy in Delhi, waiting for the monsoon in the throat of the desert heat.

We left Bram by a road that wandered through poppy-filled wheatfields and up a small hill on its way to the canal. Guislaine was striding out in her new shoes, blisters forgotten. On a long walk you fall in love with your shoes. I kept looking down at my beige boats and saying thank you.

At the top of the hill was a large farmstead of several buildings set in a grove. We walked stealthily past the barn, mindful of dogs. I sensed Guislaine's silent prayer. We had left the cover of the barn and were moving towards a clump of bushes when there was an eruption of noise and a pack of five or six baying creatures skidded out from behind the building. They bounded up to us, snapping, barking and jumping. I had the aerosol dog alarm at the ready. Guislaine stopped, paralysed with terror. I was rotating slowly to make sure one of them didn't remove the back of my thigh. An Alsatian jumped up at Guislaine and put its paws on her shoulders.

'For Christ's sake. The alarm. Use it, DO IT. Oh God,' Guislaine gasped at me.

The dogs' tails were windmilling around as they jumped and pushed. I was almost as frightened as Guislaine, but surely if they were going to attack us they would have done so already? My finger itched on the alarm but I held back. A wolfy-looking mongrel stood in front of me barking and jumping from side to side on its front paws.

'I think they're OK,' I said. 'They only want to play. Look, their tails are wagging. God knows what will happen if we give them a blast.'

'Oh God. Where are your loyalties? The dogs or me? USE IT! DO IT!'

'Give it a bit longer. Look, they're really not going to hurt us. I promise they won't bite while their tails are wagging. Look.'

Guislaine unfroze enough to start edging forward, still stiff in every movement. The dogs went on jumping around, then as we walked faster they began to drop away one by one. Soon we had left the buildings behind us, but two of the dogs stayed on, a black Labrador and an Alsatian. They would run ahead and frisk, then turn round to make sure we were coming.

'I think they were just bored. There doesn't seem to be any-one around and I expect they want someone to play with.'

'Well, why do they always go for me?'

'They sense your fear. I was pretty frightened back there but you were even worse.'

The Labrador, still no more than a big puppy, bounded up to Guislaine and stopped in front of her, tail wagging. She stiffened and then gave a hesitant smile. 'Well, I suppose you are quite sweet.'

Guislaine comes from a family of cat-lovers. When we lived

in America we got an Airedale, Sammy, whom she came to adore after a hesitant start – 'Oh I wish Sammy didn't smell so much like an old sweater.' But the affection didn't spread to the generality of dogs. I come from a dog family: we always had at least two; I have had to learn to like cats. The only one I have ever really been fond of is Kimbers, our present cat, with the colouring of a Friesian cow and the build of a small vacuum cleaner.

The Alsatian and the Labrador were still with us a kilometre later, their farm no longer in sight. Guislaine had started talking to them with a 'Gosh, look at me' expression whenever they ran up. The dogs were delighted at having people to play with. It was time to test the dog alarm. I also hoped that it would send them home, as they had come a long way by now. I took it out of the pack, pointed it at them, fifty yards away, and gave a good squeeze. 'PeeeeEEEEEEEEEyeeUP.' We shrivelled. Guislaine put her hands over her ears. The dogs paused in their frisking and looked at us with concern. Anyone giving out a noise like that must be ill. The Alsatian ran up and gave me a lick. So much for the dog alarm.

Two kilometres later we approached another farmyard. Guislaine had changed from questioning my loyalty to regarding the dogs as her personal bodyguards. We sauntered past the farm gates, sure that 'our dogs' would see off any attackers. Soon we rejoined the canal.

We were now half an hour's walk from the first farm. What were we to do about the dogs? Were they going to come with us to the Atlantic? On the way to Carcassonne we had met a farmer driving up and down the towpath looking for his dog. It had been stolen, he said, a common occurrence. He had a big club on the seat beside him and told us what he was going to do to the thief when he found him. We were now in open possession of two dogs that didn't belong to us. We had to persuade them to go home. I suggested that Guislaine speak to them as presumably they spoke French. She did a gruff *'Vas-y, vas-y'* and a lot more I couldn't understand. No good. Feeling like Judas I picked up a pebble and threw it at the Alsatian, the leader, taking care to miss while making 'go away' noises. It gave me an *'Et tu, Brute'* look but kept trotting along the towpath with us.

We were wondering whether we should call the police, which would have meant a tedious delay, when we saw a well-dressed young woman striding towards us with a small floppy-eared spaniel on a leash. A new playmate. Our two skidded over, elbowing each other aside to get at the spaniel. The more it cowered and yelped the more fun it was.

'Appelez vos chiens. Appelez-les! Nom de Dieu. Vite!' the woman shrieked.

We had reached the mêlée by now. We composed our features. 'Not ours. Terribly sorry,' I said, while Guislaine echoed in French.

The woman's shriek rose to a new peak as the spaniel took shelter between her legs, followed by the Alsatian.

'Désolés, mam'selle. Absolument désolés,' we said, accelerating away down the towpath. We didn't look back till we were round the corner. The dogs were no longer following us.

We missed the dogs. They were the first ones we had met in France that became friends. Dogs are the bane of walkers in France. Every farm has quantities of them and most of the village houses have a couple. None of these dogs is a pet; our meeting with the woman and her spaniel was one of the few times we met someone taking a dog for a walk. They are deterrents. Alsatians are the most popular breed, followed by Dobermanns and large terriers. Rottweilers don't seem to have taken hold.

Dogs are the biggest difference between walking in France and in England. We can spend an afternoon ambling around Norfolk byways with hardly a woof; in the Languedoc the house where you don't get barked at is the exception. The ones on the outskirts of towns and villages are the worst; their dogs are kept behind wire fences and skid up and down barking and growling, teeth bared, only a couple of feet away as you walk past. Their confinement turns rage into hysteria. At least the farm dogs have room to roam about and work off their frustration.

For our first few days we were terrified. I was tempted to take the universal advice and get a stick. I think I was right not to. No stick is going to ward off an angry Alsatian, and it might goad it into attacking. The best dog advice I found I scribbled down at the back of *Pendennis* because I liked it so much. It is from Frank Tatchell, an English traveller of the twenties:

> The mongrel curs are a nuisance to the wayfarer in most foreign lands. It is useless to try and 'good dog' them. Instead, abuse them in the hoarsest voice at your command and with the worst language you can think of. They may slink off utterly ashamed of themselves, but, if one comes for you, try this method. Snatch off your hat and hold it out to him, when he will snap at it and seize it by the brim. Now the length of your hat and arm is exactly the length of your leg, and, if you kick out, he will get it just under the jaw, bite his tongue and go off howling. Approaching a dog sleeping in the road, I do so whistling. This wakes him up before I get close and helps to convince him that I am human, in spite of the bag on my shoulder and my outlandish smell.

Tatchell was the Vicar of Midhurst. This and other good advice I had found in Eric Newby's *Book of Travellers' Tales*. I suggested to Guislaine that she try the hat method while I took a photograph; it wouldn't work with my sun-vizor, I said. She had no interest. She did, however, as did I, regard dogs differently after the day's incident. From then on we treated dogs like badly brought-up children.

Not long after parting with the dogs we were attacked again. This time by a swan. He was floating huge and graceful, alone in the middle of the canal. As we approached he turned towards us, arched his neck and hissed. He puffed his wings to make himself appear even bigger and began to move on us in a series of powerful thrusts, each one creating a bow wave like a barge's.

'I don't believe it,' I said, 'we're about to be savaged by a swan.' Climbing the bank would have been the work of an instant for this brute.

We braced ourselves as we came level with him. He was no more than six feet from us. I had the dog alarm out and ready. It might at least put him off his stride. I remembered all the swan stories I had been told as a boy. Was it a man's leg or a man's arm a swan could break with one blow of its wing? Why was it always a man's? Women were safe?

We were past the swan and he hadn't yet launched himself, but he was still vibrating with aggression. I didn't want to look round but I could sense him following us. Thank God the towpath began to climb – out of swan-hop I hoped. We looked back. He had stopped following us and appeared to be erect in the water, almost standing on his tail; he clapped his wings in front and behind and gave out a raucous crow.

'Well, he doesn't like to gloat, does he?' said Guislaine.

'I feel like I'm in Aesop. Enough animals for one day.'

'How much further to Castelnaudary?' she asked.

'Another twelve. All on the towpath. No more happenings I hope. I could use a stretch of serious boredom now.'

Every few kilometres we passed another lock to take us a few feet higher, and on each new reach of the canal the water-level was that much lower, leaving the banks of cracked brown clay more and more exposed. Navigation had been impossible since Carcassonne. Even fishermen were becoming fewer, though we could still see dark shapes gliding under the surface of the soupy water. Occasionally a quick deep swirl would brush the surface – pike? The fishermen sat on folding seats in the midst of their nests of equipment – spare rods, hampers, two or three nets, bait buckets, tins and boxes with floats and lures and, most important, a Y-shaped device for holding the rod while the fisherman snoozed. We never saw a fish caught.

The locks were scruffy affairs; no roses and cream teas here. Unlike on the Thames, the keepers' houses were grey and run down, as were the locks themselves. While the English lock-keeper tends his garden, the French one breeds his lunch. In addition to the inevitable dogs there were chickens, pigeons, bantams, rabbits, geese, and often a cow or two behind the house. The animals, like the locks, had a threadbare look.

'I wonder why they don't keep pigs?' I asked Guislaine.

'Maybe they can't swim.'

We came across double-decker locks, something I had never seen on the Thames. Where there was a large gradient, one lock would lead directly into the next to create a second step up for the boats. In places there were triple-deckers, and when we reached Castelnaudary we met the prince of locks, a four-decker. It must have climbed sixty feet to take the canal on to its highest reach. We had thought the canal was, like the English ones, built at the beginning of the nineteenth century, until we saw a plaque to its builder, Pierre-Paul Riquet, and the date – 1681. It was built while Wren was working on St Paul's.

The French were the first canal enthusiasts. I had recently read Trollope's *The West Indies and the Spanish Main*, in which he devotes a whole chapter to French canal mania and ridicules the ease with which promoters of hare-brained canal schemes could raise money from the French public. He wrote the book as a result of a tour of the West Indies. He had been sent there to sort out the postal system in the British Caribbean colonies and had taken advantage of the trip to nose around and see what the French, the Dutch and the Spanish were up to. He had a good laugh at the expense of de Lesseps, who was talking of building a canal from the Caribbean to the Pacific, through a bit of what was then northern Colombia. Trollope showed beyond doubt that, even though the French were probably stupid enough to put up the money for it, it couldn't be built and, if it was, it would fail. So much for the Panama Canal.

We reached the outskirts of Castelnaudary without any further disturbance other than hooting and yelling from the road that ran alongside the canal for the last bit. Cars raced past with either green or blue streamers and scarves, their occupants leaning out of the windows and making as much noise as they could. We were in rugger country. Today was the final of the Championnat du Sud-Ouest we were told later.

We panted up the steep path beside the four-decker lock. The other side, said the map, was le Grand Bassin. This would be where the holiday-hire barges lived and was bound to be surrounded by cafés and restaurants. It had been almost twenty kilometres from Bram and we were looking forward to eating lunch under a parasol and watching the movement in the Bassin. Later we could find our hotel.

We breasted the hill and found that the Bassin was deserted. Sans restaurant, sans parasol, sans bar and even sans boat. They must have moved them all down to the lower reaches before this one dried up. There were a couple of shops with ice-cream posters. It was Sunday and they were shut. There was no shade. We had prepared ourselves for a stop here and hadn't the energy to go further. We found the entrance of a clothes shop that hadn't been barred off and sat there in the shade looking at our reflections in the shop window.

Guislaine began giggling.

'What's so funny?'

'Look,' she said, pointing at the shop window, 'just look at us. Try turning up at First Boston dressed like that.'

I had on my favourite pair of walking trousers, khaki, now stained from lying in playgrounds and scrambling through bushes, a white T-shirt that was getting greyer with each wash, and the First Boston sun-vizor with bits of damp hair sticking out from underneath at funny angles.

'Yes, well. Time to find the hotel.'

We were booked in the Centre et Lauragais, another Logis.

We were learning that Logis were easy to find. Look for the busiest and noisiest corner in town. This was no exception. We checked in, left our packs in the room and went out to find some lunch; the hotel restaurant had already overflowed with Sunday lunchers. We found a café by the square where we ate sandwiches while Guislaine and the waitress agreed that rugby was a bore. The town had gone mad. Everyone was in green or blue. There was a couple in our café who had dyed their hair green.

We liked Castelnaudary. Whereas Carcassonne lives for the tourist but isn't comfortable with it, Castelnaudary takes the attitude that if you want to visit, fine, but don't get in the way, we're busy. The town has grown rich thanks to its position on the Canal du Midi half-way between Toulouse and Narbonne, in the middle of one of the most fertile plains in France. We were out of wine country now but this was the place for cereals, oils and beans and, of course, the thing you cook them in: shops in Castelnaudary that are not selling food are selling pottery, the earthenware casserole that gives its name to the great dish of south-west France, cassoulet. As with all great dishes from bouillabaisse to chilli, everyone spits on their neighbour's concoctions. Castelnaudary derides the things that people in Carcassonne and Toulouse put in their cassoulets. I can't remember what went into the local *'vrai'* cassoulet along with the beans. I think here it's pork and elsewhere they put in goose and duck, or maybe it's the other way round. Everyone agrees on sausage.

I took a stroll up and down the cours de la République after lunch, admired the variety of cooking pots in the shop windows and then returned to the Centre et Lauragais. I had spotted earlier a giant television in the sitting room on the first floor. Guislaine harumphed something about vegetating and went off to taste blackcurrant sorbets while I stretched out on the sofa and watched the finals of the French Open. Michael Chang, of whom I had never heard, beat Stefan Edberg. Afterwards he made a short speech in French (*bravo*), thanking his parents, but most of all thanking the Almighty for strength and guidance. The era of John McEnroe, hero of anyone who has ever sat at a trading desk and Shouted Down a Phone, was over.

Guislaine came back, purple-tongued, to the hotel for a siesta. 'How about making tomorrow a rest day?' she said.

'Good idea. I like it here and a lie-in would be wonderful.'

'Mmm. Up at nine, maybe ten. I wonder if we can get breakfast in bed?'

We hadn't made any rules about rest days before we started but we'd now walked for six days and we'd earned one. Neither of us liked to say it but we were both starting to believe that the Atlantic was reachable. Shhh.

We were in high spirits over dinner that night; we ate in the hotel. The restaurant, overcrowded at lunch, now had only three other tables occupied. That was the pattern in the South-West: lunch was the big meal of the day and supper was eaten in front of television at home. Jean-Pierre Campigotto, the owner of the Centre, was also the cook. He had a hang-dog face behind a trim beard. Every quarter of an hour or so, he walked purposefully through the dining room, head down, and out into the street wearing his toque and monogrammed chef's bib. He had the air of a man going to place a bet. A minute or two later he was back looking disgruntled. The third time he did it we peered out of the window to see where he went. He just stood on the front doorstep and looked up at the trees and the sky.

'Do you think he's bored?' I said.

'It's not that. Chefs dream. Ask my father; half his friends own restaurants. If they're in the country, it's the place they're going to own in the *septième*, and if they're in Paris, it's that little auberge in the South.'

'And I bet they're miserable once they get it.'

'Oh maybe. Not that different to the City really . . .'

'*Touché.*'

After dinner we took a stroll round town. We didn't

have to get up in the morning. I could spend all day in moccasins. We could laze, maybe take a swim. I could wash my trousers. We had a muscat at the bar opposite the hotel to celebrate. We talked over the Walk, veterans now. I felt like an orbiting spaceman, the London of suits and dinner parties a receding speck.

Last stretch, a yawn, one o'clock and time for a long night's sleep.

The room was hot and stuffy. We could open the shutters and let in the flashing neon, the noise from the bar opposite and the beeping and revving of cars and mopeds up the cours de la République celebrating Castelnaudary's famous victory in *le rugby*, or we could keep the shutters closed and suffocate. We opened them. Sleep was impossible so I got out my torch and book while Guislaine tried to sleep.

What a prig Pendennis was.

By three the noise was lessening although the neon still flashed and every minute or so a motor *vélo* went past like a buzz-saw. I forced myself to lie still, determined to sleep. At five they began putting up the market. Monday was market day in Castelnaudary. First singly and then in groups, vans drew up in the street outside our window and started unpacking their stands. The cafés reopened to catch the market trade. Cries of *'Salut'* and *'Ça va?'* drifted up in between the banging of hammers.

Finally, at six, I fell asleep. At 6.15 the phone rang. I jolted awake and reached out, instantly alert. What was it? The children?

No. Monsieur was doubtless unaware that today was market day and if Monsieur had by any chance parked his car outside would he mind moving it.

I never did get back to sleep.

Nothing went right on our rest day.

By 7.30 we were downstairs for breakfast; at least it was quiet in the hotel dining room. We bought some newspapers. I found yesterday's *International Herald Tribune* and looked at the stock prices. It took me a year to get out of that habit. In the past, whenever I had taken a holiday from work in an out-of-the-way place there had been Great Events in the market and I had spent the first week after returning scrabbling to catch up with what had happened. I found it hard to persuade myself that now it really didn't matter. Let IBM declare bankruptcy and monetary policy do a U-turn, the only thing I had to worry about was blisters.

There was one good bit of the day. We wandered round the market. That made us feel better. The market stretched from under our bedroom all the way up the *cours*, the Champs-Élysées of Castelnaudary, to the place de Verdun, a leafy square with a fountain of playful nymphs and a wrought-iron covered market. Food and flowers were sold in the *place*, while pots, pans and blue jeans occupied the *cours*. We sniffed cheeses and hams, enquired about the six different kinds of cassoulet, all on sale in sealed glass jars, and bought some cherries.

After that, a swim seemed like a good idea; today was even hotter. Yes, the pool's open, the hotel said, down the *cours* and right at the river. We borrowed hotel towels and hurried off. Open it was, but reserved for the *lycée*. This put us in a bad temper. We separated, Guislaine off with her notebook and I up the hill to inspect the Church of St Michel. This was the first 'sightseeing' I had done on the trip. When you are on the march a two-hundred-yard detour to see a church is too much. From the hill I caught my first sight of the Pyrenees. They weren't far away, no more than forty miles, but the haze had hidden them till now. I glanced between two roofs and there, caught in the angle like a cut-out, was a black, jagged-edged sweep. It took a few seconds before I realized what it was.

We met later in the afternoon outside the cinema. There was a queue of old people waiting to go in. The film was *Mississippi Burning* but the main attraction was that the cinema was air-conditioned. We felt short-changed by our rest day, and the feeling of camaraderie, so strong on the march, had turned into irritation. We had a violent row and began shouting at each other, much to the delight of the cinema queue. We were arguing about plans for the girls' summer holidays, but if it hadn't been that it would have been something else. After ten minutes of shouted sarcasm we parted, vowing to finish our walks alone.

'It'll be a relief not having you telling me what to do,' spat Guislaine.

'Oh yeah? Who's going to carry your pack?'

'I'll catch the train.'

Two hours later I crept into the hotel room. Guislaine was already there, lying on the bed reading. We looked at each other, tired and sheepish.

'I'm sorry, darling. It was my fault,' I said.

'No it wasn't, it was mine.'

'Well, anyhow. So much for rest days.'

Dinner was terrible. We went to La Fourcade, advertising itself as *the* place in Castelnaudary for cassoulet. We couldn't pass through without having one. The restaurant had seen better days. There were faded newspaper clippings above the desk and old bullfight posters round the dining room. We were the only diners. Where is everyone, Guislaine asked the waiter, in her good-as-the-natives French.

'Hah. No English. They don't come because the canal is shut. Last year in June we were full, all English from the canal-boats.'

'What about the French, don't they go on the canal?'

The waiter looked at her as if his leg was being pulled. He shrugged and walked away muttering.

My cassoulet was inedible. Guislaine makes a much better one.

CHAPTER 13

'What time does the sun rise?' Guislaine had asked over dinner in the Fourcade last night.

'Oh, I don't know. About 6.15ish. It was getting light when I finally got to sleep this morning and that must have been about six. Why do you ask?'

'Let's leave at sunrise tomorrow.'

I choked on my cassoulet. 'What? What did you say?'

'Let's leave at sunrise. There.' She giggled. 'Surprised you, didn't I?'

Surprised me? In the eighteen years we have known each other I have only once known Guislaine get up at dawn, other than to catch aeroplanes. That was to drive up a mountain in Madeira to see the sun rise. We have different memories of that occasion; she does agree, however, that she is not a morning person.

The rhythm we had adopted of walking for four or five hours in the morning, picnic lunch and a couple more hours in the afternoon wasn't working. It was simply too hot in the afternoon, with the sun in our faces and the road radiating out the heat it had been absorbing all morning. And picnic lunches were either impossible to buy or impossible to eat. We decided on a new pattern. We would get up at first light and keep going till we reached our destination. That way we would be on the road in the relative cool of the morning and when we reached our destination we could shower, eat and dissolve. I was delighted by the new plan. Watching the sun rise has always had a special romance for me. But for Guislaine to suggest rising at dawn was so extraordinary that it made me realize how hard she was finding the afternoons and also how uncomplaining she had been about it.

I had at least slept last night. I had bought some ear-plugs to keep out the noise from the *cours*. I had never worn them before. It was like being in a submarine. Even the juke-box from across the road was better than listening to cranial plumbing. I pulled them out and fell instantly asleep, and slept until the alarm at 5.30.

M. Campigotto had left us a thermos of coffee and some of yesterday's croissants. We sat on the bedside munching unenthusiastically in the semi-dark and listening to a plague of starlings in the street twittering like an out-of-tune radio. I wondered how Guislaine was doing under the strain of the early start. I looked up from stuffing the dog alarm into a corner of my pack and saw that she was standing up and strapping her pack shut; washed, dressed and ready for the road.

'Come on,' she said, big smile on her face. 'Not ready yet? Do hurry up. What's taking you so long?'

'Hmph. Just wait.'

Campigotto had forgotten to tell us how to get out of his hotel. All the doors were locked.

'Oh damn. We're going to have to wake someone up. We can't very well break out.'

Guislaine looked one way, then the other, and pulled hard on the side-door. Another violent tug. There was a splintering noise and the door was open. Did I know this woman?

It was five past six. The air was cool. Our route took us along the towpath for the last time; in ten kilometres we would turn left and tackle the first of two hundred kilometres of grey smudges on the map. The sun had just risen when we started along the canal and it shone fresh and silvery-yellow between the plane trees on the far side. The irrigation jets in the fields were already at work and throwing rainbows of spray up into the air against the sun. The silence was complete, the towpath empty. We walked hand in hand, in love with the morning and each other.

This was the highest reach of the canal. I looked at the map. We were two hundred metres above sea-level. The canal would gently let itself down lock by lock, metre by metre, from here to Bordeaux. It was a sad sight at this level. The water had sluiced down to the lower levels to leave this reach dry. We hadn't seen a moving boat since Bram, and the canal was no more than a series of muddy puddles in cracked clay.

The bridge at Segala was our turning-off point. Well before we reached it, the dawn start, lack of sleep and no real breakfast were making themselves felt. Guislaine's bright-eyed enthusiasm had given way to muttering and talk of coffee. I was lost in my own fantasies about breakfast. There had to be somewhere to eat in Segala.

'OK. I've decided what I'm going to have. First, a mammoth pot of coffee. Two fried eggs. Plenty of bacon, crisp. Fried bread. Perhaps a couple of bangers and then a toast-rack full of white toast. Cooper's Oxford . . . Or shall I have kippers?'

'Oh shut up.'

One more curve in the canal and we would be there. A pall of black smoke hung over Segala. It looked as if the Cossacks had just pulled out. But this turned out to be no more than stubble burning in the neighbouring fields. Where was breakfast? There was a decrepit shop with a sign outside. It did say 'Restaurant' but it looked more like a garage.

Inside was granny, in the perennial black dress and white apron.

'*On peut manger, madame?*'

'*Mais oui, si vous voulez.*'

'*Croissants?*'

'*Pas de croissants.*'

'*Du pain?*'

'*Pas aujourd'hui.*'

I looked at Guislaine. 'I bet they're out of kippers.'

'*Café?*' pleaded Guislaine.

'*Euh, oui.*' She shuffled off into the back.

Next door was the restaurant. It was bare but for some wobbly tables scattered with old newspapers, and a few battered chairs. First we searched the shop for breakfast. I found a banana; Guislaine a pre-wrapped loaf of gingerbread. She was delighted; *pain d'épices* carried a cargo of French childhood memories. I ate the banana and took another one to have with coffee. The old lady shuffled back in with a camp-fire coffee pot and a jug of hot milk. She gave us bowls to drink out of. Delicious. Guislaine crammed in the last of the gingerbread and went in search of a lavatory while I admired the *Sea Nymph*. This was a smart white yacht; from Poole, said the transom. It was high and dry on the mud, leaning crazily against the quay.

'Poor chap,' I said to Guislaine when she returned. 'He'll be there till October.'

'What happened?'

'He must have been making the journey from Bordeaux to the Mediterranean when they let the water out.'

'Bit careless of him.'

'By the way, how was the loo?'

'Oh, fine. Once I shooed the hen out. It's back there in the yard.'

We paid the granny.

'Looks like rain,' said Guislaine to her by way of conversation.

'*Non.* It won't rain. It hasn't rained for three months. There's no water in the canal. Look what happened to him.' She pointed at the *Sea Nymph* and cackled with pleasure.

'But it's cloudy outside,' Guislaine persisted.

'Pah. That means nothing. It only rains when you can see the Pyrenees.'

Apart from the previous day's glimpse, we never did.

We crossed the motorway on leaving Segala. Looking down on the cars whoosh-whooshing under the bridge made us feel good, perhaps even smug. Once over the bridge the road wound up the side of the hill. We came to our first corner and our first real view since Carcassonne: we could trace the green line of the canal all the way back across the plain to the grey and red blur of Castelnaudary, now more than twelve kilometres away.

Even the exertion of walking up a hill was pleasant after the tramp, tramp, tramp of the towpath. We had only half a dozen kilometres to go to our destination, the Château de la Barthe, our first *gîte*. This, said the *gîte* handbook, was in Belflou and had 'five guest rooms in a castle on a farm in the open countryside'. We didn't have directions but I had located Belflou on the map and could see the symbol for a château next to the village church. The walking was harder now that we were in the hills, but we didn't mind: the elation of following the swoop and curve of the path blew us along

> . . . in his riding
> Of the rolling level underneath him steady air, and
> striding
> High there, how he rung upon the rein of a wimpling
> wing
> In his ecstasy!

Another couple of days and I would have 'The Windhover' by heart.

We coasted down the hill into Belflou heading for the church and stopped on the green in front of it. Opposite was the château, a grey, slab-sided donjon surrounded by a swampy moat. The garden was overgrown and we could see no way in.

I pulled out the hotel sheets to check. 'Well, we're in Belflou,' I said, 'and this is the château. So much for the "castle on a farm in the open countryside". There doesn't even seem to be an entrance.'

The shutters were closed. As I spoke, one on the top floor creaked open and a man with a beaky face looked out. He scowled at us for a few seconds and then slammed the shutter closed. Guislaine walked over to the telephone booth while he went off to boil up some oil.

She came rushing back. 'It's OK. It's OK. Wrong château.'

'Thank God for that. I wasn't looking forward to spending the night there.'

'Back to the crossroads, right at the Virgin and follow the sign for Auberge des Cathars. That's their other name. She sounded nice.'

She was. The auberge was a hamlet of dignified stone buildings grouped around a courtyard. Our room was clean and airy, with curtains blowing in the breeze and the noise of cocks crowing in the farmyard outside. We ate a delicious lunch in a whitewashed dining room and drank a bottle of cold rosé from Les Vignerons d'Octaviana, Ornaisons.

'Remember Ornaisons?' I said.

'Mmm. Pâté sandwiches.'

'And the dancing bear.'

After lunch we sat and read at a table in the middle of the courtyard under an old maple. By the tree was a weather-beaten stone obelisk with an unusual cross carved into it.

'That,' Mme Cazanave, the owner, told us, 'is the Cathar cross.'

The farm had been in her family for centuries. It had descended in dog-legs down the family tree as different members had disappeared or emigrated to Quebec to avoid religious persecution.

'What a shame we wasted our rest day in Castelnaudary,' Guislaine said. 'I could spend a week here.'

I left her under the maple, hard a-scribble in the notebook, and wandered out through the farmyard. A path wound down between the fields of ripening wheat to a lake; I sat on the strip of sand that ran around it and threw pebbles into the water and tried thinking about what I was going to do when we got back to London. It didn't work. My mind refused to stay on the topic.

* * *

After I resigned, the thing people were most curious about wasn't what I was going to do but how much money we had and what we were going to live on. It was a natural question but most people were too polite to ask it. Instead they would say things like 'Well, of course, it's all right for you. I'd give up my job tomorrow if I could afford it. But then no one's giving me an enormous golden farewell. You lucky bastard.'

No one had given me a golden farewell either. First Boston had behaved decently but saw no reason to give me anything other than what I had already earned. If I had been fired I might have received a fat severance package but, having resigned of my own will, I didn't qualify for anything like that. Nor did I expect it. I had, however, saved up some money in the last few years when times had been good on Wall Street and put some aside for the children's education; but I wasn't a rich man.

And our house was on the market. When we got back together after our separation I sold my bachelor flat in Tite Street and moved in with Guislaine in her little house in Fulham. It wasn't big enough for the whole family and I felt uncomfortable in what was very much Guislaine's territory; after two months of me trying to squeeze my things into her private corners, a second divorce was becoming a possibility. We sold it and bought a tall white stucco house overlooking a garden square in South Kensington. We felt very grown-up. Grand the house may have been but we never came to love it. It was on six floors and had no heart. The sitting room was out of earshot of the kitchen.

We were lucky. Soon after the Walk ended, the house sold. It was bought by an Italian lady whose English lawyers dithered and dickered so much over the details of the contract and the price that she finally overruled them in embarrassment and told them to pay the full asking price.

We moved from six floors and five bedrooms to a houseboat on the Thames embankment with one bedroom and a cabin each for the girls. I sit in the deck-house for breakfast and watch the sun rise over the river, while a cormorant stands sentinel on each mooring post with its wings stretched out against the wind to dry like an Aztec god, and my heart sings in a way it never did in our South Kensington square.

Meanwhile our cottage in a little sailing village on the north Norfolk coast became home. We squeezed what we could in there from the London house and the rest of our furniture was sold, but for a few well-loved things which went into storage.

Buying the cottage had been a lucky accident. While Guislaine and I were separated I had been vaguely looking for somewhere to go with Tasha and Georgia at weekends, as my bachelor flat was too small for the three of us. One weekend, when I didn't have the children, some previously arranged plans fell through, leaving me with two empty days. I had never seen the great cathedrals of East Anglia so I put a bag in the car and headed for Ely. That weekend I went to Ely, Norwich and Peterborough cathedrals; I loved them all but especially Ely.

In between Norwich and Peterborough I took a loop along the north Norfolk coast. I had never been there before. The thirty-mile stretch from Weybourne to Brancaster, with its salt marshes and little flint villages, narrow lanes and church-topped hills, is a place of magic. The railway never really came here to bring it into the modern world; north Norfolk peaked in the fourteenth century when the wool trade was thriving and the harbours deep. The harbours are now silted up and not much has happened since. As I drove along the coast I explored all the little villages. The prettiest house in the prettiest village had a 'For Sale' sign.

A week later Georgia and I drove up together and went round the house. 'This one's a Yes, Daddy,' said Georgia, and we bought it. That was before the property boom came to East Anglia.

This happened during the most painful period of our separation and I would retreat to the house like a hurt

ABOVE About to shout down a phone…

BELOW The 'Dead-beetle position'   BELOW 'Fore-and-afting'

LEFT The grey ridge of the Montagne d'Alaric

BELOW LEFT The melancholy Canal du Midi

RIGHT Belflou: Madame Cazanave's Cathar Cross

BELOW The Gers – '…plotted and pieced – fold, fallow and plough…'

ABOVE 'Montgeard was famous once…'

ABOVE Head down, eyes closed…

BELOW Another château we didn't buy (this one near Noé)

ABOVE The Château de Jottes – no corpses on the lawn

BELOW Samatan: lunch inside us

BELOW Dressed for dinner, Bassoues

ABOVE Before meeting the minotaur

BELOW 'Not bad for someone sitting on a thistle'

ABOVE The yellowy-blue thing

BELOW Saubusse: the river was flowing the wrong way

'Bliss was it in that dawn to be alive' – and only 30km to go

Ça suffit

animal at weekends. It had no furniture apart from a bed, three canvas chairs, a garden bench and a garden table, but I would drive up on Friday nights, wind down the car window as I turned off the main road towards the village and smell the salt air and feel free.

At the end of that summer Tasha asked if she could have her twelfth birthday party there. She invited six friends, all girls. I rented a minibus and we set off from London on Saturday morning. They had been told they would have to sleep on the floor so they had all brought sleeping bags. That afternoon all eight of us went out in my little sailing dinghy made to take three people, and when we came back to the house we found seven mattresses piled on the sitting-room floor. Perry Long, whose father Stratton owned the village boat chandlery, had taken pity on us and been round the village collecting.

Soon after Guislaine and I remarried, we made our first trip together to Norfolk. I was praying she would like it and worried that, because she is not a sailor, the charm of its muddy little creeks and ramshackle quay would be lost on her. I took her into the village the prettiest way, down the narrow High Street winding between the flint fishermen's cottages until the road curves and there, before you, is a view stretching without limit across the wide marshes and out to the sea.

'Pretty, isn't it?' I said.

'Uh-huh,' she said uncertainly.

The house was cold and damp having been empty for a few weeks. Guislaine, who hates the cold, took two hot-water bottles to bed that night. The next day we walked out across the marshes, the winter mud of the estuary flecked white with great flocks of migrant birds – Brent geese, shelducks and, my own favourite, the oystercatchers, running busily up and down the shoreline like so many head waiters in their dinner-jackets. We looked out at the cold North Sea, brown and angry under the winter sky.

As we walked back along the dyke, Guislaine looped her arm in mine. 'Oh Matou,' she said. 'I love it. This is the first place I've felt at home in England. It reminds me of France.'

I was overjoyed that she liked it and baffled by the reason. It doesn't remind me at all of France. It reminds me of Tollesbury, on the Essex marshes, where we lived just after the War when my parents came back from India. Everyone who has been to stay with us in Norfolk likes it. Perhaps the reason is that it makes everyone think of their childhood. Now the cottage has become our home. It's a bit cramped, but I have a shed in the garden which is my 'office', Guislaine sits and works in the attic where she has a view of the setting sun over the harbour bar and, between there and the houseboat, we can imagine no finer life.

There were occasions in the years before I resigned when I said to Guislaine that I was thinking of giving up my job but couldn't do it as it would be irresponsible of me to put her and the children's material well-being at risk. She called my bluff. 'Go ahead,' she would say. 'We can get by on much less. Do what you want to do, we'll be OK.' I didn't do it. I was frightened.

Now it was done, friends in the City were congratulatory in an indulgent way. When, months after the Walk, I said that I didn't have any plans to go back to the City for the time being as I was writing and surprised at how much I was enjoying it, they smiled and said, 'Mmm. Writing. Better than working.' The only person who disapproved of my giving up a 'proper' job to write was our friend Peter. He didn't say it directly to me, but I heard that he thought it was thoroughly irresponsible. But then, Peter is a writer.

'*Pomph-a-luga*-kerplop,' said Guislaine from behind as a stone curved over my head and into the water. 'How does it go?'

'*Pa-phlas-masin. Pomph-a-luga-pa-phlas-masin.*'

It was about all I remembered from doing Greek at school. We used to do a Greek play in the summer term. One year we did *The Frogs* by Aristophanes. *Pomphalugapaphlasmasin* is the noise Aristophanes says is made by a stone being thrown into still water.

'You remember,' I said 'Pompha is the stone going into the water, luga is the ensuing spout of water and paphlasmasin the spreading of the ripples afterwards.'

'Bit like you, really,' she said. 'You've got the paphlasmasin still to come.'

'Hmm. Yes. Bit laboured, isn't it? Don't know about that, but I do know we've got a long trip tomorrow.'

'Do I want to know? OK. How far?'

Tomorrow was not only going to be our first day in the Fan, up, down, up, down, all day, but also promised to be our longest walk. There was nowhere to spend the night between Belflou and Auterive. I was going to play with the map on my way to bed to try and find the shortest way there, but it was going to be well over thirty kilometres.

'I'm not sure yet. Probably a bit longer than Narbonne to Lézignan. That was twenty-nine.'

I was secretly excited.

CHAPTER 14

Today was the day we hadn't talked about. The Distance that dared not speak its name. We had known it was there, but surely something was going to come up, someone would tell us about a closer place to spend the night. Nothing had come up. I ran the 'thermometer' over the three or four alternative routes but none of them was less than thirty-three kilometres. We both vividly remembered how we had felt as we lay in the dust at Thunder Junction in Lézignan after twenty-nine. We could only have laughed if someone had suggested doing another hour's walking then. Today we didn't even have an escape route. If Auterive proved too far there was no fall-back destination. We would go through two villages in the first half of the walk but after Montgeard, the second of them, there was nothing but empty France until Auterive.

Guislaine didn't press me on the distance. She had learnt by now that I shaded each day's distance by a few kilometres to make it seem less daunting. The fact that I had admitted to a distance of thirty-plus for Auterive told her all she wanted to know. And none of it was flat. Every time I looked at the map it got smudgier. I counted seven lines of hills and seven valleys to cross and kept the news to myself.

We had told Mme Cazanave before dinner about the Walk. She had congratulated us.

'And where do you go tomorrow?' she asked.

'Auterive.'

'Only to Auterive? That should be easy. It's less than half an hour away.'

To a car driver.

She had recommended a short cut to start the day. We had

first to return to Belflou to pick up the road; she told us of a farm track that would save us a kilometre. It was a bit rough, she said, but on foot we wouldn't mind, would we.

We left at 7.30. The track was not only rough but also near-vertical. We slipped once or twice in the steeper places and by the time we reached the Virgin of the Crossroads we were sweating. It was another day of grey beginnings and we half-expected it to drizzle. 'No Pyrenees, no rain,' I reminded Guislaine, who had rain-jacket at the ready.

The first hours of a long walk are the best. Stiffness unwinds and distance passes without a need to count the miles. Today's business was too serious for much chat. We didn't even have much to say about the ever fascinating subject of our health. Our blisters were under control – thank you Mr Mephisto – and our family of aches and pains, each one as individual and quirky as a character in a play – Guislaine's hips, my tendon, and all their little brothers and sisters – were unusually quiet.

The map had again deceived us. What looked cold, grey and empty on the map was generous and gentle countryside. It wasn't easy going, with the long traverses up the hills, a rest at the top to get our breath back – and to gaze at another view the size of an English county – and then the thump, thump of the descent. We couldn't keep a rhythm going downhill. With each step the foot landed with a jolt unless you went to the effort of checking it first. Once or twice we were lucky and we would have half an hour on the flat as our path wandered along the valley floor next to a poplar-lined stream. We walked for an hour after passing through St Michel-des-Lanes, the village after Belflou, without once seeing a car.

This was farming country, the soil too rich for vines. We tried to identify the crops, not always successfully. Maize was easy, although in most places it was still only a foot or two high. We watched it grow as the trip went on. As we neared the Atlantic it started to form cobs and put out tassels. Maize was the most common crop. Wheat we knew and that too was common. There was another cereal with a long wispy ear that we had seen often in England.

'Barley,' said Guislaine.

'Oats,' said I.

Many fields had a crop about two feet high with a broad oval leaf, pointed at the end. It looked familiar but we couldn't identify it. We agreed on tobacco. There was another crop we hadn't seen before. It was stalky and two to three feet high. Each stalk divided into a head of a dozen smaller stalks crowned with seed-pods. Lentils, perhaps? Peas were common. There were fields of them, but they had suffered badly in the drought and had shrivelled away to a papery yellow.

The sun and drought had not been kind to the crops but the farmers were choosy as to what they irrigated. They had plenty of equipment, wheeled rigs that could span a field and swivelling jets capable of throwing a spray of water fifty feet into the air. But they didn't use these on the peas. The maize always got water, the wheat sometimes. The heat had been too much for the wheat. Instead of ripening to a healthy yellow, it was taking on a red-gold sheen. Stripes of this ran across otherwise green fields. The effect was startling. I thought again of 'The Windhover':

> No wonder of it: sheer plod makes plough down
> sillion
> Shine, and blue-bleak embers, ah my dear,
> Fall, gall themselves, and gash gold-vermilion.

That was it exactly. The wheat stripes were gold-vermilion.

We reached Montgeard around noon.

'That's over eighteen kilometres,' I said. 'More than Gruissan to Narbonne. You surviving?'

'Just. I need a rest. There must be somewhere we can get a coffee and some Evian.'

We asked. The restaurant had closed the year before but there was a shop in the backstreet by the church. We hurried round in case he was one of the shut-at-nooners. Today was going to have to be a picnic; there was never a hope of reaching Auterive in time for lunch. We'd be lucky to get there for supper.

He was open. 'Looks like Omar Sharif,' whispered Guislaine. While we filled our basket he plied us with questions: where were we going, what were we doing; they didn't get many hikers here, he told us. Was there anywhere for a coffee, we asked.

'Not since the restaurant closed,' he said. 'But come upstairs. Madeleine and I will be happy to give you a coffee.'

'We're not interrupting, I hope?' said Guislaine.

'*Mais non.* I will leave the shop open. No one comes at lunch.'

The shop was cramped and dingy. Upstairs was a big, open flat like a New York loft, with white leather sofas, plate-glass windows and the biggest aquarium I had seen outside a zoo. It must have been over ten feet long. We perched on the sofa, feeling sweaty and stained, listening to Jean-Pierre, the shopkeeper, talk while Madeleine made the coffee. Their daughter came in, immaculate in white, curtseyd – '*Je m'appelle Marion*' – and almost disappeared in a big leather chair.

Jean-Pierre was delighted to have someone to talk to. His wife was from Clermont-Ferrand, one of his favourite places in France, and he was from here. Here was all right but everyone was moving to the cities. Even the people still living in Montgeard commuted into Toulouse. There was no one to talk to. But it was another of his favourite places in France.

Madeleine served us with coffee in small gold and green Limoges and offered us *langue-de-chat* biscuits. Oh for a pint of beer.

'Montgeard was famous once,' said Jean-Pierre.

'Really?' said Guislaine.

'*Oui, oui.* It was the Land of Cockaigne. Pastel. You know what pastel was? A plant. It was how they would make blue

dye. They grew all the pastel here and turned it into blue –
le bleu français. Montgeard was rich and important. Then the
Portuguese went to India and came back with indigo. Phut.
That was the end of pastel.'

Most of this Guislaine had to translate for me later. I was
fascinated by the aquarium. 'What's that one?' I asked,
pointing at an iridescent blue fish.

'Pfff . . .' Jean-Pierre put on his glasses and peered. 'I'm not
sure. They die so fast I can never keep track. Every week we
are getting new ones. That one I don't know. Only one has
survived. Old Léon we call him. He has lived for, let me see,
nearly five months now. There he is, see?' He pointed at a
dead prawn in the corner. *'Pas mal, hein?'*

'Mmm. *Bravo,*' said Guislaine. 'Tell me. What's the plant
we keep on seeing that has long oval leaves and stands about
a metre high?'

'Pointed leaves?'

'Yes.'

'Tournesol.'

Of course. Sunflowers. We felt stupid and too embarrassed
to ask about the other things we couldn't recognize. I sneaked
a look at my watch. We'd been there for an hour, and we still
had nearly twenty kilomètres to go.

'You are very kind,' I said, 'and the coffee was delicious,
but we must go. We have to get to Auterive.'

'Auterive. No problem. That's just round the corner. Relax.
We can have a good talk and another coffee. Then I'll drive
you there. It's only twenty minutes.'

We looked at each other, aghast. 'Oh my God, no, no, you
see . . . You don't understand . . . God, no. Certainly not.
Heavens, what a suggestion.' We stumbled over each other
to explain.

Jean-Pierre watched us with a polite but puzzled smile.
'Comme vous voulez.' He sounded disappointed to be robbed of
company and gossip.

Packs back on and we were off into the Land of Cockaigne.

'Let's do a bit more before we stop for lunch so we can break the back of the walk, and then we'll find a really nice place with some shade and a stream,' I said

'Good idea.'

The sun had burnt off the morning clouds. There was no whisper of wind, and heat radiated from everywhere. We kept on; we had to find that cool, shady spot. We walked for more than an hour and still there was nothing, not a tree nor a barn whose shade we could borrow.

We stopped. Montgeard was far behind. We were on top of a hill. The road stretched shadeless to the valley two kilometres away. We sat down by the side of the road on a broken concrete telephone pole and spread out our picnic. We took gulps out of a litre bottle of warm Evian. The air was perfectly still. The scent of food must have sent out a lunch-is-served signal to every insect in the Haute Garonne. I felt like one of those photographs you see in the newspaper of a man wearing an overcoat of bees. Within minutes of our breaking the baguette, wasps, bees, hornets, dragonflies, giant bluebottles, flying beetles and little black dive-bombers were fighting over the ham and cheese while a chain of ants dealt with the bread. Guislaine, despite her footweariness, was trying to eat while hopping from one foot to the other and windmilling with her free arm.

'It's no good, is it?' I said. 'Can you go on?'

Guislaine nodded. I flicked a kind of flying cockroach off my forearm. I wondered if I looked as red as Guislaine. Slowly we helped each other on with our packs and creaked off down the hill, leaving our lunch to the insects. I didn't have the heart to measure how far it was to Auterive, but a glance at the map showed it was a good ten kilometres, with two more ridges and two more valleys to cross. I chewed morosely on the remains of a peach as we walked on in silence. I could almost hear Guislaine's internal dialogue: 'No, this isn't hurting, or, if it is, I shouldn't be minding the pain. It's part of the achievement. All I need to do is to make it to the next tree and then the one after that, and then . . .' I carried her pack up some of the hills but I wished I could have done more to help her.

It was at times like this that we felt the lack of songs. Guislaine is musical. She was brought up on Fats Waller and loves 'real' jazz. She likes just about anything musical except very modern classical music and cool jazz. I am unmusical, but am often brought to tears by music that communicates a story: *Tosca*, Lotte Lenya singing Brecht, John Bunyan hymns, some Tchaikovsky and all Verdi.

My love for Italian opera started on an aeroplane. We had been flying from New York to Rome, ten years earlier. 'Listen to this,' said Guislaine, handing me the earphones. I started to say no and then changed my mind. Nothing else to do. I had never listened to an opera in my life. It was '*Che gelida manina*' from *La Bohème*. For some reason, up there, on that day, I heard something I hadn't heard before. I kept the earphones on all the way to Rome and when we got back to New York I became an opera bore. I booked tickets to everything and embarrassed Guislaine by reading the libretto before going to the performance. 'What's wrong with that?' I would say. 'At least I'll understand what's going on.' 'That's not the point,' she would reply. 'You're not meant to pay attention to the story. It's the music that matters.'

But neither of us can sing. The only songs I know are hymns from school. Guislaine doesn't even have that. And anyway, we couldn't march through the Languedoc singing 'The Church's one foundation'. To help ourselves along we did a few rounds of 'Frère Jacques' and then cast around for other things we could sing together. The best advice I can give anyone contemplating a long walk is, learn a dozen songs before you leave. We will next time.

After stumbling up a long hill we at last found real trees and proper shade. We threw off our packs and stretched out in the shadows, Guislaine in the dead-beetle position, feet in air, and I flat on my back with my pack as a pillow.

Every limb said thank you.

'Don't worry. Not much further,' I said. 'I can see a short cut on the map that will save us a kilometre, and it cuts out a hill.'

'Oh, please Matou,' small voice from the dead beetle, 'not a short cut. I don't have the energy left for that.'

'No. Really. This one's different. It's one side of a triangle and, judging by the contours, it's all downhill.'

'Oh darling. Shouldn't we stick to the road?'

'It'll be OK. Off we go. Trust me.'

I was right. It was only one side of the triangle. I was, however, wrong about the contours.

'Damn contours. How was I to know they'd be uphill?'

'I said we should stick to the road. Isn't that it over there? Look, it's practically flat.'

Perhaps it was the grumps that fuelled us home. Finally, we were over the brow of the hill and coasting along a gentle downward slope. Ahead of us, a sign read: 'AUTERIVE'.

I have the photograph Guislaine took of me. I am slumped along the top of the sign, head down, eyes closed. The sun is casting a hard shadow beneath the sign.

There was a feeling almost of anticlimax. We staggered on through the village. It was more than a village. Five thousand people, according to the map. Our hotel, the Pyrénées, was on the route d'Espagne, the far side of the town and the other side of the river. Guislaine was muttering something. It may have been that she was debating whether her exhaustion was entirely caused by my short cut or the preceding ten hours might have contributed to it. We were going in single file along the pavement.

'Almost there,' I said over my shoulder – and realized Guislaine wasn't there. I was speaking to a lady pushing a pram. *'Pardon, madame,'* I said.

Guislaine had crossed the road and was easing herself and her pack on to two chairs outside a café.

I joined her.

'I don't care what you say,' she said, glaring at me, 'I'm

stopping here. I'm not doing anything till I've had a drink. Then we'll see.'

I wasn't going to argue. And a drink was very appealing.

After it we could hardly walk. We shuffled and creaked the half-mile to the Pyrénées. I don't remember much else. I think I stood in a shower for a long time holding up first one foot and then the other to allow the water to tickle their soles. We probably had dinner. I don't remember.

Lying in bed I traced our route on the map and then ran the 'thermometer' over it. 'Thirty-seven kilometres. Jesus. That's about twenty-five miles.'

Silence. Guislaine's eyes were closed, her breathing deep and rhythmic.

CHAPTER 15

'Sleep well, darling?'

'Wonderful. Never better. Slept like a baby.'

'Oh good. I am glad.'

No I wasn't. By two in the morning, after four hours of listening to rhythmic untroubled breathing, I had been getting ready to smother her with the pillow. I remembered looking across at her with disbelief as she fell asleep while I was still folding up the map. After that it had been the usual business for me of twitching muscles, restless knees and *Pendennis* – by torchlight so as not to disturb the peaceful breathing of this person next to me. At two, just when I thought there was a chance of dropping off, the noise from the route d'Espagne had picked up, tomatoes and melons from Galicia on their way to Paris.

I felt less sour once we had started walking and the rhythm of the road began to make itself felt. Auterive was behind us. We would never have to walk that far again, at least not on this trip. We were quietly proud; we had joined the Serious Walkers' Club. Not wanting to tempt whichever gods it is that look after walkers we didn't say it out loud, but we were beginning to believe that only bad luck could rob us of the Atlantic.

We started off gingerly, testing to see how stiff we were after yesterday's marathon.

'Everything working?' I asked.

'Think so. Hips a bit sore but nothing serious. How about you?'

'OK. Pretty good actually. Had a look at the tendon this morning. It's still about twice the size of my right one,

141

but it seems to be holding up fine apart from the odd twinge.'

'Oh good. And my blisters have hardened.'

'By the way, I hope you don't mind, darling, but I thought we'd add four kilometres to the walk today.'

'Hah. Oh sure. I'll show you where you can add them. And it's not to the walk.'

'Getting a bit coarse, aren't you?'

'Well. I'm not walking a yard further than I have to.'

'Look.' I waved the map in front of her. 'We can't take that yellow. It'll be a nightmare; it's the main road west from Auterive. Let's take this little white one through the hills. We'll still make Noé in time for lunch. Unless you want to spend your day being run into the ditch by fertilizer salesmen. Look.'

I flourished the map at her like someone demonstrating a card-trick, but only once. I didn't want her coming up with an alternative idea. Maps were my department. I spent hours every afternoon planning the next day's walk while Guislaine wrote in her journal. She was welcome to have a quick look at the map to endorse my decision, but God forbid that she should start making her own suggestions about the route.

Today was sunny; there were none of the fake morning rain clouds we had had since Carcassonne. I was surprised at how cheerful I was after another almost sleepless night. It is a myth that if you're tired enough you can sleep anywhere. I can fall asleep easily enough while driving on the M4 or sitting in a tube train, but not in a French bed. Thackeray didn't help. I should have taken something more boring to read. Thackeray knows how to hook his reader. He had to, as his books came out in serial form, and he needed to make sure that the reader bought the next month's chapter. I was hooked. I would finish a chapter, determined to put out my torch, but find myself so involved in the come-and-go of Victorian social life that the trucks could thunder on to eternity along the route d'Espagne, I still had to know what was going to happen in the next chapter. Would Arthur really marry the gatekeeper? Surely not. Was Helen ever going to stop allowing herself to be used as a doormat? I wanted to tell her to stop being so damn nice all the time.

Thackeray is also very funny. Sometimes I would mark a sentence and read it to Guislaine in the morning.

' "Love is an hour with us men; it is all night and all day with a woman." '

'Hmph. Sounds a bit of a chauvinist,' said Guislaine.

'Or how about this,' I went on. 'It's about barristers; he never liked lawyers. "You may get on at the Bar to be sure, where I am given to understand that gentlemen of merit occasionally marry out of their kitchens: but in no other professions." Nice isn't it?'

'Oh very funny.'

An hour and we were across the plain of the Ariège with its maize and its sunflowers – so easy to identify now that we knew what they were – and climbing again on the white road to a rolling plateau with cows and pasture and poppies. We passed a château with pepper-pot turrets.

'That'll do. Let's buy that one,' Guislaine said.

'Done. When do we move in?'

Ever since we've been together we've been buying small châteaux in France. We've never got further than the estate agent's window but there's no more satisfying fantasy.

Our short walk was taking longer than expected; we'd had a late start. It was now midday and we still had three hours to go to Noé. Veterans of the Long March we may have been, but we wanted lunch. The map came to our rescue. We could dip south to the yellow road and have lunch in St Sulpice. I did some fore-and-afting with Guislaine's pack as her hips were starting to complain.

St Sulpice was a long time coming. We passed one signpost saying 'St Sulpice – 3.2 km.', walked for half an hour and passed another one saying 'St Sulpice – 3 km.' This would often happen. The little differences in distance might be immaterial to a motorist; to a walker they are small tragedies. At last the town sign came into view. There were two of them. The top one read 'St Sulpice-sur-Lèze'. The bottom one, 'Sent Somplesi'. Sent Somplesi? Then we both realized. Basque. Our first Basque sign; Basques live on the Atlantic. A breeze from the sea.

We liked St Sulpice. It was the prettiest town so far. The road led into a square like an Italian piazza surrounded by graceful old buildings in faded red Toulouse brick. On two sides was a shady arcade with shops and restaurants and on the other two the *mairie* and the bank, buildings both dignified and frivolous at the same time.

We had a choice of restaurants. We took the Café des Arts, where we could sit outside at a table in the arcade and watch people drawing up in expensive cars and going into La Commanderie across from us. Two months ago we would have gone there and chattered about the menu – was it to be the duck with raspberry vinegar or the *langoustines* with a *coulis* of sweet peppers? Today we ate grilled pork chops, local sausages, *frites* and ice-cream, with a couple of bottles of the local rosé.

After lunch the school playground was irresistible. It had a thick, mossy lawn under ancient cedars. Sleeping after lunch was never a problem. I stretched out under a sweeping bough, arranged my pack for a pillow and was dreaming within moments, hardly even having time to wonder why it was impossible to sleep like this in bed. In the background I heard the giggles of the kindergarten class; they had come out to play and weren't sure what to make of these two large figures snoring in their playground. When, twenty minutes later, we stretched and sat up there was a scamper of retreating feet and giggles. The more daring of the boys had crept up close to inspect us and our packs. They stood in a semicircle to watch the show as we clambered up, leaning on each other for support. When we moved off, one little boy rushed forward and shot me with an imaginary bow and arrow.

'Aaaaagh . . .' I went, clutched my chest and stumbled. More nervous tittering and some backing away, but when they saw it was safe, they followed us to the gates and watched while we creaked off to the main road.

Back in the sun we were stiff again and I was regretting the second bottle of wine. I could feel the beginnings of a post-nap afternoon hangover. On the way out of town we saw a little hotel in a quiet backstreet. Noé was still two hours away. Guislaine and I both had the same thought.

'What about it?' she said.

'Mmm. In ten minutes we could be in bed and asleep. I wonder.'

It was three o'clock. The sun was murderous.

'I suppose we ought to go on.'

'Suppose so.'

We shuffled off. Things started badly. The map was in one of its playful moods and sent us on a long loop across a steep hill looking for an imaginary crossroads. The hill wouldn't end. I felt I was on a treadmill in a sauna. My head throbbed from the drink and Guislaine's pack strapped across my front was doubling the effect of the heat. Guislaine wasn't saying much. What she did say made no sense. I assumed she was hallucinating but was too fascinated with my own misery to ask.

Guislaine is well known for never being warm enough; her circulation doesn't circulate as far as toes, hands, ears or bottom.

'Darling?' I said as we staggered up the hill, the top still not in sight.

'Uh?'

'Try repeating this after me . . . This is so gooood. At last I'm warm.'

'You've cracked, haven't you?'

'No, seriously. Say it. Ohhh, this is wonderful. My feet are warm at last, my hands are warm, my bottom . . .'

'Oh OK. My feet are warm at last, my hands are warm, my bottom is warm . . . Oh shut up. I can't believe I'm saying

145

this.' She broke into something not far from a run, chased me up the hill and began pounding on me with her fists, but she was laughing.

Finally we were on a road whose existence we and the map could agree on. We juddered down a hill. One last hairpin and we were at the Garonne.

Even in its dried-up summer state it was a big river. We leant on the edge of the bridge and watched the water swirling under us. Like us, it was on its way to the Atlantic.

Noé, said Guislaine, was the French for Noah. We never did find out how the town got its name. There were two hotels; both were called Arche de Noé, Noah's Ark. One was mentioned in the by now notorious guide that had sent us to the Grand Soleil in Lézignan, but we weren't sure which it was. Though we were suspicious that no other guide said anything, we took the first Arche de Noé we came to and were rewarded with a soft mattress, crisp cotton sheets and a private bathroom.

Over dinner that night we made two new rules:

1. No more afternoon walking.
2. No more late starts. 6.30 a.m. breakfast in future.

Accordingly, next morning, we started at nine. We justified this by saying we had our shortest walk ahead of us, only fourteen kilometres. A month earlier a fourteen-kilometre walk would have been a serious undertaking; now, we told ourselves, it was a stroll. Today we were heading for the Château de Jottes at Lherm; 'Six guest rooms in a castle surrounded by a thirteen-hectare wood', said the *gîte* handbook.

On the way out of Noé we stopped to take photographs of houses. They were, as in St Sulpice, of flat, wafered Toulouse brick, which gave them a pink, woven look. The top half often had a crosswork of timbers with bricks herring-boned in between. Many had scrollwork over the doors; there were portholes and lattice-filled eyes. Noé and St Sulpice were different to the workmanlike towns of the Aude with their serious-purposed buildings. Here there was an air of frivolity. These houses had been built by grain merchants who wanted to show off their new wealth, and wouldn't have known what to do with fortifications and ramparts. These river-crossing towns had neither natural nor man-made defences. Far easier to take out the white flag at the sight of an approaching army than to fight and risk damage to property. Not that the merchants would have been troubled too much, as the English never laid claim to this part of France. Most of the fighting took place to the west of here, where the English and the French squabbled for three centuries over whose writ was to run in Aquitaine.

We stopped for a coffee in the village of Lavernose-Lacasse. Guislaine was carrying a twig and some leaves from a tree we kept on seeing which we wanted to identify. She thought it was the same as one in her mother's garden in the Quercy. We asked the lady behind the bar in the café.

She put on her glasses and considered it. 'It's a pity M. Roland isn't here,' she said. 'He knows about trees.'

A pity, the other four people in the bar agreed. The twig was passed from hand to hand. Difficult to say exactly what it was. You needed old Roland if you wanted to know about a tree. What could this be? A fruit tree. But certainly. Not a cherry, no, nor a plum. *Un mûrier*, perhaps? A mulberry. Old Roland would have known in an instant. So much for peasant lore. This for a tree that was everywhere along the roadside.

We left, mystery unsolved. An hour later we sank down for a rest at the beginning of a drive leading up to what the map said was la Serreuille, with the symbol for a château. Thanks to our three-hours-later-than-the-new-rules-allowed start, the heat was fierce. Another cloudless day. A clear brook was bubbling by the roadside. It was as cool and inviting as an iced drink. I had a floppy green and orange sun-hat from New York, which I hadn't yet worn as I preferred the First Boston sun-vizor – it was cooler. I unpacked the sun-hat and dipped it, prospector-style, in the stream. I lifted it out, brimming with clear water, and plunged my face in. Oh God, it was good. This was in the same class as lifting your feet in the air as you fell on the hotel bed.

I filled up the hat again and took it to Guislaine, whose normally tanned face had gone the colour of entrecôte. She hesitated and then dropped her face into the cold water.

'That is so good,' she gasped. 'That's the best thing I've ever felt. Again.'

For ten minutes we filled and plunged. We sprinkled water on our forearms and necks and down our chests and felt the cold as it evaporated. I filled the hat to the brim one last time and up-ended it over my head as we bounced off down the drive.

'I've just realized something,' I said.

'What?'

'You know people always say that sharing pain and hardship brings people closer together?'

'Yes.'

'It doesn't. Sharing pain actually makes people pretty ratty. It's afterwards when you've got through it that you feel close to each other.'

Our worst pain had been anything but shared. Our separation. We had spent more than two years with our lives messed up, ending in the divorce. That too was a mess. We were given the decree nisi, but it never became absolute as I was too pig-headed to file for the absolute till we had stopped bickering about money. Naturally I blamed this on Guislaine's lawyer, a man who seemed to me to have the manners and tactics of a squid. Mine, in contrast, I felt was too much of a gentleman. I had gone to him on the recommendation of Phyllida, an old friend. He had been wonderful in her divorce. I soon realized that whereas he would work overtime for someone as good-looking as Phyllida, he found men less interesting. I would be talking to him on the telephone about the latest outrageous demands and I would hear what sounded like a long yawn in the earpiece. I never met Guislaine's lawyer face to face. I would like to because, although I haven't hit anyone since I became an adult, I think with relish of popping him one on the nose.

All that, thank God, is now another country.

My worries that the Walk might put too much strain on the marriage were wide of the mark. The opposite was proving true. Apart from our argument in Castelnaudary – which, we both pointed out, had been on the only day we weren't walking – we had never felt more of a team. A friend of mine had asked for advice before we left London. He was concerned about his marriage. Did I think a trial separation was a good idea? I didn't have any good advice at the time, but I sent him a postcard from Noé. It read: 'Go for a walk.'

Refreshed by the cold water from the brook, I set off up the drive towards the château to investigate while Guislaine did some jotting in her notebook. The map showed a path leading past the château that would save us a couple of kilometres. The path was blocked by the owner, a short man with a bristly red moustache, his wife, who had the build of a removal van, and two things that might have been long-haired Dobermanns.

I approached the man. *'Excusez-moi, monsieur. Je cherche la route pour le Château de Jottes.'*

'Pas ici. Il n'y a pas une route ici. Là-bas.' He pointed back the way we had come and gestured to the left. That was the long way round.

'Er. Mais non, monsieur. Excusez-moi mais il y a une route sur la carte ici. Près de votre maison. Regardez s'il vous plaît.' I smiled ingratiatingly and handed him the map while Madame adjusted the slip collar of one of her animals; it was making a noise like a waste-compactor.

'Pfah! La carte. Pfah!' He took it from me, glared at it and handed it back. *'Il n'y a pas une route ici.'*

Madame looked at her husband for instructions. She was leaning back against the straining leashes.

'Eh bien, monsieur,' I said hurriedly. *'Merci beaucoup. Une erreur, peut-être. Au revoir, madame, merci.'* I backed away down the drive keeping watch on the dogs.

Guislaine was waiting. 'What's wrong? Puppy trouble?'

'Puppies?' I'll give you some puppy trouble. And stop laughing. I thought we'd take the long way. I'm sure it's much prettier.'

Two hours later we saw the spiked towers of the Château de Jottes over the trees. From a distance it was impressive: four pyramid towers of grey slate, one at each corner of the house, a square brick building of classical proportions. The gatehouse leading into the courtyard was capped by another impressive tower, this one like a spiked helmet.

'Gosh,' said Guislaine, 'I hope we're dressed OK. It looks awfully smart.'

She did some patting and smoothing. I was past that. The shower from the upturned sun-hat had been the final touch to my disrepair. We walked under the spiked helmet and three giant Alsatians bounded up, barking and snarling.

'Oh God, not more dogs,' we said simultaneously.

A young woman uncoiled herself slowly from a deckchair by the steps leading up to the front door. *'Ketchup! Coca! Cola! Venez.'* Two of the dogs backed off; the third, an old bitch, lame, wall-eyed and vicious, continued to circle us, snarling.

The woman came up and grasped it by the scruff of the neck. *Ketchup! Tais-toi.'*

Close up the house looked decrepit. Windows were boarded up, shutters hung at angles on their hinges, cracks ran down the brick façade. We followed the woman into an untidy office, desk and table deep in old papers and dirty coffee mugs. She went off to find *'ma mère'*, who had the keys, leaving us to explore. Next door was a big high-ceilinged room with shutters closed behind torn brocade curtains. At one end was a trestle table with a tattered cloth on it and dozens of empty wine bottles and dirty glasses. Ribbons and rosettes were tied to the curtains and the chandeliers.

'Someone's had a party,' I said.

'Yes. They must rent it out for weddings and things.'

Madame appeared, to take us upstairs. Some of the stairs

were missing and many of the old doors had been boarded up. We were to be given the best room, Madame announced with a beam.

'*Voilà!*'

I noticed that the original door lock had been splintered off and a new one screwed over it. There were four bolts on the door. Guislaine noticed it too and raised her eyebrows.

'Here you will be comfortable.' Madame gestured at the faded curtains and a great four-poster bed leaning against the wall at an odd angle.

'I hope they catch this for "Gone with the Wind II",' whispered Guislaine. 'The return of Scarlett O'Hara.'

Lunch was not on offer, Madame said, but Lherm was only two kilometres away. A moment in a car: half an hour on foot. But we were hungry. We walked the two kilometres and ate a disgusting lunch in the back room of a dingy bar. Guislaine then announced she wanted to go shopping. We had passed a shop that sold clothes on the way in, and she liked the idea of buying a skirt to walk in: 'Less confining.' The shop was closed till four, so we went to the village church and stretched out on pews. It was cool and quiet with the scent of lilies.

When the shop opened Guislaine decided that they didn't have the right skirt; we thumbed a lift back to Jottes. That was allowed; we had done our walk for the day. But how strange to be in a car. So fast. So boring.

Our dinner *en famille* consisted of Guislaine and me alone in a gloomy dining room while *la famille* ate in the kitchen watching a western on television. From time to time Madame or her daughter would sweep silently in, plonk down a piece of limp ham or some lettuce and sweep silently out again.

'I wonder why they go on living here,' said Guislaine. 'The repair bills must be a lot more than they make from taking in occasional guests. They'd be much happier in a bungalow. That's the French for you.'

'Reminds me more of Ireland,' I said. 'It's like a Molly Keane novel. The family abandon the main house and go and live in the servants' quarters. Every year a bit more of the house falls down and the family retreats a bit further. Meanwhile they take in guests in those parts of the big house that are still habitable. Every franc helps.'

We crept up to bed by the light of one forty-watt bulb for three flights of stairs. Everything creaked. I pushed all four bolts home on the bedroom door. A full moon shone in through the uncurtained windows. Guislaine fell quickly asleep. What was her secret? I took out *Pendennis*, hoping to take my mind off all the unexplained noises. The house was groaning like a galleon under full sail. At midnight I turned off my light.

At one o'clock the gunfire started.

At first there was just a bang. Perhaps a bird-scarer, although what it was scaring at one in the morning apart from me I couldn't think. Birds were asleep. Then there were answering bangs. Soon it wasn't just bangs but a regular chatter of gunfire. It was coming nearer. I lay in bed, rigid with fear, but finally forced myself to get up and creep to the window, the floorboards squeaking at each step. I stood by the side of the window and peeped out, not wanting to show myself in the full moon. The lawns and the woods beyond were chalk-white. Nothing moved. The chatter and counter-chatter of gunfire rose in intensity; it sounded as if it was coming from the next-door field. Still I saw nothing. Guislaine slept on. The house creaked and groaned some more.

I wondered whether to wake *la famille*, but I didn't know where they were and I didn't like the thought of Ketchup springing for my jugular from a dark corner. In any case it seemed wise to keep the four bolts rammed home between us and whatever was going on outside. How had the door been splintered off its hinges last time?

I tiptoed back to bed and turned on the torch to consult the map. Maybe there was a military range near the château. Nothing. Not another building nearer than Lherm, two kilometres away. By now it was 2.30. Had the Basques risen? We hadn't read a paper since Castelnaudary. But surely we would have known if there had been an uprising? There was a crescendo of gunfire. It sounded as if it was coming from the lawn. Then two isolated bangs. Silence. The moon was casting stark shadows over the four-poster. I fingered *Pendennis* and waited.

I was fast asleep with the book across my chest when the alarm rang at 5.45.

CHAPTER 16

The alarm went, Guislaine was up and twirling around within seconds and I was left groping with memory to try and sort out what was real and what was dream. The gunfire . . . ? That was dream. No . . . *Pendennis* was still there where it had fallen from my hand, and the torch. Battery flat. That had all happened. Hadn't it? What was going on?

And Guislaine had almost finished in the bathroom. She was doing everything but whistling. Had some alien colonized her body in the night?

'Morning, darling,' she chirped, bending over to give me a peck on the cheek. 'Mmm. I slept well, although I did wake up a couple of times to some funny noises. Must have been frogs, all exes and zeds. Did you hear it?'

'You mean the gunfire. You heard it too?'

'Gunfire? What, from guns?' She gave me a funny look.

'Oh never mind.' I looked out of the window to check for corpses on the lawn. No. Just dew, undisturbed by footsteps, and a hen clucking around. I brushed my teeth as Mary Poppins put the finishing touches to her packing.

'Do you want me to wait for you?' she asked.

'No, no. Go ahead.' Oh my God. What if the dogs got her?

'OK darling,' she said, tugging at the bolts on the door, 'see you downstairs.'

'Yeah. Er, watch out for the dogs.'

Coward.

But as she groped her way down the stairs I did listen for sounds of Ketchup. Monsieur, whom we hadn't met last night, was up at six every day to make breakfast before going out to the farm, his wife had told us. What if he had decided to stay in

154

bed and Ketchup hadn't had breakfast yet? I listened carefully while pushing the last of my things into the pack. I could run downstairs with one of the blankets if there was an attack and throw it over the dog like a net . . . I heard the television . . . Monsieur was up.

Guislaine was almost finished by the time I joined her. She wasn't quite so bubbly now. 'I can't believe the way these people listen to television,' she said. 'I mean it's never off. What is it, a horse race or something? Horses don't race at six in the morning.'

'This coffee is delicious. It's a pity Monsieur didn't make dinner last night. He's a better cook than his wife. I expect the less time he spends in this house the happier he is.'

At 6.30 we were out of the house. Not a peep from the Alsatians, and a total bill for 145 francs for room and dinner.

'That's pretty good,' said Guislaine.

'They should have paid us. At least the gunfire was free.'

'What are you talking about?'

'Doesn't matter. You know, it's almost chilly this morning. Isn't that wonderful?'

The sun was just up, there was dew everywhere and a wispy mist over the stream – le Touch, said the map. We had to walk along that for half an hour or so and then we would have our longest straight, nearly six kilometres. The straight took us off the edge of 'Toulouse–Albi' and on to 'Tarbes–Auch', the third of our four maps. That gave today a half-wayish feel, although we wouldn't actually be at half-way till we were past Samatan, today's destination.

Every five minutes or so a car passed us, grizzled farmers in beaten-up station wagons or a Citroënful of hens on their way to market.

'Rush hour starts early round here,' said Guislaine.

A bread van drew up at a cottage to make a delivery; baguette smell wafted over to us. 'Shall we buy one?' I suggested. 'We could eat it on the go.'

155

'No. It's about time we lost some weight.'

We had both been expecting to lose stones on the Walk. I was disappointed that so far I had taken in just one notch on my belt – and even that felt tight. 'Oh OK. Which way is that car up there going to go at the crossroads?'

'Er, left.'

'Sorry. Straight on. I win.'

This kept us happy for the half-hour up to the crossroads and then we went back to looking at the trees and the fields. It was the only time we played a game on the trip. On long car trips we play everything from Botticelli to the five-letter-word game to pass the time.

We stopped for our usual rest after an hour and a half. I ran the 'thermometer' over the map to see how far we had come. Ten kilometres. A record. This was flying, over six kilometres an hour. I interrupted Guislaine, who was saying something about the smell of frying calf's liver drifting over from a nearby farmyard, with the news.

'Don't get over-confident,' she said. 'That was pretty easy going.'

She was right. Walking across the wide plain of the Garonne was one thing. The flatlands ended just ahead of us at the Forest of Lahage. After that, 'Tarbes–Auch' showed nothing but hills. The Fan proper. The walk to Auterive had been just a foretaste.

Walking through the forest gave Guislaine an opportunity to flex her tree-recognition muscles. This was a walnut, that was an ash, and could that be a chestnut over there?

'That's an oak, isn't it?' I hazarded, pointing at a big tree just ahead.

'Heavens no. No, no. Wrong crown. Too wispy.'

'Oh . . . What are those?'

'They're easy. They're poplars. You can always tell them. Think of a fish backbone. Well, they're just like that upside-down. Straight trunk with all the branches pointing up at the same angle. Can't miss them.'

156

This was wonderful. I was fascinated with my new poplar-recognition ability and kept trying it out. It worked.

After the forest and before our first hill we crossed one of the hiking trails, a Grande Randonnée, GR87 according to the map. All the books I had read about walking in France said how good they were. 'Forget the roads,' Frank Neyens had told us, 'you can't go wrong on the GRs.' The book had paragraphs of instructions about the variety of marks used to denote the paths of the GRs. This was the first we had met, so we were intrigued.

We reached the crossroads and began hunting for marks. We searched trees, walls and roads. Nothing. The field across which the GR was meant to run was virgin. Later in the Walk, in Bassoues, we asked our host – who, being a Belgian, had found out everything there was to know about this part of France – about this. He laughed. 'Forget it. The farmers get rid of all the marks. They plough them up or obliterate them. The last thing they want are bunches of hikers walking across their fields. I'm told the GRs are OK in the mountains where no one's growing anything, but around here it's hopeless.'

We climbed to Montgras, a tiny village astride the ridge of our first hill, and took a rest on the church steps while I played with the map.

'We're in a new *département*,' I said. 'This is the Gers.'

'Is that where Auch is?'

'That's right.'

We had visited Auch a year earlier for a weekend break from First Boston. We had flown to Toulouse, rented a car, driven to Auch and stayed at the Hôtel de France, owned by André Daguin, the most famous cook of the South-West and, like all Gascons, *un rugbyman*. The hotel celebrated rugby, *foie gras* and Armagnac, the three glories of the Gers. Dinner the first night had started with four different kinds of *foie gras*, two from a duck and two from a goose; the game was to say which was which. We had been toying with the idea of making Auch our half-way point on the Walk and taking a couple of days' rest there to mend socks and clean clothes. But we had drifted on to a more southerly route. Auch would have been too much of a detour, and the Hôtel de France with its Michelin stars and four kinds of *foie gras* didn't seem right anyway.

As we walked along the ridge of the hill we could see as far as two or three valleys on either side. The Gers was a new landscape. The fields were smaller and hedgy, the landscape patched. I had learnt 'The Windhover' by now and was on to Hopkins's next poem, 'Pied Beauty', more lyrical but less moving – 'Glory be to God for dappled things'. The country here was pied and dappled:

Landscape plotted and pieced – fold, fallow, and plough . . .

The prairie fields of the Haute Garonne were behind us. Here there was less brick and more clay in the houses; agriculture was cosier. And if we thought we had been in duck and goose land before, it was nothing compared with the Gers. Every house had a troop of fat geese, big Barbary ducks with red jowls, and plump white Pekings. Sometimes there would be a whole field given over to them. We loved to watch them. The geese in particular were fascinating. In a minute we could see the social order, who was boss and who was getting a bit above themselves, but it was an ordered society quite unlike the bad-tempered hen world and its power pecking.

We weren't sure what to expect from Samatan. We were worried about the hotel. We – that is to say, Guislaine and her fluent French – usually telephoned ahead a day in advance to make a booking. I would ask her as she hung up if they sounded friendly, on the principle that nice hotels sound friendly on the phone. And while she was making the booking, I would usually hiss in her free ear, 'For God's sake, get directions.'

She had called Samatan from Lherm; the conversation had gone on for a suspiciously long time. The Hôtel Maigné was the only clipping we had for Samatan. We had found it in the

Michelin listed as a *'restaurant simple avec chambres'*, and although I hadn't clipped the mention I remembered something in the Gault-Millau about a warm welcome and old-fashioned food.

'Well? How do they sound?'

'Drunk.'

'Drunk . . . ?'

'Yes. I could hardly understand a word he was saying.'

'Oh. Do they have a room?'

'I think so. I'm not sure.'

'Well, did you find out where they are located? We've got to walk the best part of thirty kilometres to get there and I don't fancy walking an extra three or four looking for a drunk who may or may not have a room for us.'

'I'm not sure; it was difficult. He was slurring his words so much. I asked him twice where he was in Samatan and he muttered something I couldn't make out, and then the third time he sort of roared at me, *"Madame, nous ne sommes pas la capitale de la France,"* and hung up.'

'Hmm.'

The last four or five kilometres to Samatan were the usual noonday slog. We had been hoping for a sight of the Pyrenees from a hill crest, but the heat haze had cut down visibility too much. The last bit into Samatan was downhill and made me understand why the bastinado was such a terrible punishment. Each time a foot touched the road I wanted to lift it again before the weight came on to it. Blisters were no longer a problem but, after six hours on the road, the soles of both feet were on fire.

'Where the hell is Maigné?' I asked.

'Dunno. I'm sure we'll find it once we're in town.'

'I mean there are signs advertising every other damn hotel and restaurant but nothing about Maigné. Maybe the whole thing's a drunken joke. You got a wrong number.'

'Relax.'

We passed the town sign and came to a roundabout. There, like a winning-post, right by the roundabout, was a little restaurant with a garden and striped umbrellas. Maigné it wasn't, but for the time being Au Canard Gourmand was fine. A drink, a rest, and then we'd find Maigné.

Tasting the ice-cold drinks – the usual combination of Evians, *panaché* and *citron pressé* – triggered our ritual of silent ecstasy followed by, as the cool liquids made themselves felt, exclamations of 'I can't believe how good this is.'

The sensation of pleasure became almost unbearable when I took off my shoes and put my feet up on a chair. 'This is too much,' I said. 'Let's have lunch here. Maigné can wait.'

'Yes. Let's.'

Good. Another hour before I had to put my shoes back on. A menu came. Salad, grilled duck, omelette for Madame, bottle of rosé, more Evian, another bottle of rosé and two – no, make that three – blackcurrant sorbets. The waitress, our new buddy, asked if we had a room for the night. We said we were heading for Maigné.

'You're lucky to get a bed,' she said. 'The hotels round here are getting booked up. Louis Malle is starting a new film. He is going to be based in Samatan and all the beds for miles around have been taken. He himself will be *chez* Maigné.' She gave us directions. We couldn't miss it. Down the main road, through the square and just up the hill on the right.

Lunch inside us, we marched off, conquering heroes now, down an alley of planes whose branches arched over the road a hundred feet up. The hotel was easy to find, fifty yards from the main square.

'I hope that's it,' we both said, looking at the friendly ivy-covered building with its shutters and window-boxes. It was. Our room was on the first floor, deliciously cool and dark; we opened the shutters and looked out over a terraced garden with geraniums and vines. In the middle was an old well with an iron hat and a bucket on a spindle. Steps led up from the garden to an open field beyond.

We settled in, showered, took out clean clothes – a bit crumpled now, but still able to give us a reborn feeling every time we put them on – and went out for a wander, Guislaine to find a skirt and I to buy a watch, as my last one, a Swatch, had fallen off. Samatan was the centre for the *foie gras* trade. There were three buildings like hangars on the way into town, where, on Mondays, the peasants and the housewives brought the pink shiny livers for sale. 'Volailles et Gras' said the sign. They brought the birds as well so you could buy your *foie gras* either on the slab or in the bird. We were told later how the skilful buyer, like a good diagnostician, could tell the state of the bird's liver by prodding and feeling in the right place and examining the eyes and feet.

We met at the café on the town square, where the fountain bubbled on regardless of the drought. I showed Guislaine my new Swatch. It had a white face and clumsy green luminous hands and was exactly like the watch I had when I was seven, my first. Guislaine had tried on a number of skirts and was worried. They were all either too tight or too floppy, or too frilly or too sober. Could I help? We went back to the shop. The first skirt, a yellowish thing in a floaty Indian cotton, was perfect. I bought it for her, a present, to save her the agony of having to make the choice.

'And I'll get you a shirt,' she said. 'You need one. Throw out that awful non-iron thing.'

She was right. I had bought it the day before we left and so far only worn it once, in Carcassonne. It was a disaster; it felt slimy and had been cut for someone whose shoulder blades touched. Still, throwing it out seemed a bit much. 'I can't throw it out. I mean I've only worn it once.'

'What do you think of this one? It looks wonderfully loose and light.'

'It's nice. How about the yellow? I like that.'

'No. You'll be better in this. It will suit your colouring.'

'Thanks . . .' It was purple. 'Purple? Bit, well, unusual, isn't it?'

'Not at all. It's got you written all over it.'

We had another session at the café to celebrate. 'How about

another rest day?' I said. 'I know. Let's call your mother and see if she can drive over and join us for lunch tomorrow.'

'OK. If she can come, we'll stay. If not, we'll go on and save our rest day for later.'

'Right.'

Guislaine went off to make the call and I sat back to watch the movement. An election was coming up and the *mairie* was being draped with swathes of *bleu, blanc, rouge* for the big meeting. I saw a notice pinned up in the café window inviting people to apply as extras for M. Malle's film. All ages and types would be needed. Just send a photograph. Filming would start in a month. (The film became *Milou in May*.)

Guislaine returned. She was the colour of my new shirt.

'That was a long call. Is she coming? Are you all right?' She looked as if she had been wrestling with someone. And lost.

'I got trapped. The phone-booth door jammed. I couldn't get out. It was terrible. The heat.'

'You got trapped in the phone booth? You're joking.'

'It wasn't funny. I could have suffocated.'

'Poor darling. How did you get out?'

'Oh it was terrible. I was talking to Mummy and I tried to open the door for some air. I couldn't. She thought I'd gone mad. Then she panicked too and said where was I, she was going to call the police. Meanwhile half the population of Samatan were hanging around laughing.'

I tried to look serious. 'Gosh. Poor you. How did you get out?'

'Oh, in the end some man got me out. He had to almost break the door down.'

'Heavens. Is she coming, then?'

'Yes. She'll be here noonish tomorrow. And she's bringing Dougal. He's staying with her.'

Good. A rest day.

'No arguments this time.'

'No arguments.'

For walkers, rest days have a special luxury: we put almost

162

the entire contents of our packs in the hotel washing machine
and then hung them out to dry at the bottom of the field beyond
the garden. On normal days the routine was to strip on arrival,
sloosh our sweaty clothes around in the basin and then drape
them around the window.

We dined *chez* Maigné. Meals there were serious. A figure
who looked disturbingly like Guislaine's aunt Tony bustled up
in a white apron and gave us the menu. We were expected to
eat a proper meal – no dipping about on the *à la carte* and I
think I'll just have an omelette please. I had the feeling that
if I didn't eat my greens I wouldn't be allowed any pudding.

The choice was:

110 francs	200 francs
Potage Velouté	Potage Velouté
*	*
Hors-d'œuvre	Foie Gras en
	Gelée de Madère
*	*
Saumon en Croustade	Homard Mayonnaise
*	*
Caneton Rôti	Chateaubriand
	ou
	Magret Grillée
Haricots Verts	Haricots Verts
Pommes Lyonnaises	Pommes Lyonnaises
*	*
Fromage	Fromage
*	*
Patisserie	Patisserie
*	*
Fraises Chantilly	Fraises Chantilly
*	*

'I think I'll have the 200-franc one,' I said. 'I'd like to try
the *foie gras*. This should be the place for it.'

Guislaine took the 110-franc menu and then tried to duck the fish course. Aunt Tony wasn't having any of that and slid half a foot of salmon in thick puff pastry in front of her with a cheery *'C'est très bon, madame. Très léger.'*

Maigné himself, the telephone roarer, appeared. We kept an eye on him as he went on his rounds. How drunk was he tonight, or would it be yesterday's hangover? He was in his fifties and dressed in chef's uniform. The customers all looked like locals; he would approach each with a serious face and a question and then his face would light up like an eleven-year-old's as they answered.

He rolled over to our table with the gait of a sea-captain. *'Bonzzoir. Vouzzzzh êtes anglais?'*

He wasn't drunk. He'd had a stroke. Once we got used to his slurring he wasn't difficult to understand.

'Anglais. Ah, you have money then.' He leant forward and winked while rubbing thumb and forefinger together.

We were learning that in the Gers the English are regarded as the Arabs used to be in London: loaded, and easily parted from it. We kept on hearing stories of 'You won't believe this but old Claude sold his barn/stables/chicken-coop to an Englishman for . . .'

'Not much, I'm afraid.'

'C'est dommage, hein? What do you do?' he asked.

My God. This was the first time I had been asked that since I became unemployed. For twenty-two years the answer had been automatic. But now . . .

'Umm. I'm a writer.' Why not? I hadn't written anything but maybe I would.

'Ah. I understand why you have no money,' he said, shaking his head. 'Ah well. Never mind. My son is a surgeon. He has plenty of money but he doesn't want this place. I would like to sell. It's getting too much for me. Well, maybe you have a friend with money. Remember me if he is looking for a good business. Please, enjoy your dinner.' He rolled off back to the kitchen with a parting *'Écrivain, alors,'* and an upward rolling of the eyeballs.

'People didn't behave like that when I said I was an investment banker,' I said.

'Well, this is interesting news,' said Guislaine. 'A writer, eh?'

'Oh, I don't think so. I just wanted something to say. You're the writer. Anyhow, what do you think of the purple shirt? Don't you think it's a bit much? White seems to be the in colour here.'

Guislaine smiled broadly. 'It's you, darling.'

Next morning we had breakfast at nine o'clock. Nine o'clock! Birdsong and the scent of roses drifted in through the open door; we had slept like children and could linger over fresh bread and home-made greengage jam. Another pot of coffee? Another pot of coffee.

We were alone in the dining room watching Aunt Tony and the others laying tables for Sunday lunch. I had a copy of yesterday's *Sud-Ouest* and was reading an interesting account of the Common Market's plan to bankrupt French farmers, particularly those in the South-West.

'Keep us a good table for lunch,' said Guislaine to Tony. 'This one by the window would be nice. We'll be four.'

Outside, the gardener was plucking deadheads off the geraniums. Actually, he wasn't too fussy as to whether he plucked deadheads or liveheads. *La patronne*, Mme Maigné perhaps, came out to inspect.

She looked at the healthy blooms in the wheelbarrow. 'Idiot. Fool. What are you doing?' She picked up a handful of bright red flowers and brandished them at him. '*Qu'est-ce-que-c'est que ça?* Ha! You are blind, yes? You should work in a car-park. This is dead? You'll be dead if you don't take more care. *Ah, mais non. Quelle vie.*'

She marched off into the kitchen in a fine temper. God help whoever was peeling potatoes. The gardener shrugged. He went on picking every third bloom, dead or alive. We ordered our very last pot of coffee.

After breakfast we wandered, Guislaine to the bookshop and the pharmacy and I to look for a swimming pool. A circus was in town. It was a big one, not like the back-yard affair in Ornaisons. It filled the open area by the Marché de Volailles et Gras. The big top was going up and the sides of four-axle trailers had been lowered to show the beasts in their cages. A red and blue sign read 'DANGER – TIGRES'. Tethered to a tree was a lone elephant. His trunk went constantly down to search the tarmac for water and then up as if to spray it over his back. On and on he went, like some poor crazed pendulum. The tree he was tied to gave him no shade so he caught the full heat of the sun.

I walked on. The pool was half a mile out of town. It was closed. Too early in the year . . .

I found Guislaine in the pharmacy browsing between the herb teas and the suppositories. She has a love affair with French pharmacies.

'Do you think they've got anything for my crotch?' I asked. It was chafed from walking, and Vaseline didn't seem to be working.

'Oh, I'm sure they do. Just show the lady behind the counter.'

'Show her what?'

'Your crotch.'

'Shhh. Are you mad? I'm not dropping my trousers in here. She'd have me arrested.'

'Oh don't be so silly. They're all medically trained in France. They can even identify mushrooms.'

'Yes, well I don't have mushrooms thanks. I'll keep my sore crotch.'

Later, in our room, Guislaine introduced me to E-45. This is a miracle cream that she had been keeping secret. It is less sticky than Vaseline and much more effective. Models use it, Guislaine told me. I didn't ask what for. On a three-hundred-mile walk, these are the things that matter.

We sat in the courtyard waiting for Gael.

'You know why this is such a nice town?' I said.

'Why?'

'You'd miss it if you were driving. It's not in any of the guide-books, the main road doesn't go through it and you'd have no reason to stop. That's its charm. The only people who come here are people buying or selling *foie gras*.'

Gael arrived just after one, with Dougal. He was an old friend who was staying with her. She was, as always, jumping from subject to subject, each one a new enthusiasm. How pretty the hotel was . . . Were we going to Gimont? They had driven through it on the way . . . No? What a shame . . .

We sat in the garden with a bottle of cold rosé from the Béarn while Guislaine went upstairs to fill her pack so Gael could try it on.

'This isn't too heavy. It doesn't weigh as much as I was expecting. Oh, it's so wonderful what you're doing.'

'Well, it was your idea, Gael,' I said. 'Remember, sea to sea.'

'Oh yes. So it was. I'd like to do a trip like this. But I'd need someone strong to do it with; maybe Ali's son would like to . . . Perhaps I can join you for a day's walk further on? It's not too far.'

Time for lunch. Gael reluctantly took the pack off and we went to our table by the window. It was lucky we had reserved it; the room was full. At the next table were two old matrons in pre-war hats talking in that urgent whisper that compels eavesdropping.

'. . . and then he left her in Paris. Alone.'

'*Ah non*, it cannot be true.'

'*Mais oui*. And he took the dog.'

'The dog? *Mon Dieu*.'

'I think I'll have something light, a salad maybe,' said Gael.

'*Madame, c'est pas possible*. Today is Sunday. There is no *à la carte*. Only the full menu.'

Gael focused on it. 'My God. Seven courses. I can't.'

'*Si, si, madame*. But the soup is not compulsory.'

We had some more rosé from the Béarn. *Magret* followed *homard* followed *foie de gras* across the table. This was the first real conversation we'd had with other people for two weeks.

They had to leave at five, as Gael was expecting visitors at home. It was the time of summer guests for anyone who had a house in southern France. Gael is a remarkable, brave woman. She has come through serious illness without complaint, she has written several books – one of them, *The End of a Dream*, a classic of travel writing – she paints well and above all she has the capacity to stimulate. She has the widest and most unusual circle of friends and a never-ending ability to surprise.

We waved them goodbye. Lunch had been too much. We had to have a walk. We ambled around Samatan looking at a church here, a bridge there, and ended up in the Musée de Foie Gras. We went in reluctantly, as we are both squeamish about how *foie gras* is produced. We were shown round by a charming man with a naval beard who spoke old-fashioned English. The walls were hung with farmyard photographs featuring the happiest and freest range of birds. Quite a contrast with the broiler factories that we pass on the way to the Norfolk coast. Our guide explained that the birds were left completely alone to enjoy their farmyard lives until the last three weeks, when they were force-fed with corn. Then, '*Zut*, it's over.'

CHAPTER 17

Samatan was a special place. Later I learnt that both Wellington and the Black Prince spent the night there, nearly five centuries apart, Wellington hot on Maréchal Soult's scent and the Black Prince careering through on his Grande Chevauchée of fire and pillage.

We left early, but everyone was up and bustling around for market day. As we walked up the hill out of town we were passed by a steady trickle of muddy cars and battered vans bringing *foie gras* to the market. We would have liked to stay another day to see the fun, but we had things to do. After much measuring with the roller we had decided that St Soulan, a village of two hundred people, was half-way. It was seven kilometres from Samatan.

After St Soulan we would be nearer the Atlantic than the Mediterranean.

Yesterday I had gone to buy champagne to drink as we crossed the imaginary half-way tape. A full-size bottle would have been nice, but I had become too niggardly about weight to carry anything that heavy, even for seven kilometres. I searched Samatan for a quarter-bottle. This was not easy to find. Samatan is a place of big appetites, and wine, like meals *chez* Maigné, comes in big quantities. I asked in two wine shops for something smaller than a half; looks were exchanged. That the English, with all their money, had come to this. Here was proof of their legendary meanness. A quarter-bottle? *Mais non, monsieur.* Eventually I found a split of sparkling Burgundy in the local Co-op, a self-service place, thank God. Even there, when I came to pay, I wanted to tell them that normally I bought wine in magnums.

We had decided to delay our first stop until St Soulan. We would drink the sparkling Burgundy and allow the regulation seven-minute stop to stretch. Have a party. We saw the village sign towards the top of a long hill. There was a farm and a lot of noise. Another outpost of the Dobermann Breeders' Association. We reached the sign. Guislaine was not keen to celebrate just a lunge away from a beast with bits of trouser stuck on its teeth, separated from us only by some strands of rusty wire. I stood in front of the village sign and uncorked the bottle while Guislaine took a photograph from a safe distance. The wine, well shaken by now, frothed out over the sign leaving us a minimum to drink. For this we were thankful. It wasn't quite nine in the morning. Later someone told us that St Soulan was the patron saint of drunks. We never verified this.

Four minutes later, we balanced the bottle against the road sign as a trophy, our personal flag on the South Pole, and marched on towards the Atlantic.

'Booooggghhhh. Boooooggggggghhhhhhhh,' I gurgled.

'What on earth are you doing?' said Guislaine.

'That's Atlantic surf crashing on the beach.'

'Oh do be quiet.'

Getting closer to the Atlantic was fine. What was not so fine was tonight. We didn't know where we were going. The area west of Samatan was almost empty of villages on the map and a virtual void in the guide-books – nothing in the Michelin, nothing in the *Logis de France* and just two mentions in the *gîte* handbook, both of which would have required a forty-kilometre walk. The Musée de Foie Gras in Samatan had come to our rescue. It doubled as the local tourist office; they had given us a list of accommodation all over the Gers from which we had chosen the Moulin de Mazères, a *gîte* which the list said was in Lartigue. Our problem was that according to the map Mazères and Lartigue were a good four kilometres apart and we didn't know which to head for.

'You did get directions, didn't you?' I asked Guislaine.

'Well no. I thought we could ask.' She was still shy after being roared at by M. Maigné.

We stopped at a café in Saramon for a twenty minute rest and a drink. It was the only village of any size for miles around and had a bleak, uncared-for feel, very different to the pink-brick exuberance of Samatan and Noé and St Sulpice. We asked the barman if he knew the Moulin de Mazères and its whereabouts. No problem, can't miss it, signs everywhere, you'll be there in a few minutes. So we might have been if we'd had a car.

Two hot hours later we were wishing that we had pulled him along by his tongue to show us the way.

Our route was through beautiful countryside, it was true, the Gers at its purest, but we really weren't interested. It was also uphill, then up another hill and then along the crest. The breeze had failed and the tar was melting: if we stepped in the wrong place it stuck to our shoes. Guislaine was melting too and I helped her with her pack up the hills. I didn't mind the extra weight so much as the lack of ventilation that came from having a pack strapped across my chest. I could have been wearing an electric blanket.

We passed Lartigue. There were signs to everything but the Moulin. We cursed the barman in Saramon. A long time later, Mazères arrived. It was a small village of a cluster of houses round three or four grand ones. No *moulins*. It was two o'clock and 115 degrees in the sun. We made attempts to admire the architecture of the big houses. At least we could ask the way here.

We walked down a short drive to a little farm and knocked on the front door. No answer. We went round to the back and knocked again. Nothing, although there were two cars parked outside and we could hear a television.

We tried the next house, where I tugged on an old brass bell-pull. 'That would be nice in Norfolk,' said Guislaine, fingering it. The bell clanged, but no one came to the door.

We looked for the phone box. That was always next to the

village church – but not here; and the church was in ruins. Behind it and across the green was the grandest house of all, seven windows wide and Queen Anne-ish in style. The front door was open. We knocked and went in. Perhaps they would know where the Moulin was to be found, or we could use their phone.

We were standing in a great hall; it was empty but for some packing cases and an eight-foot sculpture of a thick-limbed female. Over the stairs hung an abstract painting the size of a garage door. We tried a few timorous *'Allô'*s. They echoed round the hall. There were the remnants of a half-eaten meal on one of the packing cases. 'Let's get out of here,' I said. 'This is too like the *Marie Celeste*.'

We didn't feel like knocking on any other doors after that, and we trudged off down the hill. It was the only village in France where we weren't barked at.

At the bottom of the hill we came to a T-junction and a road running along the river Arrats, said the map. Not a *moulin* in sight. Guislaine voted for right, where we could see a bungalow half a mile away in the middle of a field. I voted for left, where we could see only trees but where the map had a cogwheel sign denoting, according to the legend, a *usine*. 'It must be hidden in the trees but, as it's by the river, it could be a mill. Perhaps that's it.'

'Let's ask in the bungalow. There's a car there and the French always come home for lunch.'

'Oh OK.' Like most men I hate asking, and I was sure we would be going in the wrong direction.

Fifteen minutes later we were banging on the bungalow door. This time a dog barked from inside, but no one came to answer. We had gone the wrong way. Guislaine sat herself down on their bench for a rest. I fought hard with the urge to say I told you so, and settled for feeling smug instead.

'We can't stop here, on their front porch,' I said. 'What if they come back?'

'Good,' said Guislaine.

'Well, anyhow, let's push on. It must be that thing on the map. Only another couple of kilometres and we'll be there.'

Thank God, it was. There were tall trees, rushing water and stables behind the mill. Madame was standing in a purple tracksuit in the courtyard, hoover in hand. She pointed it at us. *'Les Morlands?'*

'Oui, oui, madame.' We bustled up and dropped our packs at her feet.

She backed off a pace or two and suggested that we would want to shower before we did anything else. She led us off to a dark bedroom in a converted stable, some distance from the main house. We didn't like this at all. Was there a possibility of maybe something a little more cheerful? After a lot of puffing and glances at our sweat- and dust-stained clothes she admitted us to the main house. We were led into a room over a millstream, decorated Hollywood-style, all in white. This, Madame announced, was the room her mother used when she came to stay. Thank you, thank you. We showered quickly, forgot about lunch, fell on the bed and slept till dinner while the water bubbled and rushed under our room.

Dinner was *en famille* at a round table in the big mill room, which acted as kitchen, dining room, salon and study. The house, apart from our room, was modestly furnished. Monsieur was living on a pension, a retired local government official, we decided. We chatted with him while Madame cooked dinner. He gave us a *floc*, the local Armagnac-based aperitif, which neither of us had had before. It was good, like muscat but more aromatic. Conversation was slow but friendly as Monsieur wanted to practise his English. They were clearly a family of limited means. The mill was their second house – home being in Toulouse – but it and the horse farm attached to it were expected to show a profit, otherwise they'd have to be sold.

We were joined for dinner by Jean-Claude, a spoilt and sulky grandson, and Pierre, a family friend who was staying with them. Conversation was in French and I struggled to keep up. Pierre worked for the SNCF – the French railways

– as an engineer. Had we been on the TGV? Was it true that there were no fast trains in England? He shook his head in disbelief. The conversation switched to horses. Equipment was important, said Madame. She believed it was worth paying over the odds for quality. She had two saddles that had come from Hermès in Paris. They had cost 20,000 francs each. Expensive maybe, but worth it. This was said not to impress us but to Pierre the railway engineer, who nodded agreement. Guislaine and I looked at each other. Two thousand pounds for a saddle? Did we have the exchange rate right?

We talked of food. Dinner was delicious. A thick chewy steak with a wonderful sauce. But you couldn't get any food of quality in Toulouse, said Madame. True, true, her husband agreed. Again, in her opinion, if you wanted good food you had to go to Paris. Fauchon was best. More money perhaps, but better value. Was it not the same in England? Where did we shop? Guislaine and I weren't sure what to say. I had three Hermès ties, relics of City days, and I've only visited Fauchon once. In both places the prices would make a sheikh blench. Later we imagined the English equivalent of this scene, sitting in, say, a sheep farm in the Yorkshire Dales with a retired Civil Servant and a British Rail employee discussing Turnbull and Asser shirts and whether the smoked salmon in Fortnum's was better than at Harrods.

Madame had cooked two puddings. There was a lime and almond ice-cream, a new recipe from a friend, and, in case the experiment failed, a large basin of chocolate mousse. I had two helpings of the ice-cream while Guislaine finished the whole basin of chocolate mousse, muttering things about how it reminded her of Strasbourg.

After dinner Madame refused our offer to help with the washing-up. For that there was a gleaming new dishwasher. Jean-Claude flounced off upstairs complaining that his jeans hadn't been properly washed, and Monsieur rooted around in the drinks cupboard for an old bottle of Armagnac. He poured a glass for each of us and nothing for himself. Madame handed him instead a saucer with a dozen brightly coloured pills on it. He pushed the dog, a floppy yellow Labrador, out of his chair and sat down with a sigh.

He gave three pills to the dog and swallowed the rest himself. 'Ah, the dog,' he said. 'It is not how it was. Now it has, how do you say, a *crise de foie*.'

By ten we were back in the neat little bedroom over the millstream. The sound of rushing water worked its magic and I had the best night's sleep of the trip.

We had only a short walk ahead of us, sixteen kilometres to Seissan, so there was none of the now customary dawn start. We wandered into the big room at about eight. Jean-Claude had stopped whining about his jeans and was complaining that his vitamin pills had been lost. Madame searched the kitchen in vain. Monsieur, looking old and weary this morning, wheezed out of his chair and went upstairs to look for them while his seventeen-year-old grandson stood pouting in the kitchen. Guislaine muttered something in English about where she would have liked to kick him. Monsieur returned. He couldn't find the vitamin pills but here were some iron pills. They would be just as good. He gave them to the boy, who swallowed them with a glass of water and walked off, banging the door behind him.

Madame shrugged and gave us a well-you-know-how-children-are smile. Now that Jean-Claude had been taken care of, breakfast could begin. Would we like Madame's *petit déjeuner pour eekaires*?

'*Oui, oui,*' I said. It didn't sound as if there was a choice.

'*Oui, oui,*' said Guislaine.

'Psst. What the hell are *eekaires*?' I asked Guislaine.

'Hikers.'

'Oh . . . Of course.'

What a breakfast it was. A big bowl of home-made fruit salad, jars of yoghurt, fried eggs – a bit runny but good all the same – toast and cherry jam. And rice pudding. Of course, there was tea for *les Anglais*: a display of different types of tea-bag – Fauchon's best, no doubt – was produced. Madame was miffed that we opted for coffee.

We left with affectionate regret. After the *eekaires'* breakfast I felt good for fifty miles. A pity today was to be so short. Before leaving I asked if I could take a photograph of Guislaine and Madame standing in the door of the Moulin. Madame was delighted and went to fix her hair first. She was wearing her purple tracksuit top and a pair of white trousers with an Olympic badge on the thigh. She stood with hands clasped behind her back. Guislaine, next to her, was clutching her belt-bag and giggling. She had on the yellowy-blue Indian cotton skirt, a white T-shirt, Mephistos and short white socks. She was understandably irritated when we returned to London and showed the photograph to our friend Debby, who cackled and whooped with laughter till the tears ran down her face. 'Oh you are brave,' she said. 'Forget the Walk. How did you ever dare go out dressed like that? I would never have the courage.'

It was half-past eight when we set off. Our spirits were high and the sky was clear and fresh. We walked south along the river while the sun threw long poplar shadows across the road. For once we were following the valley, not forging across the Fan. After an hour or so of coasting we reached our turn-off point, Lamaguère. We stopped to watch the *lycée* children being herded into class, a playgroundful of shining morning faces, and then took an old stone bridge across the Arrats, back into the beginning of another feather of the Fan.

The Gers has few towns and here, in its southern end, there is none of any size. It is a land of rivers and streams, each one flowing down its own fold from the Pyrenees. You could almost make a sonnet of their names:

La Garonne,
La Save, l'Aussoue, la Gesse, la Gimone, la Lauze,
L'Arrats, le Gers,

The three sisters – la Petite Baïse, la Baïsole and la
Grande Baïse,
Le Boues, l'Arros,
L'Adour.

We stopped at an old church. I sat in the grass and watched
a grasshopper on a gravestone. It was transfixed motionless on
top of the chrysalis from which it had emerged a few minutes
or, who knows, a few hours before. We both peered at it,
fascinated. The grasshopper ignored us.

Guislaine went off to sketch a pagan-looking Celtic cross
while I sank back in the grass. Today we could take our
time. Seven minutes or seventeen, it didn't matter. A sixteen-
kilometre walk seemed now no more than a stroll.

We walked on in high spirits. I began to sing 'The
Windhover' to a made-up tune:

> I caught this morning morning's minion, king-
>   dom of daylight's dauphin, dapple-dawn-drawn Falcon,
>   in his do riding
> Of the rolling level underneath him steady air . . .

Seissan was a smaller Samatan, another centre of the *foie
gras* trade. On the way in we passed the Marché de Gras
and the Marché des Volailles, today empty hangars but
easy to picture on market day with a jostle of peasants and
squawking birds.

Like Samatan, Seissan had been on the Black Prince's
itinerary. 'After what he did I'm surprised we don't get stoned
when they find out we're English,' I said to Guislaine.

His route was uncannily close to ours. He had been sent
out by Edward III, his father, in response to a plea from
the local Gascon war-lords. They preferred Gascony being
English, as it gave them a good market for their wine –
the beginning of the English love affair with claret – and
also allowed them to plunder their French neighbours. The

Gascons asked Edward to send someone out to assert English sovereignty: the twenty-five-year-old Black Prince, already the hero of Crécy, volunteered and duly sailed for Bordeaux where, after a short time spent entertaining the local nobility at their expense, he rode south and west on his Grande Chevauchée, the most spectacular ride of terror since Attila. The purpose of a *chevauchée* was to punish the borderers whose loyalty was wavering, to destroy the French tax base by burning crops and towns and, most of all, to provide your followers with an opportunity for knightly deeds and, of course, plunder.

The Black Prince covered most of our itinerary in reverse. In many cases the stages were identical. He first crossed our route at Plaisance, which we hoped to reach in a few days' time. He burned that to the ground on Saturday 17 October 1355. The citizenry had scuttled off down the valley to hide till he had passed. He advanced to Bassoues, two days' march from Seissan for him and for us; then on to Mirande, tomorrow's destination, where he stayed two miles to the south at the monastery of Berdoues while his men cremated the town.

On 23 October he proceeded to Seissan and, perhaps influenced by the good monks of Berdoues, gave directions that it should be spared. But by this time the Gascons' blood was up and they burned it to the ground anyhow. Next day he took a more southerly route than us to Samatan, stopping for the night in the hamlet of Villefranche, where there was nothing worth sacking. In Samatan there wasn't any opposition, so he and the Gascons left the townspeople alone, thinking that to fight would be unsporting. This was a pity, as Samatan in those days was 'as big as Norwich'.

Our ways parted for a few days as he, unlike us, had business in Toulouse, where the French troops under the foxy old Comte d'Armagnac were holed up. The Black Prince came within ten miles of Toulouse, but decided it wasn't worth trying to smoke d'Armagnac out. He wheeled and rejoined us on 1 November at Castelnaudary, which, then as now, was a city of merchants and not well defended. The Black Prince worked off his frustration and celebrated All Saints' Day by reducing the city to rubble. There was rich plunder for the men.

How they carried it all mystifies me. They were covering France at the same speed as us. We were finding it hard work with our Mephistos and lightweight packs. The knights and men-at-arms rode, but many of the common soldiers would have been on foot. They were already carrying everything we had plus armour and supplies. Lugging along looted bits of silver and furniture on top of that and still covering the same distance as us every day is a feat that I find hard to imagine. It says a lot about mediaeval determination and mediaeval greed.

After Castelnaudary, only Carcassonne, the mightiest fortress in France, stood between the Black Prince and the Mediterranean, a sea where no English prince had ever stood at the head of an army, except when on Crusade. He quickly burned the villages in his path, including Alzonne where – more than six hundred years later – we stopped to dress Guislaine's blisters. By the time he reached Carcassonne, the rich families had bribed their way into the citadel, leaving the tradespeople to their fate in the unwalled lower town. The grocers and the butchers showed great bravery, extending chains across the streets to keep out the English. Unfortunately for them, the English cavalry – led by Sir Sancho d'Ambréticourt – thought this added to the fun and jumped the chains; in the course of a bloody battle they routed the shopkeepers, who fled across the Aude. The lower town was destroyed.

Next day the Black Prince marched up the hill and camped before the Narbonne Gate – right where our hotel, La Vicomté, now stands – to assess his chances of taking the citadel. They didn't look good. It would take months, a year even, to starve these people out. He must have been amazed by the 25,000-écu bribe they offered him to go away, as he was about to leave them in peace in any event. The Black Prince was as greedy as all mediaeval princes, so the fact that he turned down the bribe suggests how contemptible it must have been by knightly standards.

He left them holed up with their écus and headed for Narbonne, then the greatest Mediterranean port in France, now ten miles inland. The town was known to be invincible. It had stood against pirates and plunderers for centuries. Whether it was by the force of his arms or by the terror of his reputation is not known, but the Black Prince took Narbonne in a day. It was a disappointment. Most of the booty had been removed, and the garrison held out in the citadel hurling jibes at the English and lobbing dead horses into their midst.

Meanwhile his spies told him that the real enemy, the Comte d'Armagnac, had left Toulouse and was shadowing him. The Black Prince left Narbonne and wheeled north, hoping to cut the Comte off. Because all the water close to the sea was brackish, he gave orders that the horses should be given the local wine to drink. Many of them fell down dead; the ones that survived had a bad hangover. This slowed the English progress. D'Armagnac, playing grandmother's footsteps, had soon scuttled back to Toulouse and the Prince elected not to follow him.

Not long afterwards he made for home, followed by a huge train of plunder. Among the casualties was Auterive, where we ended our thirty-seven-kilometre walk: he burned it to the ground.

He was back in Bordeaux well before Christmas. The Grande Chevauchée had covered four hundred miles in forty-nine days. His troops had burned five hundred towns and villages, an average of ten a day. D'Armagnac was still at loose and the English were now hated throughout the Languedoc. There is no evidence that the Prince's armour was blacker than anyone else's. The name Black Prince doesn't occur in print before Tudor times, but he may well have become le Prince Noir in the course of the Grande Chevauchée – owing not to the colour of his armour but, in the words of Froissart, the best gossip of the fourteenth century, to 'the terror of his arms'.

*   *   *

Seissan has been handsomely rebuilt since it was burned by the Black Prince. We found *la place* and located our hotel, another named after the Pyrenees, those ghost mountains to the south. Often we peered through the heat haze hoping for a glimpse, but they remained a hidden presence.

The Auberge des Pyrénées was fresh and clean, with polished wood floors and lacquered green doors. A chic lady greeted us at the desk.

'She's from Paris,' said Guislaine as we checked in. 'I can tell from the accent.'

We were shown to our room. Guislaine stretched out on the bed. 'That's it,' she said. 'Forget lunch. I'm staying here. Not another step. I don't think I've recovered from yesterday's walk.'

'More likely last night's chocolate mousse,' I said, and ducked out of the door with *Pendennis* to find some lunch. I went back to a little restaurant we had passed on the way into Seissan and sat happily eating *poulet grand-mère* and drinking a bottle of rosé, while the old Major tried to talk his nephew into marrying Blanche Amory.

CHAPTER 18

We tried not to count the kilometres as we went. In the morning we would breeze along, oblivious of the miles; when we took our second break I would get out the 'thermometer' and would be surprised to find out how much distance we had covered – and how painlessly. The second half of the day was different. After twenty kilometres we would be doing secret sums to see how far we still had to go. It put lead feet on a walk. Six kilometres, five, then a long time till four came up. Three had a knack of coinciding with a hill and then, just when we thought it was two, a sign would appear saying 3.2 kilometres to our destination. I would curse the map. Guislaine would give me one of her looks. We would walk on in a foul temper, muttering and nursing aching feet.

It was, of course, the IGN's fault – by now they had become a convenient all-purpose whipping-boy – that we had to start our walk from Seissan along a thunderous truck route. There was an alternative, a cosy little country by-road, which was hardly any longer but according to the map had no bridge to take it across the river Sousson.

'We could always chance it,' I said. 'There must be a bridge.'

'And what if there isn't?'

'Well. We'd have to backtrack for a couple of kilometres. Or,' I added brightly, 'we could ford it Congo-style. You know. Packs on head.'

'No thanks. Let's take the truck route.'

Later, after we had crossed the Sousson on the main road and detoured on to the by-road, we looked back to see if there had indeed been a way over after all. Yes. Not far behind us was a sturdy and ancient stone bridge that the IGN had had six centuries to discover.

As always, when we left a big road, the atmosphere changed. Our senses, freed from listening for the traffic and making sure that it didn't hit us, could breathe in the countryside. Today, as we ambled up the hill away from the Sousson, two buzzards mewed and circled. There was the small, quick rustle of snakes and rodents in the hedgerow.

Guislaine's nose was ready for action. 'Look, look. Smell. Wild chervil.'

I peered doubtfully at a handful of something smelling like cut garlic and tried to look appreciative. 'Gosh. Interesting.'

We came to a crossroads with a café. This was a rarity on these little roads and, since we were making good time with only four or five kilometres to go, we decided to treat ourselves to a coffee. We couldn't see anyone, but there were two tables with chairs outside and the side-door was open. We dumped our packs on the ground and eased ourselves down at one of the tables.

'Mmm. I think I'll have a nice frothy cappuccino,' said Guislaine.

'Me too. Perhaps with a tot of rum. That brown agricultural stuff they use for cooking.'

Five minutes passed. We went to find someone. Guislaine poked her head in through the open door at the side. I peered through a crack in the shutters. It was dark inside.

'Ohé. Allô . . . ALLÔ . . .' called Guislaine.

Silence. There was a snarl like ripping paper in the darkness. Maybe we had better try the front door.

'Allô,' Guislaine shouted through the front window, slightly ajar.

'Anyone there?' I added.

At last there were some sounds of activity. A stirring. We looked in through the window, smiling. A door at the back of the room opened and a man appeared out of the gloom. He was entirely naked. Not so much as a pair of socks. He crossed the

183

room, large and angry-looking, tummy and everything else at a furious wobble. He slammed the side-door. We backed away from the window. He slammed the shutters on that too.

'I think coffee's off today,' I said.

We retrieved our packs and set off down the road.

'*Merci,*' shouted Guislaine over her shoulder. '*Merci beaucoup! Très bon café.*'

'Shhh.' I was worried that if she exercised her humour too much we might have whatever it was that made a noise like ripping paper set on us. We trotted off, chuckling. It was the only time we had the door slammed on us.

We had called from Seissan to book at the inevitable Hôtel des Pyrénées in Mirande. Mirande was, for the Gers, a big town, with over four thousand inhabitants. We could see from the map that it was laid out in a grid. In Aquitaine that meant a *bastide*.

In fact, so regular was the street plan that the green Michelin guide in describing *bastides* used the plan of Mirande as the typical example. Most of the *bastides* are relics of the long fight between the French kings and the Plantagenets in their capacity as the Dukes of Aquitaine. Both sides set to building *bastides* to mark off their territory. Usually they were square, walled towns, laid out on a grid. Occasionally, topography or whimsy would alter the shape. Bram, scene of our noise-filled night at the Auberge de la Gare, was coiled like a snail, but that was rare. Edward I was one of the most active builders, which is why many of the *bastides* have English names. Guislaine thought Hastingues sounded hilarious. Others were named after foreign cities as a mark of respect or in the hope of benefaction. There is a Cologne and a Valence, just as there is a Paris, Texas, and an Athens, Ohio.

Mirande was a French *bastide*. It was founded in the thirteenth century by Eustache de Beaumarchais, a fanatical builder of *bastides*. Perhaps he tired of their sameness: his last creation was Fleurance, near Auch, one of the few examples of a triangular town.

We were hoping that our hotel, the Pyrénées, would be tucked away in a quiet side-street, but we expected the worst. By now we had come to learn that Logis, cosy and family run though they may be, are almost always situated on the busiest and noisiest road junction in town.

'Oh God. I bet that's it,' I said as we walked into the outskirts. Half a mile away, where the road curved up a small hill, just where all the trucks would change gear, was a neat modern building. The Pyrénées . . . 'I'm not staying there,' I said. 'There must be somewhere quieter.'

We passed it by and set ourselves up at a café in the main square for further research. My hotel sheet showed another Logis in town, Le Métropole, but this, suspiciously, was missing from the Michelin. I drank a litre of Evian and a *panaché* while Guislaine ate a couple of cassis sorbets. Could sorbet be addictive? Guislaine had a four-a-day habit by now.

'I vote for the Métropole,' said Guislaine.

'Agreed. What have we got to lose? Let's see. 31, rue Victor Hugo. That sounds quiet and should be easy to find.'

'You know, this will be the first time we haven't accepted the roll of the dice,' Guislaine pointed out. 'Up to now we've always stayed where we booked, even if it has looked a bit iffy. You don't think we're tempting the gods, do you?'

'No. Just common sense. Hope they've got a room.'

We located Le Métropole. It was that rare thing, a Logis in a quiet side-street. As we didn't have a booking, I went and hid round the corner with both our packs while Guislaine breezed in to see if they had a room, trying to look as if she'd just stepped from an air-conditioned car. I waited for her thumbs-up and slopped in with the backpacks. We needn't have worried. The hotel was far too busy serving delicious-smelling lunch to a packed restaurant to notice our condition, and the owner, who handed us a key and pointed up the stairs, was even sweatier and dirtier than I. I at least had shaved.

The room was fine. Best of all, it had a full-length bath. The towels provided were two little grey things the size of dishcloths, with holes in them. Guislaine took one look at them and slipped out of the room. She was back a few moments later carrying two big pink towels.

'Where did you get those?' I asked.

'I raided the room opposite. It was unlocked.'

'You can't do that.'

'Oh don't be so English. Here's yours.'

'Thanks.'

We decided to save the hotel restaurant for dinner and, after a snack round the corner, went off for our first swim. Up to now, as the school holidays hadn't started, the local pools had been closed, although it was mid-June and the temperature was often over a hundred. In Mirande, however, the pool was open. We hurried down to the sports park, pink towels concealed in a shopping bag. It was huge: two big outdoor pools, a stadium, eight tennis courts and a park with ornamental trees; all this on the banks of the Grande Baïse. The sports facilities we saw everywhere on the Walk were impressive. Even tiny hamlets had their two championship tennis courts and a swimming pool.

We had been expecting to have the pool to ourselves since term had not yet ended, and we were puzzled as we approached to hear a roar of voices coming from the pool. There must have been five hundred children there. Guislaine suddenly remembered that, despite the French distaste for organized games, on Thursday afternoons *lycées* all over France have time off for sports. Luckily the area of grass and park round the pool was so big that it was easy to find a comfortable corner where we could stretch out and sunbathe undisturbed apart from the occasional wandering volleyball. How well behaved the children were. There was a lot of flirting and giggling and good-natured noise, but no aggressive Anglo-Saxon games.

Of course, a penchant for aggressive Anglo-Saxon games was a quality most prized in the world I had just left.

Every year, we and the other merchant banks would recruit graduates from Oxford and Cambridge and a handful of other universities. As my operation was relatively small I would ride on CSFB's coat-tails. We would try to attract the brightest and most motivated – 'motivated' was the code word for aggressive – undergraduates by means of a presentation at each of the universities. A team would then be dispatched by CSFB to spend a day interviewing the forty or fifty applicants, from whom fifteen would be selected and asked to dinner that night. I would go along to the Oxford and Cambridge dinners. There would be about eight people from CSFB and me from First Boston. We sat between the candidates and rotated round the table after each course.

I was always astonished and somewhat saddened at how financially sophisticated the undergraduates were. They knew all about discounted cash flow and convertible Eurobonds. When I had been at Oxford in the sixties, none of us had known the difference between a bond and a stock. Sometimes I would say to one of the candidates, 'Shouldn't you be out manning the barricades or protesting or something?' I would get a pitying look. 'We don't have time for that kind of thing now. It was OK when you were here, but now the competition's too great.'

The next day we would meet back in the office to compare our impressions of the candidates and decide which of the fifteen we wanted to ask up to London for further interviewing.

'I liked the little Indian guy with glasses,' someone would say.

'Forget it. Too intellectual. He'd never get off his ass.'

'Yeah. Kill him. All agreed?'

'How about the blonde?'

'Which one?'

'Whaddya mean, which one? The one Michel fancied.'

'Oh her. She's a natural. With looks like that she doesn't even need to add up. Ask her up.'

On one occasion Michael von Clemm, who was then Chairman of CSFB, stalked into the room while the review session was in progress. Dr von Clemm, to give him his full title – he was a doctor of anthropology from Harvard – took a keen interest in recruiting. He was also a forbidding, aloof figure who scared the hell out of most of his employees, including me, and I didn't even work for CSFB.

Von Clemm stood motionless by the door, like a great stork, listening. The tone of the conversation changed.

'Yes. I gave candidate number four high marks for motivation and interpersonal skills,' said the person who favoured the blonde.

'And she'd done a most interesting thesis on Liability Management,' chipped in someone else.

Von Clemm flicked through the list of candidates in silence and then suddenly interrupted. 'Gentlemen.'

'Yes, Michael,' we chorused, turning respectfully towards him.

'Gentlemen. I observe that none of these candidates is a member of Vincent's,' he intoned, and abruptly left the room.

Vincent's is an Oxford club for successful sportsmen.

'Jesus. What did he mean by that?'

'God knows. So we've got Michel's blonde. Who else?'

Haphazard though the system was, I was always impressed by the quality of the people who were finally hired. This was partly because CSFB had a glamorous, buccaneering image and attracted bright people. I seldom hired anyone for First Boston from these sessions. CSFB would have first call on the pick of the bunch, and in any case I preferred people who had knocked around more than the average undergraduate.

For me, one of the big surprises of becoming a boss for the first time, when I took over the First Boston office, was how gratifying it was to hire good young people and give them an environment where they could develop. Ironically, the three best young people I hired, Dan Taylor, David Cantor and Anthony Munk, all walked in off the street and asked for jobs. Although they were graduates they didn't come in through any of the normal channels. All three of them were hired because they were so persistent that I was sure that if they could direct their persistence at our clients they were bound to do well.

They did. So well that after five years of Shouting Down a Phone they had made enough money to leave. All three beat me out of the door. Dan has gone to outwit oil barons in Houston; Anthony, aged thirty-odd, is giving paternal advice to small companies in Canada; and David is writing film scripts.

Before I had started to hire my own people, the First Boston office was a lonely place for me. I had never been lonely at work before, being accustomed to the camaraderie of the great trading rooms in New York. When I arrived back in London at First Boston I felt immediately how different it was. For the first time in my working life I didn't have a friend anywhere in the office. It was a reciprocal thing: the people there knew I was the new broom and, although they were punctiliously polite to me, I would get an itching between the shoulder blades when I turned my back.

The loneliness at the office must have made me difficult to live with at home and must have contributed to our break-up. The reasons for the break-up still puzzle me, but one of them may have been that I was looking to Guislaine for the support I wasn't getting at the office at a time when she herself was finding adjusting to life in England difficult. And I was probably too proud to let Guislaine know how hard I was finding life in the office. 'No, no, everything's fine,' I'd say, 'going great.' It didn't help that I was also travelling a lot, trying to open some new doors for First Boston and to repair old damage.

The low point of that first year was a trip I made to the Middle East. We hadn't done business there for a couple of years, and the last person who had covered it for First Boston had left broken promises and burnt fingers behind him in the Gulf. I was looking forward to the trip. I was happy to get out of the office and its oppressive atmosphere and I relished the thought of a trip to the Gulf, where I had never been, although

I lived in Baghdad as a teenager and am fascinated by the Arab world.

I went to Bahrain, Abu Dhabi and Kuwait. It was a bad time to visit. The Kuwaiti stock market had just crashed. The Arabs, who had been seen as fat sheep for the shearing by every fringe operator in the financial world for so long, were starting to turn on their Western advisers and I was a convenient target for their pent-up frustrations.

My last meeting was at one of the big Kuwaiti Government financial agencies. I was scheduled to see Ibrahim, a sleek and Westernized Syrian, who was the number-two man and in charge of their brokerage business. He received me in an office where he sat enthroned behind an ornate French desk, flanked by six or seven acolytes who nodded and murmured assent as he spoke. He wore an expensive Western suit; they were clothed in immaculate white robes.

'Mr Morland,' he said, 'we are most glad you are here.' He gave me a big smile.

At last, I thought, someone's going to be nice to me.

'Tell me, Mr Morland. Do you at First Boston and your associates at CSFB like to be viewed as one organization, or are you separate?'

I was wondering what answer he wanted. I could give either, according to the circumstances. Before I could answer he went on.

'Morgan Stanley, for instance, they treat us like kings. They are our favourite firm. They interact with every part of our organization.'

Ah, the integrated approach. 'Yes, well, Ibrahim. Good question. Glad you asked. We see ourselves as one organization. Absolutely. First Boston and CSFB. The same to all intents and purposes.'

'I see, Mr Morland. Well in that case you might care to know that your Chairman, Dr von Clemm, is a Nazi.'

'Er . . . Well . . .'

I was still wondering what the correct response was to this

piece of news when Ibrahim continued. 'Furthermore, Mr Morland, I would like your opinion on how you expect to do business with us in view of the fact that Dr von Clemm thinks that all Arabs are monkeys.'

Much murmuring and flapping of dishdashes from the acolytes.

'Well, of course,' I stuttered, 'we're not that close. I mean, my operation really has nothing to do with Dr von Clemm. No, no. Completely separate.'

'Good day, Mr Morland.'

I was back in London, glad to be in the office for once, the next day. I asked CSFB's man who covered the Middle East what this was all about. Von Clemm was to the best of my belief a man of impeccable liberal credentials and anything but a Nazi.

'He made a speech,' I was told, 'a month ago. He said that the Euromarkets could function very well without the Arabs, which of course is true, but the Arabs all took enormous offence as if it were a personal insult. You know what they're like.'

'I'm learning.'

I decided after this that maybe I wasn't the man to cover the Middle East. I went out and hired Morgan Stanley's man, the person who treated Ibrahim like a king. The following year Ibrahim's organization was our office's biggest client.

The Kuwaiti episode was the low point. Shortly afterwards I hired Nigel Pilkington, whose affable, well-bred exterior hides the best salesman I have ever met. Nigel became a good friend and I had someone to laugh with in the office. And a sympathetic shoulder to cry on when Guislaine and I broke up a year later.

Guislaine was sitting by the Mirande pool examining her upper arm. She had been worrying that she was developing Truck Driver's Elbow – a deep tan up to the line of the T-shirt sleeve and white everywhere else. This was our first chance to even it out. We realized on inspection that the sun had been so strong that we had already acquired a slight tan through our T-shirts. The pool was too crowded for anything more than an occasional cooling-off dip, but just lying in the dappled shade of a flowering cherry, poor abused feet freed from their binding, was sweet luxury.

That evening we ate at the hotel. The restaurant, so crowded earlier, was almost empty now. We were ushered through the lunch room, deserted but for two locals sitting at a table next to each other watching a giant television set, and into the formal dining room. This looked as if it had been waiting for a long time for the arrival of the Empress Eugénie. Sèvres and Limoges lined the walls in fruitwood cabinets. We resisted the urge to blow dust off our chairs as we were shown to a table set with lace and cut glass. We gave our order to a worried-looking woman – the owner's wife, as we later discovered – and sat waiting for soup, feeling a bit lonely.

From the next room familiar music floated in: '*La donna e mobile*' sung by a voice that could only be Pavarotti. Guislaine went to investigate. I heard talking, and a minute later she was back.

'Let's go.'

We gathered up napkins, wine and just-arrived soup and rearranged ourselves in the next room at the long table facing the television. We sat next to the two locals, the four of us in a row. The older one explained that this was *la fête de la musique* that is celebrated across Europe every Midsummer Day. Eurovision darted from town to town, picking up an aria here, a concerto there. This was the best part, he said, opera time. A chorus in the Grande Place in Brussels was singing the march from *Il Trovatore*, then it was back to Pavarotti in Rome with *Rigoletto* and on to Freni in Paris in front of a huge crowd round the new glass pyramid at the Louvre.

Madame still looked worried. There was something wrong with the dining room? She cheered up when she saw how much we were enjoying ourselves. It was the first music we had listened to since England. We hummed and dah-dahed through Guislaine's *bavette à l'échalote* and my *civet de poule*. I had eaten *civet de lièvre* before, but never *poule*. *Civet* is thick and rich and not a dish to make at home unless you have a stronger stomach than I do. The essential ingredient is blood. Once I bought a hare and persuaded the local butcher to give us the necessary pint. By the end of the day's preparation the smell of blood had pervaded the house and made us feel queasy. We threw out the *civet* and ate boiled eggs. Le Metropole's *civet* was authentic and good. I spooned the last bit of sauce out of the casserole dish and on to my plate. It was dark and rich.

Madame returned with cheese. We ordered a second bottle of Madiran, almost as dark as the *civet*, and shared it with our two friends. In between arias they kept us informed.

'The soprano can't sing like she used to,' said the younger.

'But she was so lovely ten years ago.'

Silence for a duet, interrupted by explanation from the commentator in Paris.

'*Bravo. Bravo.* But that commentator. What a *pédé.*'

There was a shout from the kitchen, a scurry of footsteps and the noise of glass breaking. We looked to the men for an explanation. They ignored the commotion but agreed that if Pavarotti ate any more spaghetti his double chin would prevent him from opening his mouth to sing at all. Madame came in with a *tarte aux pommes*, her smile wan and fixed. She had a definite limp as she returned to the kitchen. A drunken male voice shouted something I couldn't understand, there was a crash of breaking crockery and a door slammed so hard that the television shook.

Even our good-natured friends couldn't ignore this. 'Ah, never mind,' said the elder. 'It's old Guibot up to his tricks again. Ever since Pauline had her operation he's had to look after the whole place. He doesn't like that. Before, she managed the hotel while he gossiped with the boys at the bar and cooked. He's still the best cook around. But Pauline has been weak since her operation. He's had to take over. Since then . . .' He mimed lifting a bottle to his lips and draining it. 'It's a

pity. This used to be the best place in town, and now . . .'
He shrugged and waved at the empty room.

Thump. Bang. Perhaps Guibot was trying to demolish the staircase. Our friends rose. On the television Verdi had given way to acid rock. It was time to go. They shook our hands and left with apologetic smiles.

'*Au revoir,*' said the younger.

'*Bonne chance,*' from the elder.

We crept upstairs, humming softly, elevated by the food, the wine and the music. The hell with Guibot. But we did double-lock the door.

We woke early, bruised only by the Madiran, and went downstairs for breakfast. Guibot was leaning on the bar reading the newspaper, a *pastis* at his elbow. A day's more growth on his chin made him look like a cross between Rigoletto and Yasser Arafat. We asked for breakfast. He grunted and pointed at a table. A minute later his teenage son came in. Guibot bawled some instructions at him without looking up from the paper and the boy hurried off for baguettes, back a minute later with an armful, coffee on a tray for someone upstairs, coffee for us and back to dusting the tables.

I paid the bill while we waited for coffee. Guibot put the money in his hip pocket, finished his *pastis* and stumped off upstairs. We were happy to be left in peace. We ate most of a baguette, still hot from the bakery, downed two cups of strong coffee and were just reaching for our packs when the door was almost de-hinged as Guibot charged into the room waving something above his head.

He thundered up to our table and shook two bits of cob-webby cloth at us. '*Ha,*' he cried. '*C'est à vous? Cette chose? Eh?*'

Guislaine and I looked on transfixed. What was going on? What had we done?

Suddenly we realized. Guibot had checked our room to see what we had stolen and had forgotten that the well-holed dishcloths provided as towels were his. He thought we had done a swap. He shook them at us again.

'*Non, monsieur,*' said Guislaine groggily. '*C'est à vous.*'

Later that day we thought of all the witty things we should have said. In view of Guibot's overheated state it is lucky we didn't. He threw the towels on the bar and clumped off, swearing.

Across the room the younger of our two friends from the night before was finishing a coffee. 'Don't worry,' he said, 'it happens all the time. *C'est tragique mais c'est la vie.*'

We donned our packs and moved off quickly. 'Let's get out of here before he comes back with our sheets,' Guislaine said.

'Yes. I'm beginning to understand why he's no longer in the Michelin.'

Today's destination was Bassoues. The map showed a tiny village on a big red trunk road. It was to avoid this road that we had drifted on to a southerly route and abandoned the plan to go to Auch, our original half-way stop. We had liked Auch when we went there a year earlier, but Samatan was better. By now we were allergic to big towns. However, we could no longer avoid meeting the big red road. The sheets gave us only one place to stay in Bassoues, the Hostellerie du Donjon. The donjon itself, I read in a guide-book in a *maison de la presse*, was one of the best surviving examples of fourteenth-century military architecture.

'Sounds like a tourist trap,' I said to Guislaine as we called ahead to make our booking. 'I bet you the Hostellerie is like one of those places in the old town in Carcassonne, all Gothic lettering and coach parties.'

At least the walk there promised well. It was the Gers at its purest. Our route went through only one village, the tiny hamlet of Monclar-sur-Losse, which straggled round a down-at-heel château on the banks of the Osse. Otherwise we followed empty lanes and paths that wandered over round-backed hills from one valley to the next. What Cyril Connolly said of the Dordogne is even more true of its neighbour the Gers. It has, he said, the quality of remembered childhood. Everything is English – the flowers, the trees, the fields, the

195

hedges – but on a vast scale and enriched by the Southern light with a kind of radiance.

Half-way to Bassoues, the map told us, we would cross one of the old pilgrimage paths to Compostela, le Chemin Historique de St Jacques, it said. I like pilgrimages, journeys with a destination, both physically and in the soul. I felt our Walk was a pilgrimage of a kind, not just a journey from sea to sea, but a crossing into a different life. Even if at some time I go back to a regular job, it won't be the same. I will be changed. Lévi-Strauss said that if you eat human flesh only once you are ever after a cannibal.

In the Middle Ages, Compostela was the third great place of Christian pilgrimage after Rome and Jerusalem, and St James second only to the Virgin Mary in his power. I'm not sure how St James came to Compostela, but the first foreign pilgrimage to 'Monsieur St Jacques' was made by the Bishop of Puy in the tenth century. Soon a steady stream of pilgrims was arriving from all over Europe, Compostela being a particular favourite of the English. Crossing the Pyrenees was the hard part and the pilgrims would converge by various roads either on Hendaye, to slip through by the Atlantic route, or on St Jean-Pied-de-Port, to cross through the high mountains by the pass of Roncesvalles.

Guislaine and I had tried to visit 'Monsieur St Jacques' some ten years earlier. We had flown from New York to Santiago for a holiday in Galicia. We rented a car at the airport and thought we'd start our holiday by following a thousand years of pilgrims and paying our respects to the Apostle. We drove into town. Every road to the cathedral was double-banked with tour buses and every shop a souvenir stand. We turned the car around and drove off into the countryside, where for two weeks we never saw another foreign tourist. We still haven't seen the cathedral.

The souvenir stands have been selling their scallop shells, the original *coquilles Saint-Jacques*, for as long as there have been pilgrims. For the first few hundred years the flow of pilgrims went smoothly. The Benedictines, the great organizers of the Middle Ages, took charge as usual and set up a series of hostelries along the way for pilgrims. To this day the route is punctuated with their Villafrancas.

After a century or two the rot set in. All these gullible peasants on their way to Santiago were too tempting. Crooks and conmen from all over Europe arrived to prey on them and, as if that were not enough, there were bands of *coquillards*, thugs dressed up as pilgrims. Things became so bad that soon the locals would bar their doors as soon as they saw anyone who even looked like a pilgrim. The migration dwindled away. By the eighteenth century, anyone wanting to make the pilgrimage needed his baptismal certificate stamped by the local magistrate, a visa from the Bishop and a reference from the parish priest.

Our path today crossed the Chemin Historique at a little rivulet, la Baradée. I chattered on to Guislaine about it as we came near. 'Just imagine,' I said, 'a thousand-year-old road. Think of all those bands of pilgrims, just like in Chaucer, trudging across the Gers on their way to Santiago. Most of them would be walking over a thousand miles, more than three times what we're doing. On foot. No Mephistos either.'

'Mmm. Yes. Interesting. How much further to Bassoues is it?'

'Here's the place. This is it, according to the map. There, by that oak and the bridge across the stream. That's where we meet the pilgrims' way.'

On one side was a field of thick maize, undisturbed by any path, and on the other a meadow empty but for three Friesian cows and the oak. No sign of a path. Had this oak once shaded pilgrims or had the IGN made it all up? We never did find out.

We now had a choice. The most direct route was straight ahead through the Bois de Bassoues, along one of the IGN's 'paths'. The alternative was to keep to proper roads and go three kilometres further. I could see the beginnings of a path going towards the wood, a couple of tractor-wheel ruts with tall grass in between.

'I'm not going up there,' said Guislaine firmly.

'Oh don't worry. It turns into a road in no time at all.' The map showed the Baradée running along the path. It seemed as likely that it would turn into a bog.

'Are you sure? Let's have a look at the map.'

'No, really. It's a bit complicated. But it will. Believe me.'

'It better.'

We set off down the path and into the wood. The tractor ruts began to accumulate puddles. It got boggier. To the left was dense wood and to the right the stream.

'This is pretty, isn't it?' I said.

Guislaine was silent.

By now we were having to hop sideways into the long grass to avoid getting wet. We were in single file, Guislaine following.

'Oh drat,' I heard over my shoulder.

'Bloody IGN.'

Silence.

I was wondering how long it would be till Guislaine proposed going back when the ruts turned a corner and started climbing. In two hundred yards they broadened out and turned into a real road. 'Ah, here we are,' I said. 'Just as I thought. What a lovely view. Are those ashes or acacias?'

It was now only three kilometres to Bassoues. After crossing another stream we stopped for a five-minute rest, as we still had a three-contour climb to the village.

'We should be just in time for lunch at the Hostellerie. If we can fight our way in through the coach parties,' I said.

'Look,' said Guislaine. 'There.'

She pointed over the field that rose to our left. Beyond it, over the brow of the hill, we could see a lonely tower, reaching up out of the wheat and commanding the view. We walked along the valley and it grew taller and squarer. The donjon.

Half an hour later we walked up the hill and into the village, thankful that the dreaded red road looped off to bypass it, leaving nothing noisier than a noonday bicycle wobbling towards us down the main — and only — street of Bassoues: an old farmer, pedalling his basket of baguette and wine home for lunch.

The donjon was the first building of the village. It was made more forbidding by the absence of any windows at ground-floor level. The first openings were thirty feet up; a giant's castle. The one little street ran along the crest of the hill behind the donjon, between mediaeval houses leaning against one another at funny angles for support. In the middle of the village was an old wooden market, just a roof of big timber beams and no walls. Bassoues was lucky when the Black Prince came through. The Archbishop of Auch had his palace next to where the donjon now stands and claimed ecclesiastical immunity. Everyone else surrendered and the Prince left them and their village untouched. Not wanting to trust to luck a second time, they began work on the donjon soon after he moved out.

The Hostellerie was just past the market. Far from being a tourist trap, it was tiny and looked as if it too had been built soon after the Black Prince rode through. There were geraniums in the windows and a warm smile at the desk. A friendly girl showed us to a room overlooking the street. It had two beds with thick, old-fashioned mattresses and brass bedheads, and a walnut chest in the corner.

Next door there was a private sitting room, a tiny den with a miniature sofa and a writing desk. 'Oh look. Come in here,' said Guislaine. 'I might have to have a dolls' tea party.'

Quick shower, unpack, sloosh sweaty clothes in the basin, put on clean clothes, and down for lunch. We were hungry. We sat on the terrace at the back, looking out over the distant countryside through the trails of a vine hanging from a trellis. 'I keep on expecting to see the Aegean,' said Guislaine.

Lunch started with soup. Every meal in this part of France started with soup. Sometimes it was on the menu and some-times not. You didn't even need to order it: a steaming tureen of *garbure* was placed on the table. Help yourself. The *garbure* changed according to what they grew locally and the time of year. Cabbage was the only constant. Everything else was optional: beans, peas, bits of pork or duck, lentils.

For the next course I had ordered *demoiselles de Gascogne*. I had no idea what this was but I liked the name so I ordered it blind. I asked Guislaine.

'Don't know. I expect it's something usually considered inedible which has been dressed up with a pretty name for the table. You know, like they call testicles *frivolités*. Probably some organ we've never heard of.'

Five minutes later Jacques Parloir, the owner, a charming Belgian whom we had met when he took our order, skittered out of the kitchen beaming and holding an oversized plate on which were balanced six duck carcasses – not the whole carcass, just the rib-cage. Along the top edge of each one, by the breastbone, was a thin fillet of meat; otherwise it was bare but for a few scraggly bits round the edges. The carcasses had been grilled on a charcoal fire. Knife and fork weren't going to be much use, so I took hold of a carcass by either end and set to work like a mediaeval peasant, tearing the scraps off with my teeth.

Later, when the bones had been picked clean, we asked the owner the origin of *les demoiselles*.

He laughed. 'Ever since *nouvelle cuisine* started it has become the traditional Gascon dish. You see, with *nouvelle cuisine*, all the fashionable people want *magret de canard*. You know *magret* – just the breast cut off whole like a steak. Of course, when you have sent the *magret* to Paris, what are you left with?' He pointed at my plate and giggled. 'Round here they eat nothing else now.'

After lunch Guislaine went off to iron. She had borrowed a board from the owner's wife. I had a siesta against a background of village sounds filtering in through the shutters, the lady across the road scolding her dog and an urgent discussion in the street below as to why Auch hadn't done better in the rugby.

Later on I walked down the hill to a lake where the village boys went to swim. I splashed about to cool off and then found an old stone bench in a grove of poplars; behind was an overgrown graveyard and a tiny ruined chapel.

I opened *Pendennis*. Things were hotting up after a flat bit. The Major was being blackmailed by his old manservant Morgan. Worse, the crafty old sod had saved up so much money that he had actually bought the freehold of the Major's house without the Major's finding out.

On the way back I found Guislaine having tea at one of the two cafés in the shade of the market. I passed on some information I had learnt from a pamphlet picked up at the entrance to the donjon. ' "*Chaque étage du donjon,*" ' I read, ' "*est muni de latrines situées dans les contreforts sud-est et nord-est.*" Two loos on every floor. Not bad for the fourteenth century.'

CHAPTER 19

The twentieth century intrudes here and there, but the Gers hasn't changed much since the Grande Chevauchée. That's its charm. It's lucky it has 'nothing' to attract visitors, no Chartres, no Corniche, no Courchevel, just countryside. Even the French hardly know it. They don't go there for holidays, as they like places where they can 'do' things – hang-glide, windsurf, ski. You can't 'do' anything in the Gers.

'If we came to live in France, do you think we'd end up here?' asked Guislaine. 'It's so lovely.'

'It is, isn't it? It's a wonderful place to walk through, but I don't think I'd want to live here. There's something missing. If we were actually going to live in France I'd want to be somewhere where you get that scorched feeling and the smell of herbs. I know it's more spoilt, but for me it would have to be somewhere where the olive grows – the Luberon, Provence, somewhere like that.'

'I'm not sure. I love it round here. No people. Provence is wrecked.'

And so we go on.

Our walk today followed a small lane along the crest of a hill with views of fields and woods disappearing into the heat haze. Sometimes we would be held up to allow cows to cross the road, or we would have to press back against the embankment while a tractor crawled past towing a muddy old rig so big that it filled the road. And there were always the postman and the baker in their little vans, Pierre the Poste and Boris the Baguette. We met them every day.

For the second day running we passed through only one village – Mondébat, where we found shade in the crumbling church and lay stretched out on pews for our seven minutes. Apart from that we saw hardly a house. There was an occasional distant farm and sometimes a château in the valley, but otherwise we were alone.

We were in open country, ambling along a deserted road between two fields. Half a mile ahead at the end of a slight rise was an untidy farmyard. On our left was wheat, on our right a big field of open pasture with a dozen or so cows, grazing peacefully up ahead of us. Then we saw it.

There.

Standing foursquare between us and the cows was the biggest animal without a trunk I have ever seen, a bull of mythic size. This was the Minotaur. His huge chest almost touched the ground and he was covered in rough, brown hair. His strength was concentrated in massive shoulders, a knotted lump of brawn and muscle.

He stood at the head of the group of cows, maybe fifty yards from the nearest part of the road. That spot was still about a hundred yards ahead of us. Between the field and the road was a single strand of wire.

'Jesus,' I said.

We stopped. The bull pawed the ground, twitched his tail and flicked his head from side to side in what looked like an irritated way. He took a couple of paces towards the road.

'Oh Matou. Do you think the dog alarm might work?'

'Don't think so. That'll really set him off. I think we're OK. That looks like an electric fence. I can see insulators.'

'Oh God, I hope so. Do you think that will stop him?'

'Let's hope.'

'Is there another way round?'

I was already looking at the map. 'Nope. Not unless we want to do an extra two hours. Let's go for it. He can't be that dangerous or he wouldn't be loose in a field by the road.'

'That's what you think. We're probably the first people who've ever walked past.'

'You're probably right. Oh well. I'll go first. Walk slowly. For God's sake, don't run.'

We started. The bull scratched at the ground a couple of times and moved closer to the road. He was now, what, twenty yards away from it. I looked around for a tree. What to do if he charged? There was nothing. A ditch and a slight bank on our left, but he would be over that quicker than we would. The farm was still way out of reach, at least a minute away at a run. And there were two of us. How would I behave? All I could hope to do was distract him when he came for us. Maybe throw some clothes at him. Bulls couldn't see very well, could they? That might at least slow him. Perhaps the dog alarm wasn't a bad idea.

'Don't run. Just keep walking.'

Oh God, he was moving closer. He raised his head in the air, horns spanning the width of his shoulders, and bellowed. This was it. This was where he would charge. He couldn't have been more than fifty feet away.

He spread his back legs. Gathering himself for the charge, presumably. His tail went up. There was a great splatter of dung on the grass.

We were past and walking faster, ten yards, twenty, then thirty. I stole a look back. We were safe. He tossed his head and wandered back to his cows.

'Don't look now but I think we've made it,' I said.

'You know what that was?'

'What?'

'BULLSHIT.'

'Oh my God.' Of course. Wall Street's favourite word. 'I'd never thought it actually meant something.'

We talked excitedly as we walked on, now that we could no longer feel the pumping of our hearts.

'Were you scared?' asked Guislaine.

'Terrified. I hope that doesn't happen again. I wonder how close he was to charging?'

We passed the farm. Fierce dogs erupted out of the barn, snarling and yowling. 'Pah. Dogs,' we both said together.

It was a dramatic farewell to the Fan. Soon after the Minotaur we came down its last slope and into the wide plain of the Adour. As we walked through flat fields towards our destination, Plaisance, the roadside was a scarlet mass of poppies.

'Could you sit down in the middle of those so I can take your photograph?' I asked Guislaine.

There was the rustle of something small and alive.

'There? It's all thistle and snake.'

I gave the undergrowth a kick or two. No more rustles.

'Oh OK,' she said doubtfully. She eased herself into the bed of poppies, switched on a two-hundred-watt smile and provided me with two enchanting photographs. 'Not bad for someone sitting on a thistle,' she said back in London when she saw one pinned up by my desk.

Today was one of the easiest days – apart from the bull. We had made quick progress along the ridge, and the plain was fast walking country. As we moved further into the Walk, our bodies became a less absorbing topic. Guislaine's hips were still hurting and my tendon reminded me it was there from time to time, but we had hardened up. Somewhere after Samatan we had come to believe that only bad luck or an accident would stop us getting to the Atlantic. I hadn't yet plotted a precise route there, but it couldn't be more than ten days' walk away, perhaps less. Today was 23 June and our plane back wasn't till 5 July. We should reach the Atlantic with time to spare. A couple of days on the beach and then back to London.

'Have you done any more thinking about what you're going to do?' Guislaine asked.

'No. Not really. I have the feeling that a decision will announce itself. Don't know when. I've found that whenever I make long-term plans, things always turn out differently. I mean I never planned to go into the City. It just sort of happened.'

'Yes. It's always puzzled me. Why did you do it?'

I hadn't meant to. While I was at Oxford I had expected to become a barrister or a journalist. I tried journalism one summer and got a vacation job on the *Sunday Express*. This was in the early days of John Junor's editorship, Beaverbrook was still alive, and the *Express* stable was at that time considered the best training ground on Fleet Street. It was fascinating and not at all what I'd been expecting. Although by then I had stopped writing to the Soviet Embassy for propaganda, I was still overflowing with idealism and a strong desire to save the world. I think I'd imagined that was what journalists did.

My final few weeks at the *Express* were the most fun. The assistant news editor was a man called, I think, Dudley Smith. He was also an MP and had to go off and get himself re-elected; this was the General Election of summer 1964. While he was away I was allowed to sit at his desk and fulfil some of his administrative functions, but I didn't have enough to do to keep me busy. The *Sunday Express* didn't have access to any public-opinion polls, so Junor decided to organize his own. As a spare pair of hands I was put in charge of organizing this under the direction of Alan Watkins, then the chief political correspondent.

I was told to send questionnaires out to the paper's stringers in the two hundred most marginal constituencies, asking who would win in their constituency and what were the most important local issues – housing, unemployment, immigration and so on. In many of the constituencies it transpired that the stringer had died or moved away; the paper had often not had occasion to contact him for years. Fewer than half the questionnaires were returned. For the others I called the local paper, which

206

was usually the stringer's last contact address, and put the questions to whoever answered the phone. Some I just filled in myself in the office, assuming that the whole exercise was no more than a make-work project to keep me busy.

I handed the completed forms to Alan Watkins, gave him a summary of the findings and then left the paper on Friday, needing to be back in Oxford by the weekend for the new term. I thought that the whole lot would be consigned to the waste-paper basket.

That Sunday I bought the paper. The front-page headline read, in letters an inch high, 'TORIES TO WIN BY 26'. The story began: 'The *Sunday Express* team of skilled political investigators has conducted an in-depth survey into voting trends throughout the country . . .' That was me and my questionnaires. There was later comment in the weeklies and on television about some of the 'surprise findings' of the poll. People were surprised to learn that immigration was an issue in East Anglia and unemployment the main concern in some of the most prosperous pockets of the country. And the Tories lost.

I remember that summer with great affection, but it cured me of journalism. That left becoming a barrister. There were good reasons for doing this. I was reading Law at Oxford, and my mother comes from the Hogg family that has provided two Lord Chancellors this century. I wasn't sure. After leaving Oxford I bummed around Greece, drove a minibus in Corfu and the Peloponnese for one of the pioneer villa holiday firms and fell in love. The summer drifted on and I arrived back in a rainy London in November, with a deep tan and no money. The romance fell apart when the girl's father, a stipendiary magistrate, gave her a lecture after meeting me. 'You're making an imperial idiot of yourself,' he told her, 'going around with this unemployed boy . . .' He was right. She dropped me and took up with someone who was already practising at the Bar and whom she later married. I think he's a judge now.

My mother and stepfather were broke at the time, having decided to become farmers in Ireland. Tom, my stepfather, had already been very generous in supporting me through Oxford. If I wanted to become a barrister that meant at least three more years of not being able to support myself. It was time to get a job. In December I went to the Oxford University Appointments Board and asked what they had left. Industry didn't appeal to me and most of the rest of what they had was in the City. All the glamorous jobs with merchant banks had gone.

I went for an interview at John Govett, a small money-management firm that had decided they ought to recruit a graduate. They had taken their first the year before – Paul Oldham, who is now running the British Steel Pension Fund – and he had been a success, so why not a second? The job title was Investment Analyst. I didn't know what that meant, but the people at John Govett were intelligent and agreeable and they offered me the post – I suspect thanks more to my rowing blue than to my latent investment expertise. I took the job. They had just put the salary up, as they no longer expected you to have a private income. It was now £900 a year.

'It was fun. Of course, there were boring periods, but it's a fascinating world. The stock market is like the most complex game in the world; it combines bits of poker, chess and bridge and whenever you think you've mastered it, the rules change.'

'Maybe,' said Guislaine. 'But I'm not sure that it was the right world for you.'

'Who knows? I enjoyed most of it. What do you think I should do?'

'That's a decision I can't help you with. But I hope it's not back into the City.'

We were in Plaisance. We had to go through it to find La Ripa Alta, our hotel. It was a sad town. Half the buildings were being renovated and there was scaffolding everywhere, giving the place rather a run-down air. We had high hopes for the hotel. This was the only hotel we would stay in that had a Michelin star for its cooking and we were looking forward to enjoying the best meals of the trip. I remembered reading before we left England, in Richard Binns's reliable little guide *France à la Carte*, that its owner – 'my old pal Maurice Coscuella' – was the most imaginative cook in the South-West. We hoped success was not spoiling old Maurice as we walked past the expensive cars parked outside with their German, Swiss and English number-plates.

Inside, we placed our backpacks neatly in the corner. After a five-minute wait a severe-looking woman checked us in, looking with a sniff at our packs. She gave us a key and pointed up the stairs, too busy to take us herself. We passed the afternoon snoozing, reading and wandering, although Plaisance didn't have anywhere much to wander. The town swimming pool was closed. Too early in the year.

At 7.30 we took our places in the restaurant. Guislaine looked wonderful, tanned and healthy in her floaty pantalons, tied harem-style below the knee; I felt good too in the Samatan purple shirt, my hair freshly washed and brushed back, and face well freckled if not exactly tanned.

'Easily the best-looking people here,' said Guislaine.

'By a mile. And the best dressed.'

The menu promised well.

Guislaine chose: *assiette gourmande* – a selection of starters; *pétoncles* – little baby scallops; *pochée de cœurs de canard*; and *Opéra Pompadour*.

I had: *foie de canard aux raisins*; *salade de pétoncles*; *panaché de poissons aux poireaux*; and *croustade gasconne*.

By the second course we had stopped trying to convince each other how good it was and sadly accepted that this was just expense-account cooking. I had avoided *foie gras* up to now, except on Maigné's set menu, but *chez* Coscuella I had to try it. Disappointing. Ordinary and a bit leathery round the edges. From time to time old Maurice came in from the kitchen in his apron. He would do a quick tour of the room, nodding to the guests, and finish at the table next to us where sat three fortyish English men in tight-fitting clothes and one English woman. They smoked long menthol cigarettes and ordered expensive champagne in a loud voice. Coscuella complimented them on their choice.

The champagne came and Coscuella was back to give them a description, in good English, of the menu. They ordered smoked salmon and steak and talked noisily of successes in the property market. Two bottles of good claret were brought to the table. The youngest and noisiest of the men put down his cigarette to taste the wine with much sniffing and swilling. 'Now that, squire, is what I call a lovely bottle.'

Coscuella was back after another perfunctory tour of the room to see if they were enjoying their steak and to receive compliments on the smoked salmon. Later, at the end of the meal, he pulled a chair up to their table while they tasted Armagnacs and smoked cigars.

'I wonder who's been cooking my dinner?' I said. 'The *pétoncles* should be sweet as sugar lumps. Mine had the taste of fish that's been too long out of the water.'

'No soul,' said Guislaine. That's as low as you can get in her dictionary.

Our room looked out on the square. Diagonally across from us was a bar where motorcyclists gathered. The juke-box blared while the bikers argued noisily and revved their machines. My French wasn't good enough to understand what they were shouting at one another. The phrase *'Enculez votre . . .'* recurred.

'Darling, you still awake?'

'Mmm.'

'What exactly does *enculer* mean?'

'Some other time.'

I dreamed of bulls.

CHAPTER 20

We hadn't meant to go to St Mont. Our intended destination after Plaisance was Luppé-Violles, partly because of its delightful name and partly because both the Michelin and the Gault-Millau said good things about the Relais de l'Armagnac. Guislaine had called them several times from Bassoues to book a room, but they didn't answer. Finally, in a state of high annoyance, she had called the *mairie* at Luppé-Violles to ask why their only hotel never answered the phone.

'Because, madame, they are bankrupt.'

Mme Parloir at the Hostellerie in Bassoues had come to our rescue. 'Try St Mont. There is a very nice inn there that is being improved. It has a new owner. He sends me people and I send him people. I will make the booking for you.' She did.

All we knew of St Mont was that they made wine. An advertisement for the wines of the co-operative at St Mont had been at the top of many of our recent menus. The co-operative was the biggest in the area, and the map showed that the village was only a few miles from Madiran, where the South-West's best wine is made.

We were happy to leave the Ripa Alta. The previous night they had told us that breakfast was impossible before eight o'clock as there was no one around to make it before then. And a thermos of coffee was out of the question. We presented ourselves downstairs on the dot of eight, annoyed that our late start meant that we would still be on the road in the heat of the early afternoon. We saw that Coscuella was already sitting at a table on the terrace in front of the hotel, finishing his coffee and wiping croissant off his lips. He gave us a perfunctory nod over his newspaper.

'Huh. There was someone up to make *his* coffee before eight,' I said sourly.

We left feeling grumpy. On the way out of town two unusually obnoxious little dogs yapped at us from a suburban garden, jumping up and down behind a low fence like enraged puppets. I bent down, put my face on the same level as theirs at the top of their bounce and barked at them. They scampered indoors, whimpering. There was an explosion of abuse from inside the house and Madame bustled out, apron aflap. She shouted curses after us as we sauntered off down the road. I felt much better.

We had two hours' walking to cross the plain to the hills of Madiran. Two hours of dark-green maize and the occasional field of ripening wheat. In the distance were grain silos the size of nuclear cooling towers. The houses here were different; brick had given way to plaster. We stopped to take a photograph of one. It had a single attic window, set in a triangular dormer like a cyclops eye. This was typical of houses in the area. We crossed the Adour, hardly more than a series of rivulets running between islands of gravel, and found ourselves on a yet bigger and busier road.

The Black Prince hadn't been the only English tourist in this part of the world. Wellington had taken this same big, busy road as he chased brave Maréchal Soult and his barefoot army down the Adour.

It was the sting in the tail of the Peninsular War. Wellington had finally, and against all the odds, broken the French in Spain at the battle of Vitoria in 1813. Napoleon's brother, King Joseph of Spain, had fled back to France, strewing booty behind him in his eagerness to avoid being caught by the English. Wellington stumbled on cartloads of Goyas and Velázquezes that had been cut from their gilt frames for easy transport and stacked in Joseph's covered wagons. Wellington had them sent to England to be cleaned and reframed before giving them back to the Spaniards.

That typified his attitude to plunder; it was the opposite

of the Black Prince's. Wellington's army was living off the land and he knew this would have been impossible without the support of the local population. Any of his men caught looting would be sentenced to bloodcurdling penalties. The lucky ones were hanged; others got one thousand lashes – usually a slower and more painful death sentence – for stealing wine. The French peasants were delighted. Local administration had broken down, so they had stopped paying taxes to finance Napoleon's lunatic expedition to Russia, and meanwhile the English quartermasters were overpaying them for anything they could sell.

Wellington's Spanish allies gave him almost as much trouble as the French. For the Spaniards, war without looting was madness. When battle was joined, Wellington complained that the Spanish soldiers fled at the sound of the first shot and would set to plundering the baggage train of their English allies who were busy fighting.

On St Patrick's Day 1814, Wellington marched south from Aire hoping to bottle up Soult before he could escape to Toulouse, which was still considered as impregnable as when d'Armagnac had hidden out there from the Black Prince. The weather was filthy. It was snowing, and the dry and dusty plain we were now walking through was a bog. The Hussars and the Light Division had spent the night in Plaisance, where they paid cash on the nail for everything, while Wellington had taken the *route du vin* through the hills.

It may have been in Madiran that his famous nose came into play. He took over an inn for the night as his quarters. The proprietress said she was *désolée* but they had no food. 'Nonsense, madame,' said old Nosy, sniffing. 'I smell truffles.' He sniffed his way to a hidden cupboard in the kitchen where he unearthed a large stuffed turkey.

He couldn't quite catch Soult. He skirmished with the rearguard and gave chase to the main army but Soult, slippery as a cake of soap, scurried away along what is now the N117 before turning north and running for Toulouse. Poor Soult.

Napoleon was back from Russia and in a terrible temper. He raged at his brother Joseph, now a king without a kingdom. The French, with an army of 200,000 men, had managed to lose Spain. Soult's orders from Napoleon now were to retake it with the remaining 30,000, only half of whom had boots.

Wellington tried to cut Soult off before he went to earth in Toulouse by taking a short cut up the Save, through Samatan, while the French took the easier way, along the Garonne and through Noé. Wellington's 18,000 men, marching through mud and snow, encumbered with heavy greatcoats and carrying muskets, ammunition and supplies, covered the same distance every day as did we with our lightweight backpacks and Mephistos.

Despite this speed, Wellington arrived at Toulouse to find the gates closed and Soult safe behind the walls. He circled round to the north, sniffing the town like an angry dog, and eventually, on 10 April, attacked. It was one of the most tragic and unnecessary engagements in the history of warfare. Neither side knew that four days earlier and five hundred miles away, in Paris, Napoleon had abdicated and that he was now on his way to Elba. The English and the French were no longer at war. The last great battle of the Peninsular campaign was fought after peace had broken out, because it took six days for the news to travel south to Toulouse. A telephone would have saved 20,000 lives.

The battle was a mess. Wellington was not clever here. A bridge collapsed, dividing his army in two, and when the dead were counted after a day of bloody fighting, more English had fallen than French. Both sides claimed victory; none the less, Soult retreated to the safety of Carcassonne the following day.

At six that morning, the Mayor of Toulouse sent a message out to Wellington, inviting him to enter the town and saying that they had, of course, been strongly against Napoleon all along. They were to a man, said the Mayor's message, loyal supporters of Louis XVIII, whom the allies had placed on the throne. At eleven o'clock the Mayor and council waited at the main gate to greet Wellington and proclaim their loyalty to the King. Wellington came in through a back way and found workmen everywhere hard at work pulling down statues of Napoleon and chipping his initials off the public buildings. At five in the afternoon, news came through of Napoleon's abdication.

Wellington gave a grand dinner of celebration for the leading citizens that night. When, after he had proposed the health of his new majesty, King Louis, the guests broke into cries of *'Vive Lord Wellington,'* his lordship said, 'They are drunk. Give them coffee,' and stalked off to bed.

Wellington hadn't had to contend with the *poids lourds* on his way through the Gers. They were too much for us. I suggested an off-road route. Guislaine forgot her usual suspicion of alternative routes, hitched up her skirt and followed me into the brambles. So keen was she to get away from the truck route that she even crossed the main railway line without a murmur. We found ourselves in a hazelnut orchard of Californian dimensions. We walked happily through it for a mile or more while the main road rumbled in the distance. The hazelnut trees were connected by an irrigation system consisting of pipes running from tree to tree at head-level. We watched it nervously and hoped that we would have time to escape a drenching if some distant hand switched on the morning monsoon. Overhead, a hawk circled so low that we could see its eyes.

Then, at last, back across the railway track, over the truck road, and we were finished with the plain and climbing a steep little hill into the wine country. As we trudged up, a group of cyclists came freewheeling down, swift and easy as gulls.

'Courage,' their leader cried.

We waved back. They and we formed a community with one enemy: the motorist.

It was good to see vines again after hectares of maize and

wheat and soya bean. We noticed that at the end of each row of vines was a rose-bush. For decoration, we decided. Weeks later, we were back in France with the children, driving down to Provence. On the way we spent a night with Alan Johnson-Hill, an English friend who lives at Château Méaume in Bordeaux and makes delicious wine. He too had roses at the ends of his rows of vine. We asked him their purpose.

'There are three theories,' he said. 'The usual story is that they attract bees to help with the pollination. It's a nice idea, but the flaw is that vines are hermaphrodites and don't need any help from bees. The second, and most common, theory is that roses are so susceptible to rot that any disease will show up on them before it appears on the vines. I don't really buy that either. By the time mildew or something like that shows up on the roses it's probably too late to do anything about it.

'The story I like is the one that was told to me by one of the old boys who's been working here for ever. In the days before tractors they used to use oxen to plough between the vines. Every time they reached the end of a row, the ox would take a bloody great mouthful of vine while he was turning into the next row. They planted the roses to give the ox a muzzleful of thorns instead.'

Thanks to our late departure we were still walking as the heat was building up. With the sun overhead, the trees gave no shade on the road. We tried sheltering under a vine when we stopped for a rest, but that didn't do much good. In the end we crept up a track to a farm and lay down gratefully in the shelter of the barn, hoping that the farm Alsatians were too hot to come and savage us.

'Well, at least there's one good thing about this heat,' said Guislaine.

'Oh yes? What's that?'

'It's dry. It's not like that awful New York heat. Remember what that was like in summer? It was so damp. We had mushrooms growing in the bedroom cupboard.'

We had spent nine years in New York. Unlike my first job

in the City, the move to New York had been premeditated. My area of expertise then had been in selling American stocks to British institutions – insurance companies and merchant banks and the like. I had been quite successful at it in London, but I wanted to see if I could succeed in New York where the competition – and the rewards – would be greater. The election of a Labour government that was vowing to do horrible things to people like me made the decision that much easier.

This time, though, I didn't want to be impulsive. I would do my homework. Wall Street was then facing their equivalent of Big Bang, some ten years ahead of London, with the ending of the fixed commission rates that had guaranteed prosperity for all but the stupidest firms. I did careful research into who would survive in the new era and decided that the firms that offered the best research to their clients would be the winners. Accordingly I wrote to the top three – Wainwright, Spencer Trask and Mitchell Hutchins – and bought myself a ticket to New York to go and see them.

I drew a blank at the first two, who had no interest in employing an Englishman with no track record in America to cover their domestic clients. My last hope was Mitchell Hutchins; they were the firm I really wanted to work for. At that time they were top of all the polls of the hottest research boutiques and they had a special aura of glamour. I had one meeting with them scheduled at nine in the morning and a plane back to London at eight that night. The meeting went well. The atmosphere here was different. This was the kind of firm I dreamed of working for. Everything, from the huge Rauschenbergs and Lichtensteins on the walls to the penthouse offices looking out over the Statue of Liberty, smelled of success and self-confidence.

I was asked to stay for a second meeting and then given a schedule to last me through the whole day and told to postpone my flight till the next morning. I didn't realize at the time that each of the people I saw would fill in one of the forms I later came to know so well, rating me as a candidate. It had on it all the Wall Street favourites – Career Focus, Motivation, Interpersonal Skills, Product Knowledge and Growth Potential.

By five that afternoon I had had nine interviews and was dizzy with exhaustion and jet lag. John Engels, the head of sales, whom I would meet again nine years later at First Boston, took me into his office. Surely after all this I would get a job offer?

'Can't talk now Miles, we're too busy. I'll meet you at seven in the Carlyle bar.'

I wasn't even sure I'd still be awake by then.

At seven John arrived with Dick Falk, his number two. 'Hey Miles, what are you drinking?'

'Er, just an orange juice will be fine.'

'Don't be a pussy. Whaddya want?'

I certainly didn't want to be a pussy. 'Well, I'll have a bourbon.'

'Good boy.'

John and Dick both had beers, which they sipped at while I nervously gulped down Wild Turkey.

For the first hour and a half the talk was about Wall Street in general and the changes taking place there. I felt I had done well at the interviews, but John gave no hint as to whether he would offer me a job. Every fifteen minutes he would order me another glass of Wild Turkey while he and Dick nursed their beers. By now the combination of the whisky and tiredness meant that I could hardly speak. I sat and nodded benignly as they talked.

Eventually we went to have dinner in a nearby restaurant. More Wild Turkey was ordered. Suddenly John and Dick turned nasty.

'Of course, we'd be crazy to hire you,' said Dick.

'Yeah. We've got all the top talent on the Street beating our door down for a job,' said John, 'and I mean these are proven producers. What would the clients think if we sent some Limey to cover them who'd just got off the boat from England? Whooo-ee.'

'Do you have any idea how tough it is at Mitchell Hutchins?'

'Where would we send you? Jesus Christ, can you imagine what they'd think if we sent you down to Texas? Hell, with an accent like yours, buddy, they'd think you were some kind of faggot.'

I smiled and said nothing, well past speech.

Later John told me how impressed he had been by my coolness under fire. The tough-guy act was the perennial last hurdle for candidates; he and Dick had practised it well.

I have no idea how long the verbal beating-up went on for. Just as suddenly, John clapped me on the shoulder as I swayed towards my drink. 'Well, feller. We'd like you to join Mitchell Hutchins.'

I nodded.

'Jesus, but you were cool,' John said later.

He was very disappointed to learn I had been too drunk to respond.

Five hours later I was in a taxi on the way to Kennedy Airport to catch the nine-o'clock morning plane to London. I had to ask the driver to stop half-way down the Van Wyck Expressway while I got out and threw up by the side of the road. When we reached the airport, I called John up and accepted the job.

My careful homework as to who would do well after the ending of fixed commission rates on Wall Street didn't say much for my judgement. Within two years all three of the firms I had gone to see were out of business and had been forced to merge with bigger firms. I had been proud to work at Mitchell Hutchins in their days of glory and stayed on after they were taken over by Paine Webber, a huge, amorphous firm of retail stockbrokers. I knew the wind was changing when Dave Williams, the head of Mitchell Hutchins and one of the brightest and most moral men on Wall Street, resigned a few months after the merger. Soon, sleazy men in stretch suits replaced John Engels and Dick Falk, both of whom I had come to like and respect, and I went off to work at Morgan Stanley, where I spent five happy years – till John Engels hired me for the second time. By then he was running First Boston's brokerage business and he needed a new person to run their London office.

When Guislaine and I had left London in 1974 we thought it would be for two years, possibly three at the most. We stayed for almost ten. They were good years and we liked living in America. But we never got used to those hot, steamy summers and the mushrooms in the clothes cupboards.

By now we had had more than our regulation seven minutes' rest in the shade of the barn. We moved wearily on for the last leg to St Mont, now only a few kilometres further. We came to a powerful rotating irrigation jet set up close to the road. Every thirty seconds or so its circle of wetness would pour down on part of the road. We looked at the cool spray and then at each other.

'Are you thinking what I'm thinking?' asked Guislaine.

'Yes.'

We stood on the wet patch of the road and waited, giggling, for the jet to swivel round. Pump, pump, pump. First our heads, then our T-shirts, then our trousers. We were soaked. And a second time. It was wonderful. We collected our packs from the far side of the road where they had been keeping dry and almost jogged down the hill to St Mont.

We passed the village sign: 'St Mont – Village de la Thérapie Manuelle'.

'Gosh. Look at that,' said Guislaine. '*Thérapie manuelle*. Yes please. Appointment after lunch. Oh my tootsies, my aching tootsies.'

When we arrived, Guislaine made enquiries. Where should she go for the massage?

'Ah no, *madame*. It is a teaching course for *la thérapie manuelle*. People come from all over France to learn.'

'Perhaps one of the students would like to make a house call.'

'No *madame*. Certainly not.'

St Mont was like a Provençal hill village, perched high above a bend in the Adour and surmounted by a ruined abbey, of which only a great façade with a small church in its shadow remained. The auberge was the centre of village life, all noise and bustle, and we were glad to learn that we were in the annexe, a little village house up a narrow lane past courtyards and laundry. We had the house to ourselves. Our room smelled of new paint and fresh linen and looked out over curved roofs and the river valley.

Early in the evening we walked down to the auberge for a quiet drink. The bar was packed full with excited teenagers getting ready for the village *bal*, which started at nine. We tried squeezing ourselves in at the end of a bench, but after ten minutes the combination of noise, smoke and inquisitive stares was too much. We walked back up the hill and sat on the stone steps in front of the crumbling church. We were surrounded by plum and cherry trees. The sun was fading into the plain from which the round, vine-covered hills of St Mont rose. The pigeons flapped and cooed as they came home to roost in the church tower. The only other noise was the distant hum of a late tractor.

I had *Pendennis* with me and was reading slowly, word by word. I had only twenty pages to read and was trying to spin them out. I was going to miss it. How many mornings had the Major, Captain Costigan, Blanche Amory, her mother – 'the good-natured begum' (Thackeray has a Homeric habit of attaching unchanging descriptions to people like nicknames: Blanche was always 'the author of *Mes Larmes*') – and, of course, that spoilt little prig Pendennis himself followed me down the road.

We slept well that night. A cool breeze blew in through the open window and from down in the valley came the faraway thump-a-thump-thump of the band at the midsummer *bal*, the noise distant enough to be soothing.

The next morning Guislaine was up at 6.30, before the alarm went off. 'You know something?' she said.

'What?'

'I'm fit. I'm really fit. I've never been fit before. Now I see what the fuss is about. I feel wonderful.'

I smiled. 'How about a song?'

'Oh why do you always have to be sarcastic?'

'Sorry. I know what you mean. It is a good feeling, isn't it?'

'Anyhow, how far have we got to go today?' she asked.

'Oh, I think it's around twenty-five or so.'

'I know your tricks, Matou. When you say "around", that means it's five kilometres further.'

'Well. Not quite five, as a matter of fact.'

We were on the road by seven. Eugénie-les-Bains was nearly thirty kilometres away; it was going to be our longest walk since Mazères. Farm workers were already out trimming vines. This was pruning time. The grapes, invisible when we started the Walk, were now the size of marbles. The wine-makers had a choice: they could leave the vine unpruned and make as much wine as possible, or they could cut off the less promising bunches and concentrate the vine's strength in fewer grapes to give a better wine but less of it. In the Corbières they tended to the first option, the more the better. It was going into the wine lake anyway, so why worry about quality? But here they were starting to take a pride in their wines and to pull themselves out of the rut. It wasn't an easy decision for a farmer in one of the newer wine areas, as it could be years before the improvement in quality enabled him to raise his price enough to make up for the drop in yield.

Like most good wine-growing areas it was hilly. Our first three hours were steep up-and-down walking. The hills here were less long but steeper than in the Fan. I was impressed by Guislaine's growing strength. Up the last of the hills I offered to carry her pack, but she waved me away with a look of tight-lipped determination. We came to the top of the hill and a great flat plateau stretched out ahead of us. I peered at the map. Today we had started on a new one; the third, 'Tarbes–Auch', had been put away, by now creased and stained, and I had unfolded the fourth and last, 'Bayonne–Mont de Marsan', still crisp and clean.

Something about the countryside here felt different. Everywhere was flat and the soil was sandy; the trees looked different, umbrella pines rather than forests of oak and chestnut. I looked closely at the map. 'We're no longer in the Gers,' I announced. 'We've just entered the Landes. Isn't that funny. We must be at least a hundred kilometres' walk from the sea, but already it looks different – sand and pine trees.'

To start with we relished the ease of strolling along on the flat. It was like being on ball-bearings, effortless motion. The road ran on straight and unbending through the endless sea of maize. I began to chant 'bor-ing, bor-ing'. Before we began the Walk, a secret worry had been that we would run out of things to say and that after a few hundred kilometres of rural France we would be sick of the sight of countryside. But this was the only time we were bored. Wheat, sunflowers, barley, even soya, all move and have rhythm. But maize is dead, a blight of lifeless green.

'Can you imagine what it must be like to live in Kansas?' I asked. 'A whole state full of the stuff.'

'I'd go mad,' said Guislaine without hesitation.

We took a detour to get away from the maize and off the plateau, even if it did add a kilometre to the journey. Our spirits lifted as we walked down the hill through straggly vines and vegetables, peas, tomatoes and melons.

We stopped for a drink and some shelter from the fierce heat in Bahus-Soubiran, a small village five kilometres short of Eugénie. It had only three hundred people but it had its own *arènes*, a bullring. We had reached the country of *la course landaise*. Bullfighting here is more graceful and less bloody than in Spain. First, they use cows. Evil-tempered brutes, but cows none the less. Secondly, they shave the horns and tie a safety rope round one of them; this allows the cow to be pulled off if necessary, ensuring that the fighters suffer nothing worse than a bruise or a sprained ankle and the cow no more than a loss of dignity. The art is in dodging the cow. I am not an expert, but I understand there are various accepted manoeuvres for dodging. Flight is not one of them. There is a second form of the sport in which a jumper plucks a ribbon or rosette from between the horns. The sport is identical to that practised by Minoan youths in Crete, two and a half millenniums ago.

The last few kilometres to Eugénie passed with aching slowness. The valley was oppressively hot and airless. We were curious about Eugénie-les-Bains. It was made famous by Michel Guérard, the inventor of *cuisine minceur* and one of the godfathers of *nouvelle cuisine*. Some fifteen years ago he bought an elegant nineteenth-century residence and created Les Prés d'Eugénie. There has always been a spring there, where for centuries people have come to drink the sulphurous waters. Guérard has made a palace hotel around it where he covers his clients in mud, feeds them colour-co-ordinated shreds of vegetables and charges them a fortune.

Guislaine and I have had an aversion to spas ever since we found ourselves in Ischia a few years ago where, quite unintentionally, we were staying in a hotel built over an evil-smelling spring famous for its healing properties. Our fellow guests all looked like Goering and came to lunch in white towelling dressing gowns.

Guérard was not for us. We were converts to simplicity. We saw several of Guérard's starving guests sitting in designer tracksuits at the village ice-cream shop and tucking into chocolate sundaes as we limped past on the way to our hotel, the Relais des Champs, on the other side of the village.

It had a SWIMMING POOL.

We checked in, grabbed the key and almost ran to our room. Routine was forgotten. We up-ended packs, tore out

224

swimming wear, ripped off clothes and scurried for the pool. We had walked since dawn, our limbs ached, we were tired and stained from the road.

We eased our bodies into the pool and pushed gently out into its cool lightness. We floated in quiet and inexpressible luxury. I paddled slowly to the deep end to hang suspended in the water without weight or motion.

Later we lay on the grass and listened to the breeze rustling the poplars. Then back into the water to float and roll and paddle again in the cool. Lunch was forgotten; the afternoon passed in a blur of ecstasy.

Three hours later, sated now, we put on clean clothes and went to investigate M. Guérard. This was how a Swiss tuberculosis sanatorium in the twenties must have felt. The lawns and gardens were immaculate and looked as if they had been tended with nail-scissors. We walked into the main building, trying to look as if we belonged. The staff wore pink nurses' coats and whispered. Guests sat in white wicker chairs and sipped pale teas. We tiptoed through the marble-floored hall and on to the lawn and the pool beyond. I half-expected to see Nabokov chase a butterfly across the grass.

'You know, it's a strange thing,' said Guislaine, 'but have you noticed how thin they all are?'

It was true. Unlike the Goering figures of Ischia, here the guests were positively emaciated. 'Not at all what I'd expected at a fat farm,' I said.

'I think that's the French for you. I don't think they come to get thin. They just love fussing over their health. They're only really happy when they're talking about their livers.'

By the side of the hotel was a steel and glass building with huge ventilation tubes coming out of it and a smell of rotten eggs in the air. 'That must be the Factory,' said Guislaine, 'where you wallow around in mud and drink smelly water.'

Later, back at our hotel, we ate a huge dinner of red meat and red wine, fried potatoes, cheese and ice-cream. We wanted to leave early the next morning and asked when they started serving breakfast.

'Five-thirty,' said the waiter.

'Five-thirty?' We gaped.

'*Mais oui*. Our guests go for treatment at the spa. The first shift starts at six.'

CHAPTER 21

We had toyed with the thought of taking a rest day in Eugénie but decided against it. Eugénie itself was a lifeless little village despite – or maybe because of – Guérard's hotel. The real attraction was the swimming pool but, with this in mind, we had chosen a hotel for the end of today's walk that also had one, La Crémaillère in Hagetmau. My photocopied sheets, now frayed from a hundred consultations, showed a number of different villages and hotels we could have gone to, but this was the only one that had a pool.

It also gave us a new destination on the Atlantic. Hagetmau, or Hatchetman as it soon became, its real name being one of those words like *pluie* that I can't get my tongue round, pulled us on to a more southerly route. Vieux Boucau, our original aiming-point, was discarded in favour of Capbreton, some thirty kilometres further south. We knew nothing of either. Guislaine had built up a mental picture of Vieux Boucau as a picturesque Basque fishing village, but the grid pattern of its streets on the map suggested it was more likely to be an Atlantic version of Gruissan-Plage.

We had been debating what we were going to do when we arrived. By now, 'when' had replaced 'if'. We had no idea what we would feel like. Celebrating? Riotous living? Or sitting on the beach for a couple of days contemplating the Atlantic rollers? There was a worry of anticlimax. I favoured a day or so at Capbreton and then on to Biarritz. Guislaine was not so sure about Biarritz; it sounded too glossy. We agreed that we would wait till we arrived and see what we felt like then; we also agreed that whatever happened we wouldn't rent a car or take a taxi anywhere after we had arrived. That wouldn't have been right at all. Foot, bike or bus.

We still had several days to go, but there was a distinct feeling that we had begun our descent. The 'fasten seat-belts' light was on. The houses had changed. We missed the flat pink wafers of Toulouse brick and the timber and clay houses of the Gers, looking as if they were part of the land. Even away from the towns, the houses here had a suburban feel, the fields were bigger, the fences in better repair and the cars cleaner and less battered.

The last few kilometres of our walk into Hatchetman took us through the Lande d'Agès, the first of those endless sand-pits held in place by pine and scrub that would become more and more frequent as we neared the sea. Most of our stopping-places up till now had crept up on us round a corner or a fold in the hills. Hatchetman filled our view for the last two hours of walking, a whole horizon of steel silos and agricultural factories.

Whatever our expectations of the place, it was worse. This was the ugliest town in France. Judging from the amount of construction, the inhabitants agreed and had decided to start again. The town was a tangle of scaffolding and newly cleared lots and we had to pick our way down the street with care between 'Déviation', 'Route Barrée' and 'Danger'.

'This is awful,' said Guislaine.

'Well thank God that in a few minutes we'll be floating in a pool. I think I might spend the whole afternoon there.'

'Mmm.'

'Did they say how far it was from the centre of town?'

'Just a kilometre. Take the route d'Orthez.'

That was easy to find. It was the main road south to Spain. The kilometre stretched on and on, into two and then three. We ploughed up a dreary hill clogged with roadworks past garages and agricultural-machinery showrooms. Truck after truck ground past on its way to the Pyrenees.

'Are you sure he said a kilometre? We must have missed it,'

I said. 'Maybe we're on the wrong road.' I caught the reflection in a showroom window of two weary figures with packs on their backs leaning into the hill. 'Attack the hill,' I added.

'Ha ha. Very funny.'

'Let's keep on to the top and telephone if we can't see it from there.'

'OK. If it weren't for the pool I'd vote for going back into town. We passed a couple of hotels in *centre ville*.'

We were just about to give up when we saw it. There, poised between two garages where the hill flattened out and just where the trucks from Spain would be changing down: 'La Crémaillère', the sign announced. I pointed. Guislaine said nothing.

At least there was a hedge in front of it and a few bits of green visible from behind. 'It can't be that bad,' Guislaine said. 'There must be a garden. And maybe our room is at the back. Overlooking the pool.'

I stood on tiptoe and peered over the hedge. 'Oh God.'

'What's wrong?' asked Guislaine.

'The pool.'

'Yes?'

'It's empty.'

There was a long pause. 'We're going to make the best of this,' said Guislaine with one of the least convincing smiles I have ever seen.

Reluctantly we checked in, asking for a quiet room. *Oui, oui*. Up one flight. Our room was on the side of the hotel that faced traffic coming from Spain. Truck headlights would light up our room all night. The room was hardly bigger than the bed and looked out over the empty pool. There was no garden; it had all been taken up by the pool. The thought of spending the afternoon cooped up here was impossible.

'I have a cunning plan,' I said to Guislaine.

'Oh yeah.' She was going through the motions of pulling things out of her pack.

'It's not on the sheets, but I remember seeing a brochure

in our hotel in Eugénie for a place called Les Lacs d'Halco or something like that. If I remember rightly it had two stars and was close to Hatchetman. I'm sure you could get the number from directory enquiries. It has to be better than this.'

'Oh Matou, I'm tired. Do we have to?'

'You don't want to stay here, do you?'

'Oh OK.'

She called. No problem. Love to have you. Just three kilometres out of town. I could see the lakes on the map. 'Cheer up. I expect it's one of those tourist complexes the French are so good at,' I said. 'There was one just outside Samatan. Nice modern buildings, swimming, windsurfing, tennis, all those things the French do on holiday.'

'I'll pass on the tennis, but it sounds nice.'

We had lunch first. Even if the hotel was a disaster it was still a Logis and, as always, the food was good. I had *civet de lièvre* and a bottle of Madiran. Guislaine had adopted a new no-drink-at-lunch policy so I had to drink the whole bottle.

After eating we told the owner that we had decided to leave as we had only come for the pool.

He was annoyed and astounded. Fill the pool in June? What an idea. They waited till July. When it got hot . . . But, in any case, even then the pool wasn't for transients like us but for the *pensionnaires* who came for a fortnight's holiday.

I looked at him and then at Guislaine in disbelief. Maybe I had misunderstood. 'People come here for their holiday?' I hissed at her in English. It was hard to imagine anyone voluntarily spending more than one night at La Crémaillère. It was so close to the road that the lights on the ceiling danced every time a truck went past.

We stepped out cheerfully towards Les Lacs. I was feeling terrific after the *civet* and the Madiran, and took Guislaine's pack; her footsteps were starting to drag, something I attributed directly to the no-drink policy. I kept this opinion to myself. We were following some vague directions about 'through the *zone industrielle* and follow the signs'. In Hatchetman you couldn't tell where the town stopped and the *zone industrielle* began. We decided it was the bit without roadworks.

After forty minutes' backtracking and trying blind alleys in a maze of distribution centres and furniture warehouses, we were out in the country again. Les Lacs lay at the end of a long alley of umbrella pines. We passed the sign for the hotel. The pines had been cut to stumps and bulldozers had been cutting up the land. The earth was raw, red and bare. There were two stagnant lakes and a powerful stench of sewer. We held handkerchiefs to our faces.

Through pines we saw a chalet-style building with wooden balconies. 'Looks quite nice,' I said.

The lakes, with all their raw earth, were new and artificial. We saw, as we got closer, that the hotel certainly wasn't. Built in the twenties, it looked as if it had been untouched since. 'Could be the Adirondacks,' muttered Guislaine.

There were drawn curtains, damp, rotting benches, broken *pédalos*, decaying balconies and no guests. All it needed was Anthony Perkins at the check-in desk. Three staff were watching television in the dark dining room. Mademoiselle, after a lengthy search for the ledger, assured us that the hotel was '*presque complet*' as she opened doors that had been closed since September.

Upstairs, two out of three light bulbs needed replacing. Everything creaked. Our room was dark and smelled of mushrooms. Guislaine looked doubtfully round the room. 'That's what comes of arguing with the dice,' she said. 'We should have stayed at La Crémaillère. I'm sure this place is haunted.'

'That's the least of its problems.'

We spent the afternoon in our room after a brief look around the grounds. Somehow, despite the fact it hadn't rained for weeks, everything reeked of damp. The only excitement came when we went to hang our washed clothes out to dry on the balcony. It swayed under my weight. Somehow it failed to collapse.

We went down to dinner early. The echoing dining room had tables laid for 150 people. It was empty but for the same three staff watching television behind the bar. We moved out on to the *terrasse*, a gloomy verandah facing the mini-golf course. It was furnished with plastic dinosaurs, giraffes and elephants, all broken and tilted at crazy angles. There was one other person at dinner, a small, dapper man with a leather handbag, eating alone. After half an hour another solitary man came in and, later, a third. They sat at different tables and eyed one another.

'Something going on we don't know about?' Guislaine asked.

On our way to bed a three-legged dog limped past. 'A black cat maybe, but a three-legged dog?' I muttered to Guislaine.

We double-locked the door.

We woke the next morning surprised that we had slept like children and that the night had passed without incident. Anthony Perkins must have been busy elsewhere. I had borrowed Guislaine's *Moby Dick* now that *Pendennis* was finished. Ishmael and Queequeg's night at the inn in New Bedford had taken my mind off all the spooky things that might have been going on at Les Lacs. By seven we had had breakfast, the bar looking strange without the three staff watching television, paid our bill, put handkerchiefs over our noses as we walked past the Smell, climbed over the earthworks left by the bulldozers and set off through the pine trees almost at a jog, feeling our hearts lighten as we put distance between us and Les Lacs.

Early though it was, the roads were busy, even the small ones. This was the agricultural rush hour. Unlike in the Gers, farming here was too serious a matter to be left to peasants. This was agri-business country, a land of mortgages and machinery. The farm workers commuted to work in their Peugeots and Citroëns, just like office workers. At eight o'clock they climbed on to their outsize tractors, closed the door, put a cassette on the stereo and rumbled out to the fields.

Perhaps our luck was changing. It was goodbye, for now at least, to the prairie lands of Hagetmau, and the countryside was reverting to something more like the Gers and its familiar patchwork of

. . . plotted and pieced – fold, fallow, and plough . . .

Guislaine was still going like an express in her eagerness to put Les Lacs and Hatchetman behind her, so fast that she walked straight past a farmyard without noticing a Dobermann the size of a small donkey which grinned and shadowed us silently along the fence.

We came to a crossroads with a *relais routier* at the junction. We have always found it hard to walk past a restaurant in France without stopping to take a look at the menu. This one had a big photograph outside of their speciality – a heaped *plateau de fruits de mer*, with oysters, mussels, *crevettes*, *langoustines*, *bigorneaux*, *palourdes*, clams and crabs, all sitting on a bed of seaweed. After three weeks of duck this was the first sign of the oasis ahead, a sniff of the sea. The *fruits de mer* joined the crash and roll of Atlantic surf in my daydreams.

Guislaine had relaxed now that Les Lacs was well behind us, and was becoming chatty. Conversation was governed by the busyness of the road. When there was frequent traffic, anything over a car a minute, we walked one behind the other, Guislaine in front so she could set the pace. On the small roads we walked side by side. Talk was seldom deep or philosophical. Thoughts wandered over landscape and weather, our route and the Walk. London and Shouting Down a Phone were a world away.

First Boston had a toll-free line from France to their French desk in London. This was manned by Michel Rostaing, a big, burly Gascon, and Julien Uribe-Mosquera, a tall Colombian with that particular elegance that well-educated South Americans have. Mussing up Julien's immaculately brushed hair was a favourite game in the office. He and his wife Anne have been our friends for ever; they had appointed themselves honorary godparents to the Walk. They were both super-fit and ran in the London Marathon; our lack of training and generally flabby way of life they regarded with indulgent disapproval.

I had called in on the French line from Eugénie to find out if there were any emergencies in London we needed to know about. Julien had agreed to be our contact point.

His partner Michel had answered the phone. 'How are you doing walking through my country?' he had rasped in a voice as thick as *garbure*.

'Fine, thanks, Michel. We're getting a bit fed up with your food, though. I never want to hear about another *magret de canard*. We're ready to join the Duck Liberation Front.'

There was a noise like a truck starting up. 'Forget the *magret*. There is only one way to eat in Gascony. Eat *foie gras* at every meal. That way you will do very well. Hang on, I will pass you Julien.'

Julien asked how we were doing in the manner of a fond but concerned parent, following this up with much sensible and detailed advice on taking care of ourselves.

I promised to follow it all to the letter. 'And what's happening at First Boston?'

'Luis is gone.'

'What?'

'Yes. Two days ago. He resigned.'

'What's he going to do?'

'Go fishing. In Florida.'

I remembered Luis's last words to me when I said I was going to go for a walk, not get another job: 'You're crazy. Good luck, chief.' Not that crazy, it seemed. Luis had survived me by less than a month. I asked Julien what had happened. Luis had made enemies on the way up. Recently he had been unlucky, too unlucky, and it was looking careless. His enemies had come for him. They hadn't actually taken him out and shot him in what had become the new style on Wall Street, but they had left him in a room with the loaded pistol. Luis had resigned. Julien was delighted. As fellow Latin Americans they had a hearty dislike for each other.

I was sad for Luis.

We reached our destination, Montfort-en-Chalosse, by lunch-time. It had been a lovely walk. 'Just like old times,' said Guislaine.

La Chalosse was a jumble of little hills and streams; it could have been a pocket of the Gers between the prairies and the great sandy Atlantic plain of the Landes.

We had had low expectations of our hotel, anticipating another noisy Logis, but today we could do no wrong. The Aux Touzins was the only quiet Logis in France, set back from the road and a few minutes out of the village. No pool was advertised, but just below our little baclony with its two deckchairs was a square of turquoise water. They had just finished building it.

Guislaine was so pleased by these blessings that she relaxed the no-drink-at-lunch policy enough for a couple of glasses of rosé. Afterwards we strolled into Montfort – like Bassoues an ancient *bastide* – and mooched around the shops. Guislaine browsed in pharmacies and I surreptitiously read guide-books in the *maison de la presse*. I picked up a green Michelin to see what they said about Hatchetman: '. . . *ambitieux monuments publics de style 1950 temoignent de la prosperité d'Hagetmau, centre de collecte pour les graines et les porcs de la Chalosse et siège de fabrique de chaises*.' Ah.

I caught up with Guislaine in a pharmacy, where she was standing at the counter holding a new cake of *savon de Marseille*, for washing our clothes, and a toothbrush. I was examining a mushroom poster detailing the different degrees of toxicity when I heard her ask for a tube of *crème anti-moustique*.

Good Lord. I had never noticed. 'I never knew you had a moustache,' I whispered. 'You've kept that a bit of a secret, haven't you?'

Guislaine looked at me as if I had just barked. 'What? What moustache? What are you talking about?'

'You know. I heard you. The *crème*. *Anti-moustique*. It must work pretty well. I've never noticed.'

'You idiot. *Moustique*. Mosquito, not moustache. *Merci, madame.*'

'Oh. Of course.'

Guislaine gave the pharmacist a big smile and me a kick. 'You didn't really think I had a moustache, did you?'

'Well I was a bit surprised.' Just in case, I took a good look at her upper lip. You never knew.

'Stop staring.'

We strolled back to the hotel, enjoying the luxury of walking with nothing on our backs. The rest of the afternoon was to be spent at the pool. There was one other couple there; they were sunbathing and sharing a copy of the *Herald Tribune*. We started talking to them and discovered that he was American and she French. They were on a cycling tour of the area; we swapped notes. Tomorrow they would be at the Atlantic, seventy kilometres away, a distance that would take us three days. Such speed was disconcerting.

He was an industrial psychologist specializing in the problems of entrepreneurs who ran small companies that were getting too big for them. I debated whether to ask him for a free consultation, having run an office that grew from fourteen to well over a hundred people in six years, but decided not to. I borrowed their *Herald Tribune* and looked at the stock prices. I had a quick look, curious to see what it would feel like. After a minute or so I lost interest and went on to the funnies.

CHAPTER 22

We left Montfort just after seven, the sun a shy yellow in the morning mist; no grey woolly clouds today. The village was already bustling, shutters opening, housewives queuing for baguettes, the smell of warm bread wafting down the street and shopkeepers unwinding awnings and shaping their piles of oranges, tomatoes and melons.

Only three days to go.

'We can never do this again,' said Guislaine. 'Not in this way.'

'Now you're saying it. I thought that was my line.'

We talked about other walks we might take and wondered what it would feel like the second time. Strasbourg to Basle through Alsace; across the Apennines in Italy; Guislaine even announced that she would like to walk somewhere in Africa. She dreams of Africa and its wide places. I wasn't particularly interested. I prefer Asia and Europe, places where you can see the debris of civilization. Guislaine wasn't sure what bit of Africa she wanted to walk through; I suspected that geography took a back seat to the dream. A few weeks before leaving London I had finished Wilfred Thesiger's autobiography and I remembered vividly his stories of growing up in Ethiopia and later working as a young District Officer in the Sudan. He had covered half of Africa on foot. I am too soft for that kind of walking.

The twisting descent from Montfort was the last real hill we would come across. It would be flat from here. We saluted the hills behind us: la Clape on the first day; les Hauts de Narbonne where we got lost; the vine-covered swells of the Corbières and the Montagne d'Alaric; the Fan and all its folds and creases from the Garonne to the Adour; and the last choppy jumble of the Chalosse.

'I'm glad we didn't take the short route along the Pyrenees. I don't think we could have handled the mountains,' I said.

'Forget it. The Fan was quite bad enough.'

The walk to Dax was unmemorable. The houses were frequent and of little interest. We dodged on and off the main road; at times we could have been in Surrey. Here, the ducks and the geese had no broad fields to roam in; they were shut up in overcrowded pens of bare earth. Today was a day for covering distance, when walking was just another form of locomotion and not food for the spirit.

But we were looking forward to Dax. My previews in various *maisons de la presse* suggested wide, leafy boulevards and elegant fountains. The map showed parks and lakes. Dax has been a spa since Roman times and, despite our memories of Ischia, I felt sure we would both like it. Reading between the lines in the guides I imagined it would have a pleasant pre-war feel, the sort of place where we could install ourselves at an old-fashioned pavement café, sip a muscat and watch the movement while Guislaine scribbled in her notebook – by now almost full. We had booked not in Dax itself but across the Adour in St Paul-les-Dax, where the Hôtel du Lac merited a rocking chair in the Michelin and sat by the side of the lake. What could have been better? We wondered about taking a rest day in Dax but decided against it. We were too close to the sea now.

I was rather pleased with my map-reading. Instead of coming into Dax the obvious way, on the main road, we followed a network of little by-roads that brought us in through what could have been part of the Appalachians. We walked past squalid smallholdings of mud and bog fenced in with chicken-wire. Children played in the mire while their parents leered at us.

We burst from this scene, which my distant ancestor George Morland the eighteenth-century pig-painter would have found familiar, on to a six-way roundabout clotted with traffic. Ahead of us was a towering block of flats painted in ice-cream colours, billboards the size of tennis courts, and hypermarket parking lots.

I couldn't locate exactly where we were on the map. Dax had grown a new suburb since the map was made. Next to the hypermarket was the Blue Hawaii Bar and Disco, its sign topped with a neon guitarist, possibly Elvis.

'Would you mind if we took a rest?' asked Guislaine.

'What, here? You must be joking.'

One look at her said she wasn't. Her hips had been giving trouble all through the trip. She had borne the pain cheerfully, but now I saw that the old brave smile was back. I hadn't seen that since Mazères. It might perhaps have made a brief appearance as we were toiling up the hill in Hagetmau, but otherwise it had faded as Guislaine got fitter. Since the Walk, whenever we have rows I think of Guislaine with that smile and I melt.

A ten-minute sit-down might not be such a bad idea after all. But where? We didn't feel like going into the Blue Hawaii and asking for – what would you drink there, a Purple Fog-Cutter? The only patch of grass was the centre of the roundabout and that was as accessible as an ice-floe.

'Just another couple of minutes and we'll find somewhere. Let's get out of Mount Kisco first,' I said.

We had lived for ten years in Bedford, forty miles north of New York. Between us and Mount Kisco had been one of those sprawls that are on the outskirts of every American town. Two miles of Adzam Motors, Caldor, Dunkin' Donuts, Radio Shack, Mr Fixit, Kalaydjian Pontiac, ShopRite, BonBon Box and Vinny's Auto for a Square Deal. We always called these sprawls Mount Kisco – quite unfairly, as the village of Mount Kisco itself was a dignified little community. Here, on the outskirts of Dax, was the first Mount Kisco we had encountered on the Walk.

We stumbled on, dodged the traffic and came to rest on a

concrete bench by the stadium parking lot. We didn't stay long, as it smelled like a urinal and the leafy boulevards of Dax were calling. Guislaine had got her breath back and we saddled up again. Much of the traffic was private ambulances taking people from the outlying hotels and caravan sites to the baths and treatment centres.

Two kilometres further into this traffic-mad city, and super-markets began to give way to pharmacies. There were two or three on every block; the advertisements on the bus shelters told of breakthroughs in the treatment of arthritis and rheumatism.

'How much further to *centre ville*?' asked Guislaine. 'Where are all those nice leafy streets and pavement cafés you were talking about?'

'Not much longer. We have to wait till we get to the park and the Fontaine Chaude. The guide-book said that was the centre of the old Roman town. Apparently it's been spewing out warm water ever since then.'

I looked at the map. There had been so much development it was impossible to locate where we were. We hurried across the street in a break in the never-ending traffic and looked about. Everything seemed to be made of concrete.

'Oh look,' said Guislaine, pointing.

There, trapped in an enclave not much bigger than a squash court was an ordinary-looking fountain set in a stone wall. Over it was a sign: 'La Fontaine Chaude'.

There was a park. That was hidden behind a stone wall.

'Not a surfeit of leafy boulevards,' I said, looking at the mess of new buildings and flashing green crosses.

'No. Well at least we won't be tempted to walk back here for dinner.'

We looked around disconsolately to check if we were missing something, decided we weren't and headed for the bridge across the Adour. So much for Dax.

I pulled the map out once we were across the bridge. I hadn't bothered to check how far St Paul-les-Dax was from

Dax, having assumed they were next door to each other. It was one big urban splotch on the map. To my dismay I saw that we had another five kilometres to go. Should I come clean with Guislaine? 'Er. I don't think we're quite there yet. It might be a bit further than we thought. We turn left somewhere, up there past the railway bridge, and it's down there a bit. I could work out how far if you wanted.'

'Don't bother. Let's just get on with it.'

We walked on in single file, past Algerian butchers and cheap clothes shops spilling out on to the pavement. At last we came to the turning; the street became less shabby. Shops gave way to offices and furniture showrooms. The road dipped up ahead. That had to be the lake.

It was. The lake itself was lovely, the size and shape of the Serpentine; it was set in a woody park of oaks and poplars. There were other trees too, but my tree recognition hadn't made any advance since Guislaine introduced me to the concept of the poplar being an upside-down fish-bone. Our hotel was on a rise at the side of the lake. It had been made out of Lego and advertised itself with a huge purple sign on top. To reach it we passed Le 24-Lane Bowling and a *centre de loisirs* shaped like a white doughnut.

'Well, at least the hotel should be clean,' I said, 'and I see the rooms have balconies. Who cares about charm? I think Wimbledon has started. I'm going to spend the afternoon watching that on the box. Hope they show it in France.'

'Good. And I'm going to have a nice long massage. Everyone in the hotel must be there for the cure. That's one thing they'll do well.'

We entered a lobby like an airport terminal. The Hôtel du Lac did not welcome walkers. It liked guests to come packaged, preferably in a wheelchair, and to do what they were told. The staff at the reception desk greeted us with the patronizing hostility of air hostesses. Our room wasn't ready. We sat with our packs, hot and sweaty, in the main lobby, getting some funny looks from the towelling dressing gowns shuffling past. Ah, maybe a room could be found after all. No, a balcony was impossible. We were shown to a dark little back room. Could we see another room? Heavy sighs and exchanging of glances.

Finally we were installed. No balcony, but the room looked clean and comfortable. The bathroom was enormous and equipped with chrome handles for levering yourself out of your wheelchair. Guislaine turned on the bath while I examined the television and read the list of the things guests were prohibited from doing. If you hung anything out to dry from your window or on your balcony it would be removed by the hotel staff and locked up. It could be reclaimed 'on payment of a service fee at the front desk between 1700 and 1730 hours'.

I went into the bathroom and reeled back, wondering what private intestinal complaint Guislaine was suffering from. 'Excuse me. Phew. Er, darling . . .'

'The smell?'

'Well, yes.'

'It's the water. Sulphur. Look.'

There was a notice above the taps saying that the hotel baths took water from *la source*. It smelled like a school chemistry lab.

Guislaine hurried through her bath, trilling things about the massage she was going to have. Pamphlets in the room told of the benefits of Dax water and the various treatments available at the hotel. Massage was a speciality and was available on room service.

Our last – and only – room-service massage had been at the Hotel Okura in Tokyo ten years before. We spent the night there on the way to Hong Kong and were bleary with jet lag. Guislaine called the desk for a massage and we stretched out on our beds in anticipation. I was hoping for something mildly erotic and wondered what Guislaine's reaction would be. Five minutes later, two female sumo wrestlers came into the room and gave us a terrible beating. Guislaine claimed it made her feel better. I have avoided massage ever since.

I lay back in the bath telling myself that there were people who actually liked this smell. Guislaine called the health centre to arrange her massage.

A minute later I heard the phone being slammed down and she kicked the bathroom door open. 'Pigs, idiots, shits,' she spat. Up to now she had been telling me not to be so critical of the hotel. 'Bastards. Bloody French. Typical.'

'Something wrong?'

'Stupid bastards. No massage. Jeepers. Only for people on one of their packages. *Vous n'êtes pas une pensionnaire, madame?*' She imitated the whine of the air hostess on the desk.

At least Wimbledon was on.

Nothing would have made us eat in the hotel that night. We went past Le Bowling and round to a restaurant on the other side of the lake, where we sat on a wooden platform built out over the water and ate steak grilled on charcoal and a good salad. The water was calm and dark in the late-evening shadows.

'You know, damn near half the places we've stayed have been disasters in one way or another,' I said, 'and I don't think we'd recommend any of them to a friend apart from Bassoues and Maigné, and maybe Montfort, yet it really hasn't mattered.'

'And the first *gîte*, the Auberge des Cathars at Belflou,' added Guislaine. 'That was my favourite. But you're right. When you think of all the time we spend trying to find the best place to stay when we're travelling by car, and half the time we end up disappointed. On the Walk we've just taken what's been dished up, and even the bad ones have given us something to laugh about.'

'Let's have another bottle of wine. It's a short one tomorrow.'

The next morning we left as early as we could. We paid the bill and said we would have breakfast downstairs in the dining room. Quite out of the question. Breakfast downstairs was not permitted. In that case we would go back to our room

243

and have breakfast there. Absolutely impossible. The bill had been paid; we couldn't go back to the room.

'I see what they mean,' I said. 'We might steal the towels. Let me deal with them.' Up to now Guislaine had been doing the talking.

'No, no, don't worry,' she said. She could see I was preparing for one of my bluster acts, a combination of subtle irony and clearly expressed demands that reminds her of Basil Fawlty. To avert this she organized a compromise. We were given breakfast in the ironing room on the third floor, under framed pictures of flamenco dancers.

Leaving Dax was as difficult as arriving. St Paul too had grown a new suburb, a commercial zone of which the map was ignorant. Our first attempt to get out into the country took us into the Peugeot dealer's storage-park, then a curved road ended up at International Harvester and next we found ourselves in the hypermarket delivery area. The fourth road was a dead end and then, at last, we broke free. Suddenly we were in open countryside. There had been nothing this pretty since the road into Montfort.

We paused to feel the warmth of the sun breaking through the morning mist on to our faces. It was quiet. We were on the edge of a small road, near to a level crossing. Guislaine was standing a few paces from me.

ByyyyyyyooooOOOOONNNNNNGGGGGGG.

A small white car hurtled round the corner at race-track speed. Three inches closer and Guislaine would have been dead. We stood dumb and motionless for a few seconds trying to realize what had happened.

We gasped. Guislaine began to pant. I felt rage mounting inside me and wanted to run after the car, drag the driver out and . . . and . . . shout at him, hit him, something to make him understand what he had just done. We stood motionless for a few seconds. I put my arms around Guislaine, pack and all, and hugged her. She was still shaking and gasping. She began to calm. I told her about a shoot I had been on a few years before. I had slipped after reloading my gun. The gun had discharged with the barrel end a few inches from my nose and pointing upwards. A fraction closer and it would have blown my face off. My mind went on revisiting that single instant of the explosion for hours afterwards, but it didn't take long for gratitude to replace shock.

The road led on to the Adour, here a broad and tranquil river, quite unlike the weedy trickle under the bridge in Dax. We abandoned the road for the old towpath, which ran along the northern side of the river on an embankment probably as old as Dax. There were few houses and almost none close to the river. On our right the fields were cosy patches of vegetables; below us on the left the Adour bubbled along a wide gravel path picking the easiest way through small jungly islands.

We discovered afterwards why this area was so unspoilt and why there were no houses close to the river. The name Barthes kept appearing on the map: les Barthes, la Barthote, Quartier des Barthes, perhaps even the St Barthélemy further down the river. Neither of us knew what it meant; later we asked at a café in Saubusse. *Une barthe* is a flood plain. All these fields would be inundated when the Adour was in spate. And that explained not only the lack of houses but also the fertility of the land.

The towpath ended at the walls of an important-looking house, built on an elevation; in late spring when the snow was melting in the Pyrenees it would be an island in the flood. We left the riverbank and followed an avenue of chestnuts towards a straggling village. Ducks and chickens fussed around the railway line at the level crossing leading into the village.

We stopped for a coffee at a place in the village that was at the same time a café, a restaurant and a shop supplying the necessities, cigarettes, drink and newspapers. Everything inside was brown, including the grizzled inhabitants sitting over their *pastis*. One, who entered Guislaine's notebook as the Lizard, was complaining. His daughter was in hospital; it was a long way to visit; and the ducks . . . breeding them had become a luxury – how could an ordinary man hope to make money at it? His companion had heard it before. He nodded encouragingly but was more interested in trying to read the headlines in *L'Équipe* without moving. It was lying on the table at an angle and he had to turn his head sideways to read. From time to time he would give a *'mais oui'*, or a *'bien sûr'*. I was soon drawn into their lives. I couldn't follow every word as the accent was too thick, but I kept up with the subtitles of hands, eyebrows and shoulders punctuated by the banging of glasses. Guislaine filled in the details later.

'The French give such force and emotion,' I said, 'to the telling of everyday tales. I wonder what they do when something really serious comes along.'

'They shrug.'

Guislaine had been exchanging badinage with the owner, who persisted in referring to us as *'les Espagnols'*. He and his son, who was acting as waiter, kept on looking at our packs or our Mephistos and then whispering. *Le patron* disappeared into the kitchen. We finished our coffees and followed him to pay the bill. He was rolling out dough and Madame was preparing quiche Lorraine. *'Une vraie quiche,'* she emphasized, not one of those things you bought in shops. Guislaine quizzed her about eggs and things. Madame, glad to be taken seriously, imparted the recipe, bit by bit, making sure Guislaine knew that she didn't do this for just anyone. Guislaine copied it down in the notebook and we set off in high spirits.

Le patron came to the door and waved us on our way with a loud *'Au'voir, les Espagnols. Bonne route.'*

'Et bonne quiche,' Guislaine shouted back.

Soon after the village we heard the noise of an aerodrome. As we approached the next village, Angoumé, a crocodile of five military helicopters buzzed overhead and dipped in sequence behind the trees and out of sight. A minute later they popped up into view again and continued their circuits and bumps. We could see two men in each helicopter, presumably an instructor and his pupil.

We came to the big open field that the helicopters were using as a landing ground and stopped to watch, fascinated, as they slipped down at an angle like snow sliding off a roof and then checked, to hover motionless for a few seconds fifty feet up. The nose would rear and the machine would slide in to land, nose cocked. Each time I was sure that the tail rotor would hit the ground first and each time, just before touchdown, the helicopter levelled slightly, enough to allow the undercarriage to touch first.

They waited on the ground, one behind the other, until all five had come in to roost. We waved. One of the men in the last one waved back. We watched the machines shuffle as the engines built up speed and then spring into the air, off on another circuit. We waited for them to come round and waved again as they approached, particularly to our friend in the fifth one. He gave us a circled-thumb-and-forefinger 'A-OK' sign. We felt like children at the circus who had had a handshake from the ringmaster.

We walked on. From time to time we would look back, secretly disappointed that none of the helicopters had followed us.

Saubusse, our destination, was unmentioned in the guidebooks; after Dax we had low expectations. The approach was dreary, past modern houses and a Vietnamese restaurant. But our hearts danced when we came to the village square.

'Looks like a set for *La Bohème*,' said Guislaine. On one side was a quirky church with two towers, one a square, chunky thing and the other a pointed fairy-tale spire; opposite was the Bar des Sports, the Café Alsace and a handful of sleepy shops with striped awnings. In the middle was a painted bandstand of curlicued metal.

We found our hotel, a crooked old house by the river, which was being done up by its enthusiastic young owners. The menu outside was aimed more at the *fins becs* of Bayonne and Dax than at the locals. We stepped over ladders and paint-pots on the way upstairs. Our room was so small, with a miniature double bed, that we took two rooms next to each other, ninety francs each. Guislaine's was on the side of the house looking out at the fine stone bridge and mine was at the front, with a view of the river.

We went back to the Café Alsace for lunch. I gave myself to a mound of *choucroute paysanne* and a cold bottle of Alsatian Sylvaner while Guislaine gossiped with the owner's daughter, the waitress. We had been followed into town by a prancing young man with a handbag who had skipped in front of us chanting little snatches of song. When we returned to the square for lunch he was sitting on a bench talking distractedly to himself and playing with his handbag. He was mourning, said the waitress, mourning his lost sister who had drowned in the river. He wasn't homosexual; he thought he had become his sister.

I finished lunch with a *tarte au citron* and a glass of *poire*; I had just taken in the second belt-notch of the Walk and felt I would never be fat again. Guislaine and the waitress talked about Alsace and Strasbourg, a city of misty school memories for Guislaine. She often says how much she liked it, but the sadness in her face when she talks of it suggests otherwise; I am sure her memories are happier than was her life there. In the next room we heard the waitress's father settling down with the boys for a serious afternoon of politics and eau-de-vie.

We ambled back along the riverbank towards our hotel for a siesta. The ancient stone bridge spanned a majestic curve in the Adour, here a broad dark stream, almost black. On the shore, drawn up in front of the hotel, were a handful of yellow and green fishing boats with flat bows like Norfolk punts. Two old men stood drowsily holding their rods while a small terrier ran busily back and forth between them as if bearing news. We could see the grey torpedo shapes of big fish stirring below the surface of the water.

Guislaine approached one of the men. 'Caught anything?' He laughed and shook his head. 'Only the sun.'

Beside him was the usual jumble of equipment. We had seen

the same all along the Canal du Midi. The French love their equipment. Next to the Café Alsace was a shop for *la chasse* and *la pêche*. The window was crammed with rods of wood and plastic, rifles with telescopic sights, pump-guns, duck-shooting boots, camouflage jackets, torches, aerosol contraptions for imitating birdcalls, fur-flapped hats and, of course, knives – a whole section of the window just for knives: short ones for gutting and skinning, folding knives, Swiss army knives, penknives with thick bone handles and daggers in leather sheaths.

We had our nap and went for a slow wander round the village, into the church, across the bridge. This was the last afternoon of the Walk. We had known for some time that we would reach the Atlantic and now we were both quiet, sorting through our emotions. It was like the feeling I had had sitting in front of the church in St Mont while the evening sun went down and I was trying to stretch out the last few pages of *Pendennis*, turning the pages as slowly as possible and hoping to prolong the moment. I wished that Saubusse wasn't so perfect.

I revisited with an ache some of the special places, Samatan, Bassoues, Marseillette, Montfort, St Mont, Belflou, Bram. I even felt nostalgic about the unshaven Rigoletto of Mirande waving his cobwebby towels at us, and about M. Campigotto sidling through his restaurant in Castelnaudary to stand outside and curse the starlings. I wondered if he'd repaired his door yet after Guislaine had forced it open.

I thought with love and respect of Guislaine's achievement. This woman who had never owned a pair of sports shoes had just walked across France.

Usually I spent much of the afternoon with the map, plotting routes and rolling the distance 'thermometer' over the alternatives. By seven o'clock I had often done and redone the route three or four times. Today I put it off. I had a shower and washed my hair. The sun was lowering across the river. I opened the shutters and leant out towards the Adour, peaceful in the evening light, 'too full for sound and foam'. The river was flowing the wrong way, upstream. The tide was coming in. The first sight of Atlantic water. The fishermen were gone and the boats were pulled up on the bank.

Oh well, better get out the map.

CHAPTER 23

We had decided over dinner to start at first light. Capbreton was nearly thirty kilometres away and we agreed that arriving on a crowded beach wouldn't be right. Having to pick our way through lilos and volleyball players to dip our toes in the Atlantic wasn't how we saw the climax of our epic. We even toyed with the idea of leaving at four in the morning so as to arrive on an empty beach.

We compromised and asked Madame after dinner for breakfast at six. She pulled a face. That would be difficult. They didn't start that early, they were up too late every night clearing up the dinner; we would understand. We did, and were thinking that we could get breakfast on the way instead when one of the waitresses spoke up. She didn't mind getting up early to make our breakfast and let us out. She could always go back to bed afterwards. Bang on her door if we didn't hear her moving about by quarter to six. It was the door at the end of the corridor upstairs. We were touched and I felt guilty. During the meal I had been making fun of the two waitresses' lack of polish. 'More at home milking a goat than serving wine,' I had said.

'Are you sure you don't mind getting up so early?' I asked.

'Not at all.'

We accepted with gratitude, feeling even guiltier.

We woke at 5.30. Ten minutes later we were ready, packs filled, eager and excited. There was no noise from the end of the corridor.

'You go,' I urged Guislaine, 'your French is better than mine. It's the door at the end of the corridor.'

'Hmph. You don't need much French to wake someone up.'

'Oh go on.'

She had just set off down the corridor when a clock radio erupted behind a door; she knocked hesitantly.

'Don't worry, don't worry. Breakfast at six.'

Over coffee and *pain grillé* we thanked the waitress for her kindness. 'You see, it's a big day for us. We're on a *grande marche* and today's the last day. We've walked all the way from the Mediterranean.'

The waitress smiled, unimpressed. Maybe the Mediterranean was somewhere near Dax.

I gave her a thank-you tip as she let us out.

'*Bonne chance,*' she said, '*et bonne route pour, er, la Méditerranée.*'

We paused on the bank of the Adour before beginning; the dawn mist swirled over the water.

'"Bliss was it in that dawn to be alive,"' floated through my mind. I said it aloud to Guislaine.

'That's lovely. What is it?'

'Wordsworth.'

'Is there more? How does it go on?' The notebook was out.

'I'm not sure. I've got a nasty feeling the next line is "But to be young was very heaven!"'

'Hmm. Well, we're young enough.'

The river shone like a salmon's skin. I photographed Guislaine half hidden in the mist. We kissed and, hand in hand, set off for the Atlantic.

For the first hour we walked in silence along the towpath watching the changing luminescence of the river as the sun chased away the long wisps of mist. To begin with we passed grand houses with colonnaded porticoes, high-shuttered windows and formal lawns marching down to the river. Then the gardens grew unkempt and soon they give way to fields and woods and nothing but the urgent noises of small animals and birds going about their dawn business. I half-expected to see Badger and Mole pop up at the next turn in the river.

After an hour's walk we went under a bridge, whose rush-hour traffic brought us sharply back to the present, and our route curved away from the Adour. We were taking a longer way than necessary so as to avoid main roads and to cut down to a minimum our walk through the pine forest of the Landes, which runs along the Atlantic from the Spanish border to Bordeaux. In some places it is twenty miles wide. We hoped to escape with four or five kilometres. Guislaine and I share a dislike of pine woods; they feel dead.

I had only seen the Landes once before. Twenty-five years ago, as an undergraduate, I had driven through with three Oxford friends on our way to Spain. We were in a 1954 Hillman Minx borrowed from one of the friends' parents. The Landes was the only place where the car did not break down, so we saw less of it than we might have as we sped through at forty-five miles an hour.

Eight o'clock. Time for our first stop. We found a bar at a crossroads, already busy serving *café et croissants* to commuters on their way to Bayonne. I wanted to tell the owner that we had walked over five hundred kilometres to have coffee in his bar, but didn't. It was a quick stop. We shouldered our packs and moved out. We were still in oak and chestnut country, a few miles yet to go before the pines.

'Good heavens. Look. I've never seen that before.' I pointed at some animals in a field on our right.

'What?'

'Woolly pigs. Amazing.'

'Gosh. Woolly pigs! They are strange-looking, Funny heads.' Guislaine peered at them intently for a few moments and was just reaching for the notebook to record this phenomenon when she came to the realization that she was looking at a flock of sheep. 'Oh ha ha. Smart-ass. Pleased with yourself, I suppose.'

I smirked.

We were back in agri-business land. Ahead of us a steel barn rose sixty feet out of the prairie. It was set back a hundred yards from the road. A single man in a Mercedes drove up and parked on the apron in front of it. He sat in his car with the windows closed and made a short call on his car telephone. Two minutes later a big, black Citroën saloon sped up from the opposite direction and parked fifty feet away on the apron. A man and a woman stepped out of it, dressed for the avenue Montaigne. The first driver got out and started walking towards the Citroën. He was carrying a slim, black briefcase. Avenue Montaigne went to meet him while the woman stayed by the Citroën. They met on neutral territory and talked briefly. They paused to look quickly at us, walking by a hundred yards away, and went back to their conference. The briefcase was handed over. They hurried back to their cars, Montaigne said something to the woman, doors slammed and both cars drove off in the directions they had come from.

'What do you think? Drug dealers or the mortgage man from Crédit Agricole?' I asked.

'The women don't dress like that at the Crédit Agricole.'

A few minutes later, Guislaine caught me by the arm. 'Look, look. There.' She pointed to our left.

There, filling the southern horizon, was the vivid black cut-out of the Pyrenees. It was the first time we had had a real sight of them. Now, even when we looked away we were aware of their presence. It seemed fitting that they should come out of hiding as we reached the sea.

'I'm sure I can smell salt in the air,' said Guislaine.

The pines became more frequent. Today's walk had been much prettier than we expected, particularly the magic of the first silent hour along the Adour. We talked of all the things on the Walk that had turned out differently to our expectations. We made a list of surprises as we walked along, crossing from one side of the road to the other to keep in the shade.

We thought of these:

254

1. The number of dogs in France.
2. How boring Gascon cooking was. How many different things can you do to a duck?
3. How hot it was in the afternoon.
4. The lack of boredom. How quickly time passed, both on the road and afterwards.
5. How easily we put up with discomfort. After years of a soft life we hadn't been sure how we'd take to living for a month out of something half the size of a laundry-bag.
6. The prices. Our average hotel room cost only 130 francs, and the bill for a four-course dinner with a couple of bottles of wine was usually 180 francs for two.
7. How hard it was to get to sleep. And how little sleep we could survive on.
8. The three great pleasures:
       a cold glass of water,
       a rest by the roadside,
       putting on clean clothes.
9. How melancholy was the Canal du Midi.
10. How empty the hotels were in June.
11. How long it took to lose weight.
12. How far we'd walked. Our total distance covered would be 550 kilometres, 350 miles.

'You know the biggest surprise of all,' said Guislaine.

'Yes, that you could get up before seven every day for a month.'

'Oh ha ha. No. The biggest surprise was how much I've enjoyed it.'

We had one more obstacle to cross before the final leg through the pine forest to Capbreton: the autoroute. It was fenced on both sides, and it took us half an hour of searching to find a little tunnel that went under the road. We stopped to look and shake our heads at the six lanes of traffic whining past from Bordeaux to Bayonne and back, and ducked into the tunnel.

Before entering the forest we stopped on its edge for a glass of water at a ranch campsite. It was staffed by a group of girls in Levis and tight T-shirts. ('No of course they're not all lesbians. Try and control your fantasies till you get on the beach.') There were no guests. No one came till 1 July. That was tomorrow. The way to Capbreton? No problem. Just follow that path there, take a right and then go left when you cross the other path. We thanked them and set off. When we next stopped, it would be to get our feet wet.

Their instructions and the map were useless. The paths multiplied into half a dozen which rode up and down sand-hills under the pines in a random fashion. I had to admit that, for the first time since Narbonne, we were lost. We sat down near a gypsy encampment. I cursed the IGN for the last time and Guislaine suggested asking the gypsies the way.

'No, they look a bit sinister to me,' I said. 'Don't worry, if we keep the sun on our left we can't go wrong.'

'Where have I heard that before?'

We picked a path and marched on. We heard traffic in the distance. We prayed that we hadn't doubled back on the autoroute and were relieved to pop out on a small but busy road. It looked the right size. After a minute we came to a junction next to a sneaky aerospace factory hidden in the woods. I located where we were on the map. Right road, wrong place – but only another couple of kilometres to go.

I didn't want to walk straight into the centre of town and on to the town beach, which would be packed by now, so I aimed south where I hoped we would find it less crowded. The town went on and on, pavements, streets, pretty little villas, well-kept gardens.

'Where the hell is the sea?' asked Guislaine, after half an hour of walking round Capbreton.

All the streets looked the same. Although we kept seeing signs to *les plages*, we didn't seem to be getting any nearer. We had been hoping for a view of the sea before arriving, but the flatness of the Landes and the height of the great dunes running along the beach would deny us that. Later Guislaine told me that she was getting furious at the fact she couldn't see the sea. She wasn't aware of the height of the dunes and kept on hoping for a preview of blue to lead her home.

There was sand on the road. Then more sand, and ahead of us the houses petered out as the road rose and lost itself in the back of the last and biggest dune.

The next dune was Cape Cod.

We ran up through the drifting sand and the marram grass to the top. The crash and roar of the great surf was in our ears, the noise I had dreamed of on so many hot, airless afternoons.

We paused for a moment on the top. Eighty feet below us the beach stretched wide and yellow from the lighthouse of Capbreton to the endless south, a beach all but empty. We looked at each other, our feelings too complicated for talk, and, joining hands, slalomed down the dune. At the bottom we kicked off our Mephistos and ran into the sea, packs still on our backs. I stopped on the way to thrust the camera into the hands of a puzzled Senegalese student, one of the few people on the beach. 'Please. Photograph us. We have walked from the Mediterranean.'

We stood in the ocean up to our knees and felt the cold water surge around our legs. We hugged each other and kissed and exulted as the surf thundered about us.

The Senegalese looked on doubtfully. '*Ça suffit?*' he shouted across the waves.

'*Oui. Ça suffit.*'

CHAPTER 24

That was two years ago.

We spent a couple of days in Capbreton, lazed in the sun and ate huge plates of seafood. We played in the surf and watched the trawler fleet setting out from the harbour for its Midsummer blessing from the Bishop, who stood, cross aloft, in full robes on the bow of the police launch. We rented bicycles and explored Hossegor, the neighbouring town, set primly around an inland lagoon.

'Do you miss walking?' I asked Guislaine.

'No. How about you?'

'I've never been happier to sit on a beach in my life. I don't care if I never walk anywhere again.'

We took the bus to Biarritz and sat on the beach there for another two days, happier, healthier and browner than we had ever been.

Guislaine and I retreated to our little house in Norfolk after the summer holidays and wrote a book together about our Walk. It didn't work as a book, but I enjoyed writing it so much that I decided to put off the decision of what I was going to do and try writing another one.

When people ask why I gave up my job, I know now that it wasn't the office politics or the pressure; I quite enjoyed those. It was that I had stopped learning. When you stop learning you start to grow old fast. We don't have as much money as we used to, but every day of the last two years has been a gift.

When I had finished my part of the book we tried to write together, I went to Victoria Station and bought a train ticket. Thirty-one hours later I was in Prague. It was the day before the Berlin Wall was opened. On my first evening I wandered in the yellow November mist from the hotel to Wenceslas Square and found myself in the midst of ten thousand students who had surrounded two police cars. It was the first demonstration in Prague. The following week I was ordered off the Budapest–Bucharest train by Ceauşescu's leather-coated thugs with a sub-machine-gun in my back and deported back to Hungary. Ceauşescu had decided to close his border to foreigners and I couldn't get into Romania. But six months after that, a magazine sent me back to write a story about the country and I spent two weeks driving around Moldavia and Transylvania; the longest queues were not for bread but for newspapers. It was infinitely moving to be at the birth of a country's struggle for freedom.

The Walk was the best thing Guislaine and I have ever done. Now I like to think we can see over things that stopped the view before. A bit like 'The Windhover'.

THE WINDHOVER
To Christ our Lord

I caught this morning morning's minion, king-
   dom of daylight's dauphin, dapple-dawn-drawn Falcon, in his
     riding
  Of the rolling level underneath him steady air, and striding
High there, how he rung upon the rein of a wimpling wing
In his ecstasy! then off, off forth on swing,
   As a skate's heel sweeps smooth on a bow-bend: the hurl
     and gliding
   Rebuffed the big wind. My heart in hiding
Stirred for a bird, – the achieve of, the mastery of the thing!

Brute beauty and valour and act, oh, pride, plume here
   Buckle! AND the fire that breaks from thee then, a billion
Times told lovelier, more dangerous, O my chevalier!

   No wonder of it: sheer plod makes plough down sillion
Shine, and blue-bleak embers, ah my dear,
   Fall, gall themselves, and gash gold-vermilion.

Gerard Manley Hopkins

One Summer's Grace

A Family Voyage Round Britain

Libby Purves

In the summer of 1988 Libby Purves and her husband Paul Heiney set sail in their cutter *Grace O'Malley* with their children Nicholas, aged five, and Rose, three. They sailed the 1,700 miles around Britain, from the offshore labyrinths of the sandy south-east to the towering stacks of Cape Wrath and back home through the North Sea. Her account of the voyage is a new classic of the sea.

'It is that rarest of all books on the yachting shelf – a work of acerbic realism. Libby Purves is wonderfully sharp on the woes of containing a marriage and a family inside their pressure-cooker of a small boat. Her portrait of coastal Britain in the 1980s is wise, affectionate and sceptical; her pleasure in our scary seas rings true because there is not a word of cant or overstatement in her story. This is how it is – and Miss Purves tells it beautifully'

Jonathan Raban

'A delightful book, warm, wise and candid'   *Sunday Telegraph*

Fontana

Fontana Non-Fiction

Fontana is a leading paperback publisher of non-fiction.
Below are some recent titles.

- ☐ EUROPE BY TRAIN Katie Wood & George McDonald £7.99
- ☐ CHEAP SLEEP GUIDE TO EUROPE Katie Wood £7.99
- ☐ ON THE WATERFRONT IN BRITAIN 1993 Alice Hart-Davis £8.99
- ☐ ON THE WATERFRONT IN FRANCE 1993 Gill Charlton £8.99
- ☐ HITCH-HIKER'S GUIDE TO EUROPE 1993 Ken Welsh £5.99
- ☐ FAMILY WELCOME GUIDE Malcolm Hamer & Jill Foster £5.99
- ☐ OBSESSIVE TRAVELLER David Dale £4.50

You can buy Fontana Paperbacks at your local bookshops or
newsagents. Or you can order them from Fontana, Cash Sales
Department, Box 29, Douglas, Isle of Man. Please send a cheque,
postal or money order (not currency) worth the price plus 24p per book
for postage (maximum postage required is £3.00 for orders within
the UK).

NAME (Block letters)_____

ADDRESS_____

_____

ARE YOU READY FOR YOUR
Twisted Journeys®?
THE PLACE: AN OLD, SPOOKY HOUSE THAT JUST MIGHT BE HAUNTED.
THE TIME: A VERY DARK HALLOWEEN NIGHT.
THE HERO: YOU!
EACH PAGE TELLS WHAT HAPPENS TO YOU AS YOU EXPLORE GHOST MANSION, DISGUISED IN YOUR MUMMY COSTUME. YOUR WORDS AND THOUGHTS ARE SHOWN IN THE YELLOW BALLOONS. JUST FOLLOW THE NOTE AT THE BOTTOM OF EACH PAGE UNTIL YOU REACH A Twisted Journeys® PAGE. THEN MAKE THE CHOICE YOU LIKE BEST.
BUT BE CAREFUL...THE WRONG CHOICE COULD HAUNT YOU FOR THE REST OF YOUR LIFE!

'I should just take you home,' Barry growls from the driver's seat. He's angry that his parents are making him take his younger brother Tim, you and your friend Sue to a big Halloween party. Plus, it's just started raining.

'Look out!' Tim screams.

'Whoa!' yelps Barry, jerking the steering wheel to the right. Through the car window, you see a boy standing in the road, lit by the headlights.

The car skids on the wet pavement. It slides into a ditch.

You all scramble out. Everyone seems okay.

'Where's the boy?' asks Tim.

'We didn't hit him,' says Barry.

'Probably got scared and ran home,' you say.

Barry tries to use his mobile phone to call his parents. It isn't working.

Up the hill, you see a light flickering in the window of a big house. Pointing, you say, 'Maybe they can help us up there.'

GO ON TO THE NEXT PAGE.

TWISTED JOURNEYS®

Tim really wants everyone to stay together.
But would that make Dr Hale angry?
What if he sends you back out in the storm?

WILL YOU . . .

. . . say you should stick together?
TURN TO PAGE 36.

. . . say you should each
go to your own room?
TURN TO PAGE 54.

You creep down the stairs as quietly as you can. You're grateful that they're stone. No creaking boards.

At the bottom of the steps, you find another round room. This one has several big leather chairs with little round tables next to them.

A heavy wooden door with iron bands across it seems to be the only exit.

Very carefully, you lift the latch on the door. Pulling it open just a little, you peer through the crack.

It opens into a games room. In the centre is an old-fashioned billiard table, with nets in the corner for pockets. The balls are all inside a triangle-shaped rack sitting in the middle of the table.

Past the table, there's a set of doors that slide into the wall on either side. Pocket doors, you think they're called.

There's no sign of the . . . the ghosts.

You don't hear anyone. Maybe you're safe here. It doesn't look like anyone has been in the tower for a long time. Then again, it's not like ghosts would leave footprints.

WILL YOU . . .

. . . try to sneak out through
the games room?
TURN TO PAGE 80.

. . . try hiding out in the tower?
TURN TO PAGE 105.

'Tim's right!' you scream. Rushing over to the curtains, you grab the glass chimney off the candle. Then you put the flame right up next to the dusty, dry cloth.

'Hold it right there!' you shout at the ghosts. They're just a step or two away from Sue. 'Let us out of here or I'll light these curtains and your house will burn down!'

Dr Hale looks almost impressed and says, 'I see only one flaw in your plan.'

'Oh, yeah?' sneers Tim. 'What's that?'

'I can light small fires,' the doctor replies. 'And I can put them out.'

He snaps his spectral fingers. Suddenly, your candle and all the lamps go out. The whole house is plunged into darkness.

You hear Sue gasp.

Tim calls out for his brother.

Then, right next to you, a voice says, 'Boo!'

You stumble away from the noise. In the dark, you don't get far.

THE END

11

As you look across
your room, you see the
lightning flashing
beyond the window. It
occurs to you that if you
climb out and stretch
down, holding onto the windowsill, it will only be a metre
or so to the ground! The ledge
behind the house isn't very wide,
but it should be wide enough.

You grab the chair and straining with
the effort, toss it through the glass.

The window explodes into a million shimmering shards.

You rush over, brushing away the last of the glass with
your bandaged hands.

Your heart pounds as you look down. Your eyes can't help
looking past the ledge below, down the deep, dark chasm
beyond.

Maybe you should try to use the bedspread to let yourself
down?

You're not sure you have the time to grab the bedspread and tie it to something. Still, it's a long way to the ground.

WILL YOU . . .

. . . grab the bedspread to use as a rope?
TURN TO PAGE 25.

. . . forget about the bedspread and climb down now?
TURN TO PAGE 48.

GO ON TO THE NEXT PAGE.

You look around the room. It's a parlour with nice chairs and flimsy tables. The windows are dark. A flash of lightning just barely shows beyond the heavy wooden shutters.

There's an archway that opens into the front hall! You run that way.

'I thought there was another one of you.'

The boy from down in the road is standing in the front hall. He crosses his arms and scowls.

'I didn't get you to come here to play with my mother!' he grumbles.

You skid to a stop, the floor creaking beneath your feet. You look for another way out. You look at the staircase. Then you see a tall, thin man standing on the balcony. 'Now, now, Chester,' he says. 'You know your mother isn't well. Besides, she's busy in the kitchen now.'

The ghost boy gives you a nasty smile. 'That means you're all mine!'

THE END

The door pivots open with a gentle push, but it scrapes and creaks as it opens. You cringe, hoping no one heard. You push it closed, cringing again at the noise.

The flickering light of your candle lights up a round room with bookcases from the ceiling to the floor. The shelves are crammed with books of all shapes and sizes. In the centre of the room, there's a big wooden table with more books lying open on it. The whole place smells musty. There's dust on everything.

There are two stone staircases. The one on the right leads up. The one on the left leads down.

You remember that there was a tower on one end of the house. This must be it.

GO ON TO THE NEXT PAGE.

There are no exits from the tower, so going up or down these stairs won't get you any closer to escaping. But it might be a good way to hide.

WILL YOU . . .

. . . go down the tower stairs?
TURN TO PAGE 8.

. . . go up the tower stairs?
TURN TO PAGE 69.

. . . go back into the secret passage?
TURN TO PAGE 109.

'You must be crazy if you think I'd trust a ghost!' you yell. Then you dart through the nearest doorway, away from her.

'Come back,' she hisses. 'They'll get you for certain!"

You ignore her and look around the room you've just run into. It's a parlour, with dainty furniture and doilies all over everything. There's an archway to your left leading to the front hallway.

Dashing through the archway, you skid to a stop in front of the doors. The floor creaks under your feet. Grabbing the doorknob of the nearest one, you twist it and tug with all your might. It won't budge.

'There you are!' says a voice behind you.

You turn to see the pale little boy drifting down the stairs. 'My father has shut the house until morning. You can't leave.'

You might have made a mistake not trusting Iris. Is it too late? Maybe she can't help you now that the ghost boy is right behind you.

WILL YOU . . .

. . . make for the kitchen and hope Iris can still help?
TURN TO PAGE 45.

. . . try to find a place to hide?
TURN TO PAGE 65.

Yanking the glass cover off the candle, you set the sofa on fire! Old and dry, it catches quickly.

'Put it out!' Mrs Hale shrieks at her husband.

'It's too much!' he screams back. 'I can only control small flames!'

The front door flies open. 'Go'! shouts the ghost. 'Push the sofa out of here and you're free! But try to leave first and the door will shut. You'll burn with the house!'

Grabbing the far end of the sofa, you all heave it towards the front hall. Little by little, it scrapes along the floor.

A cold breeze fans the fire as you shove the sofa out of the door and off the porch. You're safe . . .

. . . until the boy you almost ran over floats out of the house!

'Father lied,' he says. 'Now we can play.'

'Run!' you shout.

You don't stop until you're far, far away from the terrors of Ghost Mansion.

THE END

Barry runs to the front door. The floor in the front hallway creaks and moans under his feet.

He pulls with all his strength, but the door won't open. 'It's locked too!' he screams.

'What do we do?!' yells Tim.

Just then, Mrs Hale comes drifting through the door leading from the dining room. She looks just as pale and ragged as the doctor.

'Poor frightened bunnies,' she groans. 'Running and hopping and scurrying away. Not for long. Not for long.'

'They're all ghosts!' you shout.

'Hurry!' cries Tim. 'Upstairs!'

'The doctor said that the little guy is up there,' you remind him. 'That's probably who we heard in the hall'!

Beyond Barry is an archway leading into another room. 'Through there!' you say.

Both Mrs Hale and her husband drift nearer, closing in.

GO ON TO THE NEXT PAGE.

You don't know which way to go,
but you'd better decide fast!

WILL YOU . . .

. . . run into the next room?
TURN TO PAGE 42.

. . . take your chances upstairs?
TURN TO PAGE 98.

You run back to the bed. As you grab the bedspread, a shiver runs down your spine.

The ghost of Dr Hale is oozing through the wall.

'What a MESS,' he grumbles. 'Now Hiller will have to clean this up.'

Dropping the bedspread, you run to the window.

You climb out as fast as you can. As you lower yourself from the windowsill, Dr Hale smiles down at you.

'I have good news and bad news for you,' he says. 'The good news is that I cannot leave this house, the place where I died. I can't even reach out the window.'

You let out a sigh of relief.

'The bad news is that when I was alive, I learned a few tricks with fire.'

Suddenly, the bandages on your hands burst into flames!

The pain makes you let go of the windowsill. You tumble down, falling into the dark chasm behind Ghost Mansion.

THE END

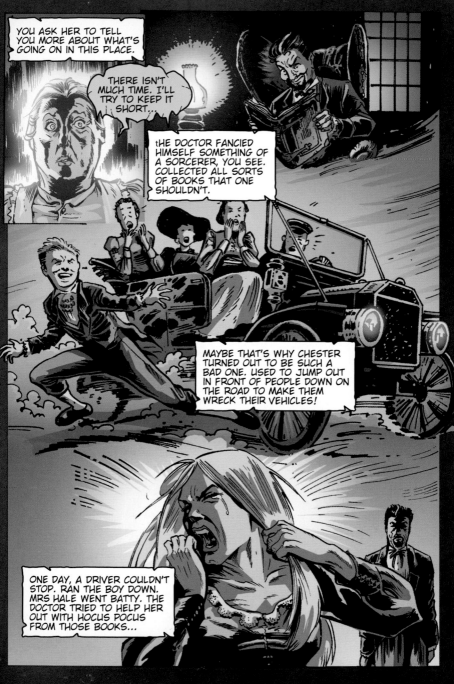

GO ON TO THE NEXT PAGE.

'Iris!' a shriek interrupts her story.

You turn to **see** Mrs Hale standing in the room, her arms thrown up in outrage. You didn't even hear her come in.

'How dare you share my husband's private business!' she moans. 'How could you betray us like this?'

Clutching her hands to her chest, Mrs Hale starts to wail.

'I'm so sorry,' Iris sobs to you as she fades away.

The wailing gets louder. It's like nails on a blackboard, but ten times worse. You clamp your hands on your ears, but it doesn't help.

Your head pounds with the thumping of your heart.

The pounding stops, but the screaming doesn't.

THE END

'What do I do?' you ask.

'The sunroom is on the other side of the dining room there. Lots of windows and no shutters at all. Smash a few and get out of here!'

You thank her and dash through the door.

The dining room is huge, with a long table set with plates, silverware, platters and glasses. There's no food. No one here has eaten in a long time.

Back in the kitchen, you hear a woman shriek, 'Iris! Where did the little scamp go?'

Then you're out of the other door and into a room with a whole wall of tall windows.

The chairs here are wicker. They look frail from all the years they've been sitting unused. Small wooden tables sit near a few of the chairs.

From the next room, you hear a child's voice calling, 'Mother! Where's my toy?'

GO ON TO THE NEXT PAGE.

The scary child is really close! Maybe you should just take a running jump and smash right through the glass. But can you do that without getting cut?

WILL YOU . . .

. . . go ahead and jump?
TURN TO PAGE 62.

. . . take the time to smash the window?
TURN TO PAGE 102.

'Tim's right!' you say, grabbing the candle from the table. You slip inside the fireplace. Tim is right behind you. After a couple of seconds, Barry and Sue follow.

Inside, there's a lever. When you pull it, the back of the fireplace slides forwards, shutting you in.

'This is daft!' says Sue. 'Now what are we supposed to do?'

'Just follow the passage,' says Barry. 'There's got to be another way out.'

'I just want to find the door that gets me out of this creepy place!' says Tim.

You lead the way down the passage. There are other openings like the one you came through, each with its own lever. You're fairly sure they just lead into the rooms your friends were supposed to stay in.

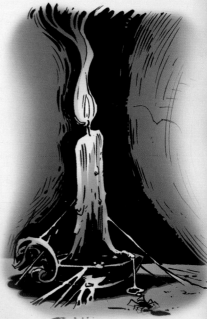

You pass them by. The four of you walk quietly down the passageway by the flickering light of your candle.

GO ON TO THE NEXT PAGE.

HANG ON, WHAT'S THIS?

THAT'S STRANGE.

BARRY MOVES OUT OF THE WAY SO YOU CAN LOOK TOO.

WHERE HAS SWEET LITTLE *CHESTER* GONE, FREDERICK? I GET SO SAD WHEN HE GOES AWAY...

NEVER FEAR, BEVERLY. HE'S JUST GONE UP TO PLAY WITH OUR GUESTS. HE'LL BE DOWN WHEN HE'S DONE WITH THEM.

GO ON TO THE NEXT PAGE.

31

After Tim and Sue have had a chance to look too, Barry closes the panel.

'I wonder if Chester was the boy down in the road?' whispers Barry.

'How come they're dressed like that?' hisses Tim.

'Its obvious,' Sue says quietly. 'It's Halloween. Maybe they just got back from a costume party? We should just go back to our rooms and stop acting like scared little children.'

'I don't know,' you say. 'That lady seems very odd. Let's just follow this passage and see where it goes.'

You continue down the dark, cramped corridor for what seems like forever.

Eventually, you come to a set of narrow stairs, leading down. There's also a door off to one side.

'What now?' you ask.

GO ON TO THE NEXT PAGE.

Barry wants to take the stairs. Tim is getting twitchy about being stuck in such a cramped space. 'Let's use the door!' he says.

WILL YOU . . .

. . . go down the steps?
TURN TO PAGE 93.

. . . get out of the passage right away?
TURN TO PAGE 106.

GO ON TO THE NEXT PAGE.

As you run across the dining room, Mrs Hale rises from the chair at the other end of the table.

'What are you doing?!' she shouts.

Suddenly she changes, like her husband did.

'NO RUNNING IN THE HOUSE!' she howls. Then she begins to moan and wail. The sound is awful! Tim stops, but Barry runs into him. They both fall.

On the floor, Tim rolls into a ball, covering his ears. Barry grabs hold of his brother and tries to drag him away.

Sue spins around and crashes into you. You stumble back. Suddenly, you feel an icy cold fill your chest.

You fall to the ground. As everything goes dark, you see Dr Hale over you. Behind him, high on the wall, is a life-size portrait of the doctor himself. It's in just the right place for his eyes to be the ones you looked through from the secret passage.

It seems funny, but you're too cold to laugh.

THE END

'Tim's right,' you say. 'Something strange is going on. Let's stay together.'

'Fine,' says Barry. 'Everybody in.' When you're all inside, he closes the door.

Still nervous, Tim starts poking around the room, looking at the books on the bookshelf and checking the dresser drawers. They're empty.

'He wasn't joking about the dust,' Tim says. 'Yuck.'

Sue points at the fireplace. 'Talk about 'yuck!' she says.

In the middle of the fireplace mantle, a short stone statue of a gargoyle grins down. Tim tries to haul it down for a closer look. It tilts forwards, as if on a hinge, and a hollow click surprises you.

Inside the fireplace, you hear a slight scraping sound. The back slides slowly away, revealing a narrow passage-way off to one side.

'That's strange,' you say. Just then, you hear quiet giggling out in the hall.

Tim is really scared. Even Sue looks a little nervous.

WILL YOU . . .

. . . try to hide in the secret passage?
TURN TO PAGE 30.

. . . see who is in the hall?
TURN TO PAGE 82.

You push the door closed behind you. 'Let's just stay here,' you tell the others. 'If anyone comes, we'll just say we got lost.'

Sue snorts but doesn't say anything.

You all sit down and try to get comfortable.

Suddenly you shiver, like someone's dropped ice down your back.

'W-what was that?' Tim asks.

The candle flickers.

'So THERE you are!" says a high-pitched voice behind you.

You all spin around. The boy from the road is standing there, a wicked grin on his lips. You didn't hear him come in.

'Father doesn't like it when people come here,' he says.

As he comes towards you, you notice you can almost see THROUGH him.

'H-he's a g-g-gho . . . ' you stammer as the boy's pale hands reach INTO your chest. It feels like he's jabbed an icicle through your heart.

The last thing you hear is your friends screaming your name.

THE END

TWISTED JOURNEYS®

You know that you need to get to the ground floor eventually, but that's probably what the ghosts are expecting you to do. Maybe you should just go out the door?

WILL YOU . . .

. . . go through the door?
TURN TO PAGE 16.

. . . go down the stairs?
TURN TO PAGE 47.

'I think he's just trying to scare us,' you whisper to the others. 'Maybe if we're not afraid, we'll be okay.'

Sue stops screaming. She looks embarrassed. 'Really?' she asks softly.

Barry frowns. 'I don't know.'

Tim stares at you for a second. Then he laughs. 'Cool.'

Taking a deep breath, you walk over to the little ghost.

'L-look,' you say, 'we're not scared of you. Why don't you go find someone else to spook?'

He looks up at you with sad eyes. 'Really? Are you sure?'

You cross your arms and try to look confident. 'Absolutely.'

'Oh well,' he says. Then he reaches out his small, pale hand and sticks it right into your forehead! Gasping, you try to pull away. It's like icicles in your brain!

The others start to scream. You can barely hear the ghost boy say, 'Maybe they'll be more fun.'

THE END

'I don't know what happens when a ghost touches you – and I don't want to find out!' you say, pulling Sue along with you into the next room.

It's big, with a couple of sofas and lots of chairs. There's even a piano.

'We have to get out of here!' shouts Barry. He picks up the piano bench and throws it at the window.

Glass shatters as the bench hits the window. There's a loud *crack* as the bench bounces off the closed shutters beyond the broken glass. The bench tumbles to the floor in pieces.

Suddenly, a shiver runs along your spine. The butler fades into view, a sad look on his face.

'I'd better get something to clean that up,' he says. Then he drifts off towards the back of the house. 'Perhaps you should have stayed in your vehicle,' the butler sighs.

Maybe Tim's plan is the best one. But you suddenly wonder how the ghosts lit all these candles in the first place.

WILL YOU . . .

. . . follow Tim's suggestion and threaten to start a fire with your candle?
TURN TO PAGE 10.

. . . forget the threats and use the candle to start a fire as quickly as you can?
TURN TO PAGE 21.

. . . let Sue prove that ghosts can't hurt people?
TURN TO PAGE 46.

. . . help Barry throw the chair at the shutters?
TURN TO PAGE 71.

You run towards the kitchen as fast as you can. Maybe Iris can help you hide or something.

Behind you, you hear Chester whining. 'I'm getting bored!'

You just run faster.

You rush through the kitchen door, calling out, 'I'm sorry! I should have trusted you! Help me!'

Then you see who's waiting for you.

It's the ghostly man and woman from the upstairs hall, Dr and Mrs Hale. They look angry.

'We had a little talk with Iris,' says Dr Hale. 'She should know better than to interfere with Chester's fun.'

Mrs Hale spreads her arms wide as she lunges towards you. 'Run along and play!' she shrieks.

You stumble back through the door you just came in. Chester is right there. You run right through him.

Icy cold washes over your whole body. Your legs stop working. You tumble to the floor.

Chester peers down at you, grinning madly. 'That was funny,' he says.

THE END

'Relax, everyone,' you say. 'Sue's probably right. They just pass right through stuff!'

Sue wags her finger at the ghosts. 'You should be ashamed, frightening us like this.'

'That's what ghosts do,' Dr Hale replies.

'Well, it's not going to work anymore!' Sue tells him, jabbing her finger at him to make the point.

The ghost reaches out, grabbing Sue's wrist. The ghostly fingers seem to sink into her arm.

She was right!

Then Sue starts to shiver. Her arm begins to turn bluish grey. 'Wha – ?' she gasps. She tries to pull away, but the ghost just moves with her.

The other ghosts swoop towards you, Barry and Tim, laughing.

'It seems we're not so harmless after all,' the doctor chuckles.

THE END

You make your way cautiously down the stairs. At the bottom, there's a narrow door.

Slowly, you push it open. The hinges don't squeal. Much.

You step through and find yourself in a kitchen. Slowly, carefully, you swing the panel shut.

There's a woman standing behind it!

You gulp.

She raises a finger to her lips. You realize she's shorter and heavier than the ghost lady from upstairs. She's wearing a white apron over her plain dress.

'I think they're still upstairs,' she whispers.

You realize you can almost see through her. 'You're one of them!'

'Don't be afraid of old Iris," she says quietly. 'The doctor done something unpleasant to keep me and Mr Hiller around. Doesn't mean we have to like it! You can trust us.'

'I can show you how to get out,' she says, 'but I'd appreciate if you'd help us first.'

TURN TO PAGE 49.

YOU MANAGE TO GET OUT OF THE WINDOW.

THERE YOU ARE! WELL, I HAVE GOOD NEWS AND BAD NEWS FOR YOU...

YOU DON'T WAIT TO HEAR WHAT HE HAS TO SAY. LETTING GO, YOU HOPE YOU WON'T MISS THE LEDGE.

YOU HIT THE LEDGE AND STRUGGLE FOR BALANCE.

YOU CLING TO THE WALL, SHAKING, THINKING ABOUT WHAT COULD HAVE HAPPENED.

48

TURN TO PAGE 61.

You wonder if this is some kind of trick. Iris seems nice, but how can you know for sure?

WILL YOU . . .

. . . just try to get away?
TURN TO PAGE 18.

. . . trust her, but ask her to help you leave right away?
TURN TO PAGE 74.

. . . try to help her before you escape?
TURN TO PAGE 111.

'I'm sorry,' you say, 'but I'm worried that they'll find me before I do what you ask.'

Iris nods, sadly.

'Maybe I can come back,' you tell her. 'But right now I have to get away. My friends . . . our parents . . . '

'I understand, child,' she says. 'Come along. I'll get you out of here.'

She gestures for you to follow her. Her head hangs low as she drifts slowly towards the door to the dining room. Then she pauses, turning back to you.

'It's just that we've been here for so long,' she says. 'And there have been others, like you and your friends. But if Hiller and I try to help, and the Hales find out . . . ' She shudders. 'They do awful things to us.'

'Iris!' a woman's voice calls out from the kitchen. 'Where are you?'

'Mrs Hale!' gasps Iris. 'We have to hurry!'

You lie on the floor, shivering, unable to stand or crawl. The ghost boy drifts into the room, frowning.

'Mother and father are going to be very cross with you, Iris,' he says.

Wailing in despair, Iris drifts out of sight.

Chester sits down, cross-legged, in mid-air.

'She went through you very quickly,' he says, 'and she didn't want to hurt you. I bet you'll be able to move before very long.'

He puts one elbow on his knee and then rests his chin in his hand. 'Maybe I'll just wait so I can chase you again.'

For a few long moments, he sits quietly, watching you.

'This is boring,' he sighs. 'I don't think I want to wait after all.'

Reaching down, he plunges his pale hand inside your chest. You can almost feel ghostly fingers clutching at your heart . . .

THE END

This is starting to sound more complicated than you expected. What if the other ghosts catch you before you can do what Iris asks?

WILL YOU . . .

. . . ask her for more information?
TURN TO PAGE 26.

. . . tell her you think
it's too risky?
TURN TO PAGE 50.

. . . just do what she asks?
TURN TO PAGE 85.

'Come on, Tim,' you say. 'It's only a few hours. What could happen?'

Tim opens his mouth to reply, but Barry interrupts.

'Worried about the bogey-man, Tim?' He laughs.

'I don't know about the rest of you, but I'm more worried about what my parents are going to say tomorrow than staying in a spooky house overnight,' says Sue.

'Maybe Barry's mobile phone will work when the storm passes,' you say.

One by one, your friends leave. Soon you're alone in a room lit only by candlelight and the occasional flash of lightning. You wish you could take off your costume, but you've got nothing else to wear. Funny that the butler didn't at least give you some towels to dry off.

Despite what you told Tim, you're too nervous to sleep. You walk over to the window and look out into the dark.

GO ON TO THE NEXT PAGE.

You head for the door, then pause. Maybe you should take something with you. Something you could use as a weapon. Do you have time?

WILL YOU . . .

. . . find something
to defend yourself?
TURN TO PAGE 66.

. . . go straight into the hall?
TURN TO PAGE 104.

You shove frantically against the door. It pivots open, creaking and scraping loudly. The sound echoes down the passage and in the room you stumble into. You run into a heavy table, knocking several books to the floor.

Dim light is filtering in from somewhere. You can just make out a round room, with bookcases that go from the floor to the ceiling. They're crammed with strange-looking books of every size and shape. It smells musty and the thick dust makes you think no one has been here in a long time.

You can just make out a stone staircase leading upwards and another leading down.

Suddenly, a thin man in a dark suit oozes through the door!

He's between you and the staircase leading up. You plunge down the other stairs.

Behind you, you hear him shout, 'Here, now! I don't allow anyone in my private library!'

GO ON TO THE NEXT PAGE.

GO ON TO THE NEXT PAGE.

With the ghostly man right behind you, you stagger into the games room. You don't even try to go around the billiard table. You just dive underneath.

Scrambling to the door, you glance back to see the man floating THROUGH the table!

Desperately, you throw open the doors, hoping you can stay ahead of him.

You stop.

A thin, ghostly woman in a frilly, white dress is standing on the other side of the door, looking sad. She opens her mouth and begins to wail.

The noise is awful and terrifying. You clap your hands over your ears, but it doesn't help.

Falling to the ground, the only thing you can hear besides the scream is the pounding of your heart. You just wish it would stop.

The screaming doesn't, but your heart does.

THE END

'What happened to my friend?' you say, reaching down to grab the creepy little guy by his jacket. 'Did you do something to him?'

Your can't believe your eyes when your hand passes right through him. It feels like you just dunked it in icy water.

'W-what ARE you?' you manage to sputter.

'What do you THINK?' he replies. Then he starts to laugh.

Reaching out a small, pale hand, he pushes it against your stomach. You feel it sink beneath your skin!

A wave of cold washes over you.

You try to call out, to tell Barry and Sue to run. You can't make a sound.

THE END

You're not sure if you can make your way along the ledge without falling. Maybe you should wait a little while and calm yourself down. After all, you're outside. Ghosts can't leave the place where they died, can they?

WILL YOU . . .

. . . take a moment to calm down and catch your breath?
TURN TO PAGE 70.

. . . take your chances going now?
TURN TO PAGE 88.

You struggle to lift the chair. You stagger a few steps and toss it through the glass.

The window explodes into a million shimmering shards.

Then you run back and slip into the passage, hoping they'll think you climbed out the window!

There's just enough light leaking in from the room for you to make out a lever on the wall. You pull it. The fireplace starts to scrape closed.

Then you hear a man's voice say, 'What a MESS! Where . . . ah, the secret passage! Clever child! But not quick enough!"

In a blind panic, you stumble along the dark passageway, occasionally bumping into walls. An eerie wailing echoes behind you.

After what seems like forever, you see a dim light shining under the crack of a door. It's just enough to reveal that there's a staircase leading down, too.

GO ON TO THE NEXT PAGE.

What should you do? To get out of the house, you'll have to go downstairs eventually. But in the dark, cramped stairway, you might not see something coming.

WILL YOU . . .

. . . use the door and get out of the passage now?
TURN TO PAGE 57.

. . . go down the stairs?
TURN TO PAGE 91.

The only place you see to hide is on the other side of the china cabinet. You duck around there and put your back to it. You just hope that the ghost boy will think you ran all the way to the kitchen.

You can't help thinking you should have listened to Iris.

A minute passes. Two. The boy hasn't gone past.

You peer around the edge of the china cabinet. There's no sign of him.

A wicked laugh rings out from INSIDE the cabinet!

As you jump back from it, the ghost boy oozes out. 'Looking for me?' he giggles.

He moves towards you.

Lurching back, you thump into a chair.

'Did you really think you could hide from a ghost?' he asks.

THE END

You look around desperately for something you can use to defend yourself. The chairs are too heavy. Everything else looks too light.

Then your eyes fall on the small gargoyle that sits in the middle of the fireplace mantle.

Reaching up, you try to pull it down. It tilts forward but then stops. You hear a loud 'click' and then a scraping rumble from inside the fireplace!

Looking down, you see the back of the fireplace slide away, revealing a narrow passageway leading off to one side.

Out in the hall, you hear Sue call out softly, 'Tim? Are you alright?'

Then Barry says, 'If he's playing some kind of joke, I'm going to kill him.'

Suddenly, it seems silly to be looking for a weapon.

As you step into the hall, you hear Sue say, 'Why is he so still?'

Then Barry stammers, 'Is he . . . is he . . . '

You duck back into your room, not sure what
to do. It's too late to help Sue.

WILL YOU . . .

. . . break the window and try to climb down?
TURN TO PAGE 12.

. . . try to trick the ghosts by breaking the window,
then hiding in the passage?
TURN TO PAGE 63.

. . . run straight into the secret passage?
TURN TO PAGE 81.

Maybe you'll find something in the tower to explain what's happening in this house. You go up the stairs. They end at a trap door.

Cautiously, you push the door open. It's heavy, but you manage to raise it.

You lift your candle and peer inside. The room is empty, except for a closed book on a wooden lectern in the centre.

Curious, you climb up and ease the trap door back into place.

At the lectern, you open the book to a place marked by a velvet ribbon. Reddish dust sprays in your face. Coughing, you wave your hand to clear the air. There is only one sentence on the page: 'It was a trap.'

You turn to run, but you stumble and fall to the floor, gasping.

TURN TO PAGE 78.

You decide you'd better get a hold of yourself. Hugging the wall, you take deep breaths. After a few minutes, you feel better.

Carefully, you start to move along the ledge. Step by step, you get nearer to the edge of the house.

Finally, you grasp the corner of the house. You pull yourself around it.

'What took you so long?'

You can't believe it! It's the boy from the hallway.

'H-how?' you gasp. Then you remember – you saw him down on the road! He must be able to leave the house...

He reaches for you. You step back quickly, thinking about the screams of your friends.

Your foot slips off the ledge behind you. For a moment, you teeter there.

Then you topple over the edge, falling into the deep, dark chasm behind Ghost Mansion.

THE END

71

'No one yells like that in their sleep,' you say. Reaching out, you grab the doorknob. It feels cold.

You swing the door open and go in. Sue and Barry follow. The room is dark, except for the light coming from the hall.

Tim is huddled on the floor in one corner of the room, his knees drawn up against him and his arms covering his head.

'Tim?' you call out quietly. He doesn't answer.

'What's wrong?' says Sue. 'Why is he so . . . still?'

You realise she's right. He's not moving at all.

'Is he . . . is he . . . ' stammers Barry.

'Yes,' says a voice behind you.

You all jump, startled. When you spin around, there's a small boy standing in the doorway – he same boy from the road. He has a nasty grin.

'Who's next?' he laughs. Then he comes towards you.

GO ON TO THE NEXT PAGE.

You wonder if the boy knows something about what happened to Tim. He couldn't be the one who hurt Tim, could he?

WILL YOU . . .

. . . try to avoid the boy and get out of there?

TURN TO PAGE 11.

. . . try to question the boy?

TURN TO PAGE 60.

'I'm sorry,' you say. 'I have to get out of here now. They've already got my friends.'

Iris nods. 'I understand. It was too much to ask.'

'How do I get out?' you ask.

She leans towards you, talking softly. 'The doctor has done something unnatural to the doors and shutters. They won't open before the sun comes up.'

'Then how – '

She smiles. 'I don't think the doctor's trick works on plain old glass, though. See, there's one room in the house with plenty of windows and no shutters at all,' she says.

She starts towards a nearby door. 'Come along,' she says. 'Quiet as a mouse. We don't want them to hear!"

You pick up one of the tables and toss it through the window. The shattering glass sounds tremendously loud.

'Now run, child,' says Iris. 'Don't you stop until you get well away from here. Remember that Chester can go all the way down to the road!'

You try to thank her, but she just says, 'GO!'

She doesn't have to tell you twice. You climb out the window and start running.

As you reach the road, you hear an awful wailing echoing down from the house. You keep running, wishing you had tried to help Iris.

There was at least one good spirit in Ghost Mansion.

THE END

Tim does play stupid jokes sometimes. Do you want to give him the satisfaction of falling for this one? Then again, something could really be wrong.

WILL YOU . . .

. . . go inside?
TURN TO PAGE 72.

. . . suggest that you leave him alone?
TURN TO PAGE 100.

78

'We have to get to the stairs!' you shout. 'Follow me!'

You run right at the boy, who just smiles. Then you jump, diving over his head. You just hope you don't break anything when you land.

As you sail over his head, he reaches up. His hand goes THROUGH your foot.

Your leg goes numb from the knee down. You try to roll when you hit the floor, but your useless leg sends you sprawling.

From the end of the hall, you can hear Sue pounding on the window, unable to get it open.

The boy comes up to you, makes a face and sticks out his tongue.

It's the last thing you see.

THE END

You tiptoe across the game room and around the billiard table. At the door, you stop and listen.

Not hearing anything, you ease open the pocket doors a little and peer through.

A pale, cold eye stares back at you.

You stagger back, trip and fall. You just barely keep the candle from falling.

The ghost woman from upstairs steps through the doors, without even opening them.

'Oh, that's so sad,' she cries. 'Did it hurt?'

Scrambling back, you get some distance from her and leap to your feet.

The ghostly man is standing there!

He laughs and smiles. 'Did I surprise you, youngster?' he says. 'Were you expecting a ghost to make a noise? Silent as the grave, you know.'

Then he comes towards you, his face suddenly looking gaunt and his eyes hollow and dark. 'Speaking of which,' he whispers, 'you must be dying to join your friends!'

THE END

YOU GRAB THE CANDLE, HOPING NO ONE WILL NOTICE IT'S GONE.

PULLING ON THE HANDLE SLIDES THE BACK OF THE FIREPLACE INTO PLACE AGAIN. NOW, YOU JUST HOPE THIS PASSAGE WILL LEAD YOU TO A *WAY OUT*!

A DOOR! BUT IS IT SAFE TO USE?

AND A STAIRCASE. WHICH ONE SHOULD YOU TAKE?

TURN TO PAGE 40.

'Let's just see who it is,' you say. Reaching up, you tip the gargoyle back. The fireplace closes.

'Wait,' says Sue. 'Listen.'

The four of you stand absolutely still. Moments pass.

Barry whispers, 'I don't hear anything.'

'That's what I mean,' Sue says. 'What happened to the noise?'

'I'm going to check the hall,' you say softly.

'We should get OUT of here!' mutters Tim.

You, Barry, and Sue all turn towards Tim.

'We get it,' Barry says. 'You're scared. Now shut up!'

You and Sue nod in agreement.

Tim scowls and starts to argue. Then he looks surprised. His lips move without a sound. He points behind you.

You turn and gasp!

GO ON TO THE NEXT PAGE.

Tim finally manages to speak. 'Run!' he yelps.
But do you really need to? Can a ghost even touch
a normal person? He seems excited because
Sue is afraid. Does that mean something?

WILL YOU . . .

. . . try to convince the ghost he doesn't scare you?
TURN TO PAGE 41.

. . . try to escape through the passage?
TURN TO PAGE 97.

. . . try to slip past the ghost and go
through the door?
TURN TO PAGE 110.

You give her a nod. 'Let's go.'

She leads you back into the secret passage and tells you to close the door. She drifts up the stairs ahead of you, quiet as the grave.

Iris goes past the door at the top of the stairs, to one of the fireplace entrances you passed on your way down. She points at the lever and then oozes through the wall.

You pull the lever and wait for the fireplace to open. Your heart is pounding.

Through the walls, you hear an awful wail of frustration. You freeze.

'Where did the child get to?' a woman's voice calls out. 'Come out, come out, wherever you are!'

You can just barely hear a young boy's voice reply, 'Quiet, Mother! They get more frightened when you sneak up on them!'

Quickly, you slip out of the passage.

GO ON TO THE NEXT PAGE.

GO ON TO THE NEXT PAGE.

You step back to watch the papers burn, hoping the fire won't spread too fast.

An awful scream echoes through the house! Suddenly, the three Hales appear in the room.

'Too late!' cries Iris. 'I'm free!'

'We can still punish your rescuer!' Dr Hale growls. 'You can't stop all of us by yourself!'

The butler appears and grabs hold of the doctor. 'She won't have to!' he shouts.

Chester tries to get at you, but Iris has him by the arm. Then she grabs Mrs Hale too.

'Run!' she shouts. 'The doctor can't fight Hiller and keep the doors closed too!'

Dodging around the ghosts, you rush into the hallway and down the creaking stairs to the front door.

It opens!

Halfway down the drive, you stop and look back. The flames have spread, engulfing Ghost Mansion and burning it to the ground.

THE END

Remembering that you saw the ghost boy down on the road, you decide you'd better keep moving.

You creep along the ledge. Closer. Closer.

Finally, you come to the corner of the house and heave yourself around to safer ground.

You want to throw yourself down and hug the ground. Only you keep thinking about that scary boy. You start to run.

As you reach the road, you hear a small, mean voice howling in frustration behind you.

You run past the car, thinking about your friends.

You keep running in the rain, hoping they won't become more spirits in Ghost Mansion.

THE END

'Sue's right,' you say. 'Let's go.'

Reluctantly, Barry and Tim agree. It doesn't take long to get back to your room.

As you come out of the fireplace, a high-pitched voice exclaims, 'You're not supposed to use the passages!'

The boy from the road is in your room!

'Don't get cross,' says Sue. 'We didn't mean any harm.' She walks over to him and holds out her hand. 'I'm Sue. What's your name?'

'I'm Chester,' says the boy. He puts his small, pale hand into hers.

Sue shivers. Then her arm starts to turn blue!

Chester starts to laugh. That's when you realize that you can almost see THROUGH him.

You rush over, trying to pull Sue away. Chester just lets go – and puts his hand right into your throat! You try to swallow, to breathe, but you can't.

You fall.

The last thing you see is Chester's smile.

THE END

90

You rush down the stairs as fast as you can in the dark. At the bottom, you shove open the door you find there.

You step out into a kitchen.

Then you realise that someone is standing nearby. With a yelp, you duck away.

A short, plump lady in a plain dress with a white apron over it looks down at you. Her eyes are kind.

'Don't be afraid of old Iris,' she says quietly. 'I mean you no harm.'

You give her a closer look. You can see the door to another room behind her. Through her.

'Y-you're like them,' you say. 'A ghost.'

'A ghost, yes,' she says, 'but not like them. You have to trust me, child.'

Next to you is a door leading further into the house. Across the kitchen, you see another door that leads outside.

GO ON TO THE NEXT PAGE.   **91**

She looks nice, but she's a *ghost*. You can't help thinking about what happened to your friends. Can you trust any ghost?

WILL YOU . . .

. . . ignore her advice and try the outside door? TURN TO PAGE 14.

. . . take a chance and trust her? TURN TO PAGE 28.

You make your way carefully down the steps, flinching every time one creaks. With four of you, it happens a lot.

At the bottom of the steps, there's a narrow door.

'Ready?' you ask. The others nod. Slowly, you push the door open, hoping its hinges don't squeal.

You step out into a big, old-fashioned kitchen. Holding a finger to your lips for quiet, you swing the door back into place.

'Well, now, what have we here?'

Tim lets out a yelp, and you all jump back. Someone was standing behind the open door!

A short, plump lady in a plain dress and a white apron looks the four of you up and down. You hold your breath.

She gives you a warm smile.

'Don't be afraid of old Iris,' she says quietly. 'I mean you no harm. Unlike some I could mention.'

She leans forward and whispers, 'But we better keep quiet. Otherwise the doctor and the Mrs might hear.'

GO ON TO THE NEXT PAGE.

GO ON TO THE NEXT PAGE.

'What do you mean?' you ask.

'It started a long time ago,' she says. 'That boy, Chester, was a bad one from the start. Used to go down to the road and jump out in front of vehicles, trying to make people crash them!'

'Like he did to us!' you say.

She nods. 'One day, he dodged one way when he should have gone the other. The driver brought him up to the house, but the doctor couldn't save him.'

'B-but, we saw him,' says Sue. 'He . . . '

'Haven't you guessed?' Iris interrupts. 'Everyone here – '

'So there you are!' a voice booms behind you.

Turning, you see the man from the dining room standing in the kitchen doorway. This must be Dr Hale! He gives a strange smile.

'Chester just went up to see you!' he says. 'Come along. You mustn't disappoint him!'

GO ON TO THE NEXT PAGE.

The doctor wants you to go upstairs,
but the cook said to avoid him.

WILL YOU . . .

. . . try to get away?
TURN TO PAGE 22.

. . . do as he asks?
TURN TO PAGE 34.

'The passage!' you shout. You pull the gargoyle forwards, activating the hidden door.

The thing seems to move in slow motion. Terrified, you look back. The ghost boy is still standing in the same place, looking puzzled.

You pile into the secret passage with your friends. Behind you, Barry throws the switch to close the fire-place mechanism.

In the darkness, Tim lets out a sigh. 'We . . . we got away.'

Then a soft glowing light forms ahead of you. The ghostly boy has stepped into the passage. He looks at you, still puzzled.

'I can go through walls, you know. Just like I went through the door to the room.'

You try to turn, to go back the way you came. But the passage is narrow and Tim, Sue and Barry are blocking the way.

You feel icy fingers pushing through your back. 'That was too easy,' says the ghost boy. 'No fun at all.'

THE END

GO ON TO THE NEXT PAGE.

'Jump!' yells Barry. He leaps over the banister. You follow him, hoping for a good landing.

Barry hits the floor just a second or two before you do. A cloud of dust swirls up around him, the floor creaks and you hear a loud *CRACK!* A floorboard gives way, and one of Barry's legs pushes through it.

Your feet slam into the floor.

More floorboards snap beneath you and Barry. The old dry wood can't take the strain of two people dropping down on it so hard!

You slide into the hole in the floor. Ignoring the jab of splinters, you try to grab onto the edge as you fall. You think you might almost . . .

Barry's hand clamps onto your leg. 'Hang on!' he shouts, desperate and frightened.

His weight is too much.

You both scream as you fall into the damp, cold darkness beneath Ghost Mansion.

THE END

'Maybe he's playing a joke,' you say. 'Or having a nightmare.'

Sue turns back towards her room and says, 'I'm going to try to get some sleep.'

Barry hangs back for a second. 'Maybe I should check.'

Behind him, you see something strange happening to Tim's door. Smoke or something is drifting off the wood. It almost looks like . . .

'A hand!' you shout, pointing behind Barry. He turns around and stares. Behind you, Sue gasps with surprise.

A pale figure steps THROUGH the closed door. It's the boy from the road!

He scowls at the three of you. 'You're no fun!' he says.

'This can't be happening,' whispers Barry.

The little guy flashes a wicked smile. 'Of course it can!'

'This way!' Sue shouts. 'There's a window at the end of the hall! We can climb down from there!'

GO ON TO THE NEXT PAGE.

Sue waves for you to come. But can you really climb down from a second-storey window? Maybe you should just try to slip past the ghost and head for the stairs.

WILL YOU . . .

. . . make a run for the stairs?
TURN TO PAGE 79.

. . . try to climb out of the window?
TURN TO PAGE 90.

Remembering the view from your room, you decide to play it safe. The house stands on a cliff. Crashing through the window could send you over the edge.

Picking up one of the small tables, you hurl it through the window. Glass explodes in a shower of shimmering shards.

Very carefully, you ease out of the broken window onto the narrow ledge behind the house. You look down into a deep, dark ravine. It's a very long way down.

Seconds after you begin creeping your way along the house, awful moans and shouts echo through the shattered window. Looking back as you ease around the corner, you see Mrs Hale glaring at you from inside, her fists clenched as she snarls at you.

As you run towards the driveway, you wonder why she isn't coming after you. Maybe she can't leave the place where she died?

GO ON TO THE NEXT PAGE.

103

TURN TO PAGE 77.

You squat down behind one of the chairs in the round room, but you can't bring yourself to blow out the candle. Minutes tick by slowly.

You can't help thinking about your friends. What will you tell their parents? Will you even see your own parents again?

Finally, you can't stand the waiting. You get up and . . .

The ghost man from upstairs is sitting in one of the chairs across the room!

'Hello there,' he says. 'I'm Dr Hale. I was wondering just how long you could stay back there. You didn't do badly for a youngster.'

'W-why are you doing this?' you stammer. 'What did we ever do to you?'

He drifts up out of the chair, coming closer.

'Nothing at all,' he replies. 'It's what we do. Bad ghosts, I mean.'

He drifts closer, reaching for you. 'This is the closest thing we have to fun.'

THE END

There doesn't seem to be a handle on the door, so you push on it gently. It pivots open, creaking and scraping. You can feel your friends cringe, wondering if someone heard.

Beyond the door is a circular room. A stone staircase to your right leads down and another to your left leads up. The walls of the room are covered by bookcases crammed with books of all sizes. Several more are open on a large wooden table in the middle of the room. The whole place smells musty, dusty and unused.

Tim pushes past you. He looks back with a sheepish grin. 'I don't like tight places, okay?'

'What is this place?' asks Sue. She wanders over to the table and peers at the books there. She looks puzzled. 'I can't read any of this.'

You look over her shoulder at the strange characters filling the pages.

'Me neither,' you say.

GO ON TO THE NEXT PAGE.

You wonder if Sue could be right. Maybe the stormy night and the spooky house are making you all nervous for no reason. Then again, the people here do seem sort of strange.

WILL YOU . . .

. . . stay in the tower library?
TURN TO PAGE 39.

. . . go back through the secret passage and to your room?
TURN TO PAGE 89.

You decide that you're better off in the secret passage. If the ghosts don't know that you know about it, they might not look for you there.

Stepping into the passage, you pull the door closed behind you. As you turn to the stairs, your candle reflects off something white. Suddenly, the woman from the hallway lurches out of the shadows right at you!

You jerk back, out of her reach. Your foot hits empty air. The stairs!

As you fall backwards, you hear her laughing. 'Oh, no!' she cries. 'Poor little thing.'

You hear her begin to wail as you tumble down the stairs. The candle flies from your hand and goes out. You finish your fall in darkness.

At the bottom, your head smacks onto the floor.

Then you don't feel anything at all.

THE END

The ghostly boy drifts forwards, his hands stretched out to grab you. Just barely, you manage to dodge his pale, grasping fingers.

'Come on!' you yell back to your friends.

You throw open the door to the hallway. Terrified, Tim pushes past you and runs for the stairs.

By the time you reach them, he's halfway to the bottom. Behind you, Sue screams!

You turn to go back. Then you hear Tim yelp with fear. Looking downstairs, you see a tall, pale man in an old-fashioned suit clutching at Tim.

There's another scream in the hallway. The ghost boy is standing over Barry, smiling.

You turn back towards Tim. The man is right next to you!

'Boo!' he says, smiling.

You stumble. Your foot slips on the top step and you tumble down.

At the bottom, your head hits the floor with a loud crack.

THE END

TURN TO PAGE 53.

READY FOR MORE ADVENTURES?

WHICH TWISTED JOURNEYS® WILL YOU TRY NEXT?

#1 CAPTURED BY PIRATES
Danger on the high seas! A band of scurvy pirates has boarded your ship. Can you keep them from turning you into shark bait?

#2 ESCAPE FROM PYRAMID X
You're on an archaeological mission to an ancient pyramid, complete with ancient mummies. Unfortunately for you, not everything that's ancient is also dead...

#3 TERROR IN GHOST MANSION
Halloween's not supposed to be this scary. You and your friends are trapped in a creepy old house with a family of ghosts. And they definitely aren't wearing costumes...

#4 THE TREASURE OF MOUNT FATE
Plenty of people have braved the monsters and magic of Mount Fate in search of its legendary treasure. But no one has ever lived to tell about their quest. Will you be the first?

This book was first published in the United States of America in 2007.
Text copyright © 2007 by Lerner Publishing Group, Inc.